THE DIVERSIFICATION OF SECOND TEMPLE JUDAISM

An Introduction to the Second Temple Period

Jeff S. Anderson

University Press of America,® Inc.
Lanham · New York · Oxford

Copyright © 2002 by
University Press of America,® Inc.
4501 Forbes Boulevard, Suite 200
Lanham, Maryland 20706

12 Hid's Copse Rd.
Cumnor Hill, Oxford OX2 9JJ

Library of Congress Cataloging-in-Publication Data

Anderson, Jeff S.
The internal diversification of Second Temple Judaism :
an introduction to the Second Temple period / Jeff S. Anderson.
p.   cm
Includes bibliographical references and index.
1. Judaism—History—Post-exilic period, 586 B.C.-210 A.D.
2. Religious pluralism—Judaism—History. 3. Bible. O.T.—Criticism,
interpretation, etc., Jewish—History. 4. Jews—History—
586 B.C.-70 A.D. I. Title.

BM176 .A54 2002
296'.09'014—dc21   2002020369 CIP

ISBN 0-7618-2327-1 (paperback : alk. ppr.)

For B.J.

Kamoni kamoka, ke'ammi ke'ammeka

Contents

List of Tables

List of Abbreviations

Ag. Ap.	Josephus' *Against Apion*
Ant.	Josephus' *Jewish Antiquities*
Bar	Baruch
2 Bar	*2 Baruch*
B.C.E.	Before the Common Era
b. Sabb	Talmud, *Shabbat*
C.E.	Common Era
1 Chr	1 Chronicles
2 Chr	2 Chronicles
Contempl. Life	Philo's *On the Contemplation of Life*
1 Cor	1 Corinthians
Creation	Philo's *On the Creation of the World*
Dan	Daniel
Deut	Deuteronomy
1 En.	*1 Enoch*
1 Esd	1 Esdras
2 Esd	2 Esdras
Esth	Esther
Ezek	Ezekiel
Gen	Genesis
Hag	Haggai
Heb	Hebrews
Isa	Isaiah
Jer	Jeremiah
Josh	Joshua
Jub	*Jubilees*
1 Kgs	1 Kings
2 Kgs	2 Kings
L.A.B.	Liber antiquitatum biblicarum, (Pseudo-Philo)
L.A.E.	*Life of Adam and Eve*
m. Ab.	*Sayings of the Fathers*
1 Macc	1 Maccabees

2 Macc	2 Maccabees
Mal	Malachi
Matt	Matthew
Nat	Pliny the Elder, *Natural History*
OTP	*Old Testament Pseudepigrapha.* Edited by J. H. Charlesworth, 2 vols. New York, 1983.
Pss Sol	*Psalms of Solomon*
4Q169	The Nahum Pesher
4Q184	*Wiles of the Wicked Woman*
4Q285	*Sefer Hamilhamah*
4Q416	*Instruction b (A Sapiental Work)*
1 Qap Gen	*Genesis Apocryphon*
1QpHab	The Habakkuk Pesher
4QmessAp	*Messianic Apocalypse*
1QS	Community Rule
11 QT	The Temple Scroll
1 Sam	1 Samuel
Sanh.	Mishnah, *Sanhedrin*
Sib. Or.	*Sibylline Oracles*
Sir	Sirach, Ecclesiasticus
Ta 'an.	Talmud, *Ta 'anit*
T. Levi	*Testament of Levi*
Wis	Wisdom of Solomon
Zech	Zechariah

Preface

This present work is the result of many years of personal captivation with the Second Temple period. Raised in a Protestant tradition, my own experience proves that this particular period has typically suffered from benign neglect. As I began to personally explore the literature of the period, I soon discovered that this unwieldy collection provides the reader with a look forward as well as a look backward. Looking forward, Second Temple Judaism lays the historical and theological groundwork for the influential writings of the New Testament and Rabbinic Judaism. Looking backward, much of this material directly reflects on the teachings and traditions of the Torah and the Prophets, shedding light on how the Hebrew Scriptures were interpreted at the turn of the Common Era.

During doctoral studies at Vanderbilt University, I chose Early Judaism as my minor concentration. Under the able direction of Professor Peter Haas, I devoted time and energy to serious study of the literature and history of the period I had previously neglected. Professor Walter Harrelson's course in the Intertestamental Period capably introduced the literature of the Apocrypha and Pseudepigrapha. Shemaryahu Talmon, Visiting Professor of Hebrew Scriptures, led lively classes in the Dead Sea Scrolls and Post-exilic Judaism, and James Barr introduced us to the intricacies of the Septuagint. Each of these individuals contributed to my interest in Second Temple Judaism.

For ten years on the religion faculty at Wayland Baptist University, I have had numerous opportunities to teach an "Interbiblical Period" course. This present work emerges directly from my experiences in the classroom, as one always in constant search for a text that might provide a general overview of the period and that would also be sensitive to the many advances in scholarship over the last several decades.

I am grateful for those at Wayland Baptist University who have provided assistance with this project. Ms. Sheri Denison read and reviewed several chapters prior to initially submitting them to the publisher, and Dr. James Waller painstakingly edited the entire manuscript. I am thankful for their patience and assistance with this project. Wayland Baptist University's Vice Chancellor, Dr. Bill Hardage, provided professional support and allowed the time required to complete this project in the midst of my responsibilities as Dean of the Anchorage Campus.

It is my hope this book will stimulate other students of this exciting period to explore its profound mysteries.

Chapter 1

The Second Temple Period: Terminology and Misconceptions

The period of Israel's history from the return from the Babylonian Exile in 538 B.C.E. to the destruction of the Second Temple in 70 C.E. is an enigma to many students of the Hebrew Bible and the New Testament. This era has been often overlooked as unimportant or been the victim of strongly confessional overgeneralizations. Many biblical scholars, particularly prior to the latter decades of the twentieth century, casually referred to this expanse of time as the "centuries of silence," or a "time of darkness, " and found it only significant as a lifeless spiritual vacuum from which a vibrant and triumphal Christianity arose. The disdain for this period is well documented in scholarship. Until relatively recently, historians of religion relegated post-exilic Israelite life and faith to be a pale reflection of the vigor of earlier Yahwism. The result has been a sharp distinction in much of the literature between biblical *Israel* and post-exilic *Judaism*. In Christian and Jewish polemical rhetoric, Christians often have touted the absolute uniqueness of their faith as a spiritual phenomenon that replaced a jaded, outmoded Jewish religion. Jews, on the other hand, at times have tended to identify Christianity as something entirely unique, a movement wholly unrelated to Judaism. Consequently, one often learns more about the interests of the observer than the observed when reading works dealing with this troublesome period of history.

The fact is, however, that the period in which the second Jewish temple flourished (515 B.C.E. to 70 C.E.) was one of the most prolific and creative in all of Israel's history. It was a time of unparalleled literary and theological diversity. Rather than positing a rigid contrast between biblical Israel and post-exilic Judaism, it is now recognized that numerous socio--religious communities during this era envisioned themselves as the sole legitimate expression of post-classical Israel. This work attempts to explore that new creativity by examining three essential elements of Second Temple Judaism: the history of the period, the internal diversification of Judaism into many different believing communities, and the literary contributions of these communities to the fresh theological innovation which characterized both Early Christianity and nascent Rabbinic Judaism.

The Problem of Terminology

One of the problems that naturally arises in this discussion relates to the parameters of the historical period under consideration. What terminology should be used? For example, some have opted for the title, "Interbiblical period." But just what do scholars mean by this designation? Does it suggest the period between the Bibles? If so, this implies that the Hebrew Scriptures and the Christian Bible are two separate scriptures, an assertion that many Jewish interpreters might affirm, but Christians would not want to entertain. Perhaps the most popular designation for this era would be the "Intertestamental period." But this confessionally Christian designation has no clear set of historical parameters. When exactly does the Intertestamental period begin? Obviously it opened with the close of the Old Testament era, but students of the Bible regularly debate the date when the last book of the Old Testament was written. Does the Old Testament period end with the rebuilding of the temple, the giving of the Law by Ezra, with the prophetic challenges of Malachi and the close of the prophetic age or with Daniel's apocalyptic vision of the new kingdom? The fact that the Hebrew Bible continued to be edited over much of the period under analysis accentuates this lack of historical clarity. The historical conclusion of the Intertestamental period proves equally difficult to determine. Does it end with the life of Jesus, the composition of the gospels, or the closing of the canon of the New Testament? Or does it end with the destruction of Jerusalem in 70 C.E., or perhaps the Jewish revolt in 135 C.E.? Furthermore, the designation, "Intertestamental" period can lead to the confessional assumption that this epoch is useful only as a backdrop against the world of the New Testament, with post-exilic Judaism being a scapegoat, the last degenerative phase of an old, worn-out religion. Such scapegoating diminishes the complexities of a religious community's beliefs and practices. This distancing of Christianity from its Jewish roots may be rhetorically powerful, but it is historically inaccurate.

On a positive note, the designation, "Intertestamental period," does draw together the worlds of the Hebrew Bible and early Christianity. When a student reads the New Testament, he or she enters a cosmos with many multivalent ideas and institutions that are wholly absent in the Old Testament. Instead of a Babylonian or Persian setting, Rome dominates the age. Additionally, the New Testament assumes numerous new socio-religious bodies such as Pharisees, Sadducees, Scribes, Zealots, Herodians, and Samaritans that the Old Testament does not even mention. The institution of the synagogue, the elevated role of the high priest, and a messianic obsession develop during this period. Without an understanding of this period, these developments all arise *ex nihilo* in the New Testament.

In recent decades, "Early Judaism," has emerged as a favored designation denoting the religious innovation of the period. Fortunately, such terminology recognizes that all the socio-religious groups commonly examined in this period were essentially Jewish, even the Jesus Movement and nascent Christianity. But, while it is clearly preferable to some of the designations mentioned above, the term "Early Judaism" also lacks historical clarity, and has no clear chronological anchors. Furthermore, the written texts and the social groups that defined Early Judaism are notoriously difficult to date. Furthermore, the Judean communities of the early Persian period, for example, differed greatly from those living under Roman domination in the first century C.E. The diachronic changes complicate a careful analysis of Second Temple Judaism.

Typically, scholars of Israelite history assign the dates of 1800 to 450 B.C.E. as the Biblical period, and 520 B.C.E to 70 C.E. as the overlapping designation for the Second Temple period. In addition, Hellenistic Judaism typically refers to the period between 300 B.C.E. to 200 C.E. While all designations for the period are ultimately artificial, the preference here will be to speak of the Second Temple period or the Second Commonwealth. Such a designation avoids confessional rhetoric and has definable beginning and ending dates, since the second temple was completed in 515 B.C.E. and later destroyed in 70 C.E. Admittedly, the religion of Judaism experienced enormous transformations during this time, so it is fruitless to speak monolithically as though there were a single, normative expression of that faith during the time when the Second temple existed. Such dangers notwithstanding, the designation "Second Temple period" is preferable, particularly as a heuristic device.

Determining what is meant by the terms "Judaism," "Jew," or "Jewish" constitutes an even more difficult dilemma. Even in our present historical context, Jewish identity is very elusive. Few objective mechanisms existed in the Second Temple period to determine who was, or was not, a Jew. At what point did Judaism emerge as a religion? The Greek term, *Ioudaismos* appears for the first time among Greek-speaking Jews of the Diaspora. Given the widespread diversity of Diaspora Judaism, questions arise regarding the nature of Judaism. Furthermore, who had the authority to actually determine someone else's Jewishness? One common characteristic of the Second Temple period is that radically diverse groups made very different determinations as to whether another socio-religious entity was or was not practicing Judaism. The Samaritans, for example, followed the Torah of Israel, but were seen as outsiders to the covenant by the majority of Jews. Tensions such as this have led to a growing consensus that the Greek term, *Ioudaioi*, often translated, "Jews," should more accurately be translated, "Judean," a much more geographically-oriented term, at least prior to the Hasmonean period. Basic markers of Judaic social identity did indeed emerge, such as monotheism, observance of the Sabbath, unique dietary habits, and circumcision, but the basic diversity of Judaism was thoroughgoing and far-reaching. Philo, for example, weaved Judaism within the tapestry of Greek philosophy, and spoke of the *logos* of God as a divine revelation. The authors of the Dead Sea Scrolls anticipated a final battle between the Children of Light and the Children of Darkness. Many of the priests made peace with Rome, while the Zealots advocated open revolt. Students of Rabbinic Judasim and early Christianity should not underestimate the influence and pervasiveness of such diversity.

Misconceptions About the Second Temple Period

Several misconceptions regarding the Second Temple period prevail in both the popular and scholarly literature relating to this period. The first, alluded to above, is the mistaken notion that this period is characterized as a time of four centuries of spiritual darkness. This position implicitly asserts that nothing of importance happened during this era--it was a period devoid of major events or theological significance. Proponents of both Christianity and Rabbinic Judaism have argued that the Holy Spirit's activity diminished after the last of the Hebrew prophets. Consequently, in this view, theological reflection and literary activity was on the wane. Recent studies of this period, however, demonstrate otherwise. The discovery of the Dead Sea Scrolls has brought about a new appreciation and interest in this period. Recent interest in the Apocrypha, Pseudepigrapha, Josephus, Philo, and the early traditions of Rabbinic Judaism has evoked a lively renaissance of scholarly study of this period. Now we understand that this era in the history of Judaism and early Christianity can be characterized as a time of tremendous literary energy, religious creativity, and sociological diversification. Second Temple Judaism was, to be sure, neither dormant nor orthodox.

2 Another misconception, related to the problems of terminology cited above, essentially stems from an oversimplified dichotomy between what was "Israelite" and what was "Jewish." It is impossible to demonstrate conclusively the origins of such a dichotomy. Hypothetically, one could argue that Abraham was the first Jew, or Jeremiah, Ezra, the Hasmoneans, or even Hillel or one of the other early leaders of Rabbinic Judaism. It could even be affirmed that Judaism as we now understand it did not develop until the Rabbinic period, and only then as a direct result of the destruction of the temple in 70 C.E. Most the socio-religious groups examined in this study, including Early Christianity, envisioned themselves as the legitimate expression of biblical Israel for their day, with many claiming that they alone were the sole legitimate expression of classical Yahwism. What flourished in the Second Temple Period was not a single, fixed, "normative" Judaism, but a developing, evolving religion. Nevertheless, no straight evolutionary line of the Jewish faith emerges. Consequently, it is preferable to speak of multiple Judaisms rather than a monolithic ideology that views one brand of Judaism as orthodox and

the rest as "sects." All Judaisms, consequently, competed for an audience and for the authority that accompanies broad-based acceptance.

3 A third misconception has already been touched upon. Can we say convincingly that what follows in Early Christianity and Rabbinic Judaism is something entirely new, to be contrasted with the Israelite religion of the Hebrew Bible? This facile assumption does not stand up to scrutiny. Nascent Christianity arose out of the turmoil of diverse Jewish religious expression, with each movement creatively adapting to the historical and social environment of first-century C.E. Palestine. Each of these groups flourishing in this period grappled with the dilemmas of Israel's exile, captivity, and subservience to the world powers of Persia, Greece, and Rome. There was a breakdown of a consensus as to what really went wrong, thus causing these unfortunate circumstances. Some felt idolatry in Israelite society led to the exile while others pointed to improper cultic procedures. Some groups affirmed the entire Aaronic priesthood as the encompassing authority for the reconstitution of Israel, while others argued that the Zadokites provided the only line of legitimate priestly succession. The prophet, Ezekiel, the Covenant Community at Qumran, the Samaritans, the Jews at Elephantine, and the Herodians all had different visions as to how to build the temple, indicating that there were serious concerns on the part of the Israelites as to whether the temple cult carried the blame for the low estate of the nation. Questions also arose regarding the proper cultic calendar. Israelite society traditionally followed a lunar calendar, but some influential groups of the Second Temple period adhered to a solar calendar. Could worshiping on improper feast days have been enough to cause, at least in part, the exile of Yahweh's people, and the continued domination of foreign oppressors? These issues and many more engendered numerous tensions in Israelite society. Pressures that centuries earlier had been limited to struggles between the northern tribes of Israel and the southern tribes of Judah escalated into all kinds of in-group and out-group issues. As a result, entire communities were marginalized, excluded, and oppressed, while the struggle for religious power intensified.

- Denominationalism

Overview of this Study

The purpose of this study, then, is to provide a broad overview of the history, constituent communities, and theological innovations of the Second Temple period, in light of modern scholarship. The body of this study appears in three main units. Part One explores the history of Palestinian and Diaspora Judaism from the rebuilding of the temple from 520-515 B.C.E. to its destruction in 70 C.E. Attention will be given to major factors that led to a breakdown of the uneasy consensus regarding what it meant to be Jewish. Part Two examines the increasing diversification of the believing community in Israel by highlighting the major socio-religious groups of the period. Tensions between Israel and Judah can be traced back to the earliest days of the monarchy. After the catastrophe of the destruction of the temple, institutions such as the temple and priesthood were the source of much controversy, as were Hellenistic influence, the sacred calendar, and proper observance of Torah. Many of the socio-religious groups such as the Hasadim, Samaritans, Pharisees, Essenes, Qumran Community, Scribes, Enochic Groups, Sadducees, Therapeutae, and Zealots had radically different perspectives on what it meant to be the people of God after the exile. Even early Christianity was no exception. The Jesus Movement had its roots firmly in the same debates and issues of Second Temple Judaism. The Jewish rabbi Hillel was highly instrumental in forming what would eventually lead to Rabbinic Judaism. An analysis of Jesus and Hillel provides the historical backdrop for the origins of Christianity and Rabbinic Judaism.

Part Three introduces the prolific literary creativity that characterized Second Temple Judaism, including the development of canon, the creation of the rubrics for the interpretation of Sacred Scripture, and the resultant theological developments which sprang from these new hermeneutical constructs. The discussion of canon and canonization explores the evolution and early versions of the Hebrew Bible, and includes an introductory survey of the literature of the Apocrypha. Representative examples from Second Temple literature are classified into three categories: the Bible reworked, the Bible explained, and the Bible expanded. Innovative theological developments of theodicy, messianism, resurrection and paradise, wisdom, and apocalyptic literature also are introduced.

The ultimate purpose of this present work is to serve as a reader's first introduction to the Second Temple period. Footnotes have been kept to a minimum but a bibliography appears at the close of each of the three parts. These bibliographic works provide more specific and detailed discussions of each of these topics. The limitations of this study are similar to those present in any historical analysis. Admittedly, the end result is a portrait of the religion and faith of Second Temple Judaism rather than the actual religion and faith itself. As with any portrait, some features are exaggerated while others might seem neglected. Nevertheless, the intention is to introduce the reader to the vibrancy and refreshingly creative constituencies of a most important epoch to both Judaism and Christianity.

Part One

History of the Second Temple Period

Chapter 2

Judaism Under Persian Sovereignty

The Babylonian Exile

The fall of Judah to the rapidly expanding empire of Babylon in 587/6 B.C.E. occurred after 135 years of political uncertainty. The powerful Assyrian empire destroyed the Northern Kingdom of Israel in 722 B.C.E. Only Judah remained, but in many ways, this tiny nation was not wholly independent after Israel's destruction. The larger, internationally aggressive world powers of Assyria, Egypt, and Babylon intervened frequently during Judah's last 135 years of existence. As Assyria weakened, Egypt maintained control of the western territories, ushering in a new, yet short-lived dream of pharaonic glory. Meanwhile, Babylon also grew, and a man who would later be known as Nebuchadnezzar defeated the Egyptian army at Carchemish in Syria (Jer 46:2). With that defeat, the Assyrian army was finally and irrevocably dismembered. Judah, having suffered for over a century of its precarious existence, fared even worse as Babylon's might grew to maturity. In 597 B.C.E., Nebuchadnezzar deported a sizeable contingent of Judah's population to Babylon, along with their King Jehoiachin.

> At that time the servants of Nebuchadnezzar king of Babylon came up to Jerusalem, and the city was besieged. And Nebuchadnezzar king of Babylon came to the city while his servants were besieging it; and Jehoiachin the king of Judah gave himself up to the king of Babylon, himself, and his mother, and his servants, and his princes, and his palace officials. The king of Babylon took him prisoner in the eighth year of his reign, and carried off all the treasures of the house of the LORD, and the treasures of the king's house, and cut in pieces all the

vessels of gold in the temple of the Lord, which Solomon king of Israel had made, as the Lord had foretold. He carried away all Jerusalem, and all the princes and all the might men of valor, ten thousand captives, and all the craftsmen and the smiths; none remained, except the poorest of the land (2 Kgs 24:10-14).

Table 2.1

Key Events of the Persian Period	
539 B.C.E.	Fall of Babylon to Cyrus the Persian
538-530	Reign of Cyrus
538	Cyrus Edict
	Return of Judean Exiles under Sheshbazzar
530-522	Reign of Cambysis
522-486	Reign of Darius I
520-516	Building of Second Temple
	Ministries of Haggai and Zechariah
486-465	Reign of Xerxes I
	Ministry of Malachi
465-424	Reign of Artaxerxes I
458	Return of Ezra (traditional date)
445-433	Nehemiah Repairs Walls of Jerusalem
424-404	Reign of Darius II
410	Temple of Elephantine Destroyed
405	Persians Loose Control over Egypt
404-358	Reign of Artaxerxes II
398	Return of Ezra (alternate date)
358-338	Reign of Artaxerxes III
338-336	Reign of Arses
336-330	Reign of Darius III
333	Fall of Syro-Palestine to Alexander
332	Battle of Issus
330	Fall of Persian Capital Persepolis

He replaced Jehoiachin with his uncle Zedekiah, who eventually rebelled against Nebuchadnezzar. A decade later, in 587 B.C.E., Jerusalem and its temple were destroyed, after an eighteen-month siege. A second group of exiles were taken captive to Babylon, while shortly thereafter, another contingent fled in fear to Egypt, worried about future reprisals by Babylon. Importantly, at just this point, the Deuteronomistic History (Joshua through Kings), which narrated the eventful blessings and curses of Israel and Judah from the wilderness to the destruction, comes to an abrupt end.

How severe and extensive was the deportation? The biblical record appears to paint a picture of a land of total desolation and utter destruction. The book of Jeremiah (Jer 42-44) indicates that there was virtually no one left in the land, yet counts the exiles as less than 5,000. How do we account for this discrepancy? Unfortunately, archaeology has yet to confirm the population of Jerusalem and Judah at this tumultuous time. While Jerusalem was extensively devastated, it can be safely assumed that in the smaller towns and rural countryside, the devastation was much less pronounced. What happened, in essence, was the removal of the upper strata of society--the political and religious leaders. A remnant of Judeans remained in Palestine to put their lives back into some semblance of order.

As a result of the exile, Jewish communities now continued in three primary locations: Judah, Babylon, and Egypt. Just because the temple was destroyed and many had been removed from their homeland did not necessarily mean that the worship of Yahweh ceased for these displaced Judeans. These three representative groups now sought to determine the working-out of their religious faith in light of the new social context in which they found themselves: the Babylonian faction faced geographic displacement and removal of the source of power, the Judean survivors remained in the land of promise but had no temple and no Davidic monarchy, and those who fled to Egypt experienced shifts in the level and nature of religious innovation and political organization. Consequently, life for Judean and Diaspora Judaism was more vivid and diversified than has often been portrayed.

The Rise of Persia: Cyrus and Cambysis

Babylon's imperial strength did not last long, however, and its power quickly waned. A series of kings who followed Nebuchadnezzar were not the military and organizational leaders as was their predecessor, and as a result, morale deteriorated. As Babylon's strength withered, the rapidly expanding empire of Media threatened to

replace Babylonian influence. Cyrus, a chieftain of one of Media's
vassals, defeated the Median army and imposed himself as successor to
the Median sovereigns. A master of propaganda as well as military
conquest, Cyrus marched against Nabonidus, king of Babylon in 539
B.C.E. He presented himself to the Babylonian people as a noble king,
come to restore order and security to beleaguered Babylon. The people
of Babylon eagerly received Cyrus, and the Persians secured the
conquest of Babylonia without a single casualty.

   Cyrus spent roughly 20 years establishing and expanding his new
empire. He did not dismantle the former Babylonian Empire, but
allowed most administrators to retain their posts. By proclamation,
Cyrus allowed the Jewish exiles to return to their homeland (2 Chr
36:23, Ezra 1:2-4, 6:3-5, cf. 1 Esd 2:3-7) and sponsored the restoration
of temple objects throughout the empire. The book of Ezra records the
edict:

> In the first year of Cyrus king of Persia, that the word of the LORD by
> the mouth of Jeremiah might be accomplished, the LORD stirred up the
> spirit of Cyrus king of Persia so that he made a proclamation
> throughout all his kingdom and also put in writing: 'Thus says Cyrus
> king of Persia: The LORD, the God of heaven, has given me all the
> kingdoms of the earth, and he has charged me to build him a house at
> Jerusalem, which is in Judah. Whoever is among you of all his people,
> may his God be with him, and let him go up to Jerusalem, which is in
> Judah, and rebuild the house of the LORD, the God of Israel—he is the
> God who is in Jerusalem; and let each survivor, in whatever place he
> sojourns, be assisted by the men of his place with silver and gold, with
> goods and with beasts, besides freewill offerings for the house of God
> which is in Jerusalem.' (Ezra 1:1-4)

   The biblical text depicts Yahweh directly inspiring Cyrus' policies
of religious autonomy (Isa 45:1-7). In fact, Cyrus is directly referred to
as Messiah, the only place in the Hebrew Bible where this specific term
is used of a non-Israelite. Some have speculated that Cyrus was a
monotheist, but it is impossible to determine his own religious views.
His controlling interest in the indulgence of these religious freedoms
was the dominance of the empire, not religious freedom *per se*. The
socio-religious nature of the Persian administration of *Yehud*, an
Aramaic name for the province and their designation for Judah, is
obscure. The people of Judah or Judahites, were now known as the

Yehudim, or "Jews," part of the fifth satrapy of Persia. It is also possible that Cyrus' long-term intent was the annexation of Egypt that lay to the west of Judah, making his policy of religious freedom in Syro-Palestine of strategic importance. Information on Cyrus' rise to power and the subsequent fall of Babylon is derived from several contemporary sources from Babylon. One such source is the famous Cyrus Cylinder, a baked clay cylinder about 23 centimeters long. An effective piece of Persian propaganda, the Cyrus Cylinder lays the blame of the sudden fall of Babylon at the feet of Nabonidus, its last king. Additionally, another source, the Nabonidus Chronicle, records many of the activities of this monarch who reigned from 556 to 539 B.C.E. Nabonidus, evidently, placed severe restrictions on folk religion in the empire and its satrapies, or at least did little to support it.

Cyrus, therefore, established an empire that was to last for over 200 years, whose territory was larger than any known empire of that time. A mass migration of great numbers of Judeans back to their homeland during these two centuries is improbable. There may have been a few relatively large caravans during Cyrus' reign, but even this would represent a small percentage of the overall population of Jewish settlers remaining in Babylon. Ezra-Nehemiah (originally one book in the Hebrew Scriptures) specifies a figure of 42,360 (Ezra 2:64, Neh 7:66), but data from archaeology suggests that the number was substantially less. Josephus adds that many former Judeans who lived in Babylon were unwilling to leave their possessions in Babylon (*Ant.* 11.1.3). Regardless, a slow, steady, migration over decades resulted in a progressive influx of a Babylonian-born Jewish populace into Palestine.

During this transition, there appears to have been at least three stages to the return. The governor or prince Sheshbazzar led the first return under Cyrus (c. 538 B.C.E.), probably a son of the Davidic king Jehoiachin. He, along with a group of 50,000 returnees, reportedly carried with him some of the temple treasures, and began laying the foundation of the temple. The book of Ezra records that they had to leave it unfinished due to local opposition (Ezra 1:8). A second return transpired under Darius I (c. 521 B.C.E.) led by Zerubbabel and Jeshua. They excitedly took up the task of rebuilding the temple, due to the encouragement of Haggai and Zechariah. The book of Ezra indicates that the people of Samaria asked to assist, but summarily were dismissed by the returnees. Obviously the faction that had preserved itself in exile believed that they alone had the right to determine Judean orthodoxy. Out of resentment, the "people of the land" hindered the work by appealing to the Persians to stop the construction. The plan backfired when the Persian governor wrote the emperor Darius, and not only obtained permission to continue the project, but also garnered financial support for the construction. Consequently, in 515 B.C.E., the temple was completed. A third group of returnees was led by Ezra, portrayed in the Bible as a "scribe, skilled in the Law of Moses," who brought the Law from Babylon during the reign of Artaxerxes I (around 458 B.C.E). A possible fourth stage could have occurred under the leadership of Nehemiah, in one of his several journeys to Jerusalem during the last half of the fifth century B.C.E.

Cyrus, meanwhile, died in 530 B.C.E. during combat in central Asia. In spite of his earlier decree, no temple had been completed in Judah, presumably because of the preoccupation of the returnees with establishing their own homes and livelihood, as well as tensions with the Judean-born populace. No one knows the fate of Sheshbazzar, the first post-exilic Judean governor. It is assumed that these tensions proved to be a test of his power that he was unable to overcome. The heir apparent to Cyrus from the beginning was Cyrus' son Cambysis, who had been chieftain of the vassal of Babylonia. Following the Elamite custom of marrying his sisters, Cambysis effectively removed any chance for future brothers-in-law to vie for power. As emperor, Cambysis continued the military expansion of Cyrus, but set his sights on the West rather than the East. In 525 B.C.E. he conquered Egypt, thus occupying the entire Middle East. His hold there, however, would prove to be precarious. He no sooner began to consolidate his rule in Egypt that he heard of internal dissent at home. Reluctantly, he left Egypt to quell the revolt that was taking place, and died in 522 B.C.E. on his journey back to Persia.

It is doubtful that there was much noticeable impact on Yehud due directly to the policies of Cambysis. Cambysis' military campaign from Persia to Egypt did not pass through Palestine, but he sailed from Syria to Egypt instead, largely thanks to the support of the Phoenicians. Relative silence in the historical record may indicate a peaceful exchange between the administration of Cambysis and the Yehud. Possible administrative neglect that often accompanies military campaigns may have been the biggest burden felt by the Judeans.

There is no evidence that he reversed the lenient religious policies of Cyrus concerning Yehud. Indeed, the Elephantine papyri suggest that Cambysis destroyed the native temples of Egypt but allowed the Jewish temple there to remain unharmed.

The Reorganization of the Empire: Darius I

Cyrus and Cambysis were succeeded by a ruler who reigned over Persia twice as long as both of their reigns combined. For four decades (522-486 B.C.E.), Darius I promoted the unity and stability of the empire. After killing Gaumata, a magus who had usurped the imperial throne from Cambysis while he was in Egypt, Darius consolidated his control on the empire. Much of the information on Darius presented in his official autobiography is characterized by exaggeration and polemic often associated with royal records. It appears, however, that Darius organized the empire into twenty satrapies, large territorial units, each with Persian officials loyal to himself. He did not actually create these satrapies, but structured them so that they provided effective tax revenues for the empire, while Persia itself was exempt from the taxes. He not only promoted, but also heavily financed the rebuilding of temples throughout the empire, thus endearing himself to the hearts of many of his subjects. Like his predecessors, Darius was not so much exhibiting his benevolence, or dabbling with religious tolerance, as he was effectively reconciling his centralized power with the local populace. While it has been the assumption that Darius, like Cyrus, was a monotheist, his own religious beliefs are impossible to verify. Zoroastrianism was the national religion of the Achaemenids, the official name of the Perian royal family, but history records no specific mention of Dairus' own religious beliefs. He also attempted to standardize laws, both in the provinces and the empire as a whole, thus earning the epitaph, "Lawgiver." It is likely that this juridical function had a significant influence on the development of Israel's own legal tradition. He also is credited with the introduction of coinage and a postal system, and he planned and supervised the construction of the capital, Persepolis. When Darius ultimately entered Egypt in 518 B.C.E., the Egyptian people welcomed him with open arms, and crowned him Pharaoh, indicating the stability of the empire established by Cyrus and Cambysis. Having secured Syro-Palestine and Egypt, his appetite for conquest would only intensify. The next logical opponent of Persia could only be the city-states of Greece, and conflicts with this new opponent escalated for the next 150 years.

In was because of Darius' financial support for temple building that Zerubbabel and Joshua were commissioned in 520 B.C.E. to rebuild the ruined temple of Jerusalem, a task left unfinished by Sheshbazzar. Zerubbabel was the Persian-appointed governor for Jerusalem, and Joshua was the high priest, a descendent of Zadok, presumably having been delegated the role of regulating the religious practices of the temple. It is unclear whether Zerubbabel was of Davidic descent. The books of Haggai and 1 Chronicles agree that Zerubbabel was the grandson of Jeconiah, the last king of Judah, but they disagree as to who his father was (Hag 1:1, Ezra 3:2, Neh 1:1, 1 Chr 3:9). The silence of Ezra on the issue of royal descent may have been due to the collaborative attitude toward the Persian Empire that characterizes Ezra-Nehemiah. Regardless, two prophets, Haggai and Zechariah, gave strong support to the rebuilding of the temple, enacting an exciting new era of unbridled hope for the returnees, with the promise of prosperity and blessing. While these two important prophets do not specifically refer to one another, the chronological information in their books confirms that they were contemporaries. Haggai, in particular, promised that completing the temple would usher in a messianic age of unparalleled abundance for the Jewish people. Haggai states unequivocally,

> For thus says the LORD of hosts: Once again, in a little while, I will shake the heavens and the earth and the sea and the dry land; and I will shake all the nations, so that the treasure of all nations shall come, and I will fill this house with splendor, says the LORD of hosts. The silver is mine, and the gold is mine, says the LORD of hosts. The latter splendor of this house shall be greater than the former, says the LORD of hosts; and in this place I will give prosperity, says the LORD hosts. (Hag 2:6-9)

Furthermore, both books use similar messianic language associated with the Davidic kingdom to extol Joshua and Zerubabbel (Hag 2:20-23, Zech 3:8):

> Thus says the LORD of Hosts, 'Behold, the man whose name is Branch: for he shall grow up in his place, and he shall build the temple of the

LORD. It is he who shall build the temple of the LORD and shall bear royal honor, and shall sit and rule upon his throne. And there shall be a priest by his throne, and peaceful understanding shall be between them both.' (Zech 6:12-13)

The completion of the temple would remove God's curse from the land and usher in a new era of prosperity.

It was not long, however, before this spirit of high optimism gave way to disillusionment. When the new temple was completed in 515 B.C.E., none of the glorious expressions of God's presence were present that had accompanied the completion of the tabernacle or the first temple.

There is further evidence of intensifying internal division, over much more than rebuilding the temple. The literature of Isaiah 55-66 may suggest a possible split in the Judean community between the Zadokite priestly establishment of the returnees and the Levitical priesthood of the Judeans who remained in their ancestral land. This acrimonious controversy preserved in these texts has been judged by some scholars to portray a future judgment of the righteous and wicked of Israel. Some of the texts in Isaiah 55-66 may have been written from the perspective of the oppressed minority who deemed themselves as the righteous Judean remnant, longing for a future judgment that would alleviate the present humiliation. Name-calling and imprecatory speech characterizes this literature. While the perspective of Palestinian Jewry may be preserved, these voices are drowned out in utter condemnation.

Furthermore, there is other evidence of growing diversity in the Diaspora. The book of Jeremiah describes an exodus to Egypt after the Babylonian conquest. Jeremiah exhorted these exiles to remain in Palestine (Jer 42:7-22), warning that the strong temptation of idolatry awaited those who fled to Egypt. Against his advice, however, this group of Judeans forced Jeremiah to accompany them to Egypt. It is difficult to say what might have become of this community. Did they join other displaced Judeans? Evidence of immersion in the culture of Egypt is demonstrated by hints of religious innovation present in later literature from Egyptian Judaism.

One thriving Jewish community outside Palestine during this time was a military garrison in Elephantine, Egypt. The Jews at Elephantine originally may have fled to Egypt in the sixth century B.C.E. during the oppressive reign of Manasseh, Judah's most infamous monarch. They built a temple, and followed Jewish customs of Sabbath and Passover, but also assimilated many of the local religious customs in their worship. The temple in Elephantine Egypt was destroyed in 410 B.C.E. Attempts were made to rebuild the temple by Khnum priests with the support of the local Persian governor. A series of important but fragmentary documents called the Elephantine Papyri, found in the late 19th and early 20th centuries, recount the petitions of the Jews at Elephantine to rebuild the temple. Requests sent to the priestly head in Jerusalem had initially been ignored by the Jerusalem authorities. A second petition evoked an oral response that permitted the reconstruction as long as no animal sacrifices were offered. Such sacrifice by this time had evidently become the exclusive prerogative of the Jerusalem temple.

Rising Conflicts with Greece: Xerxes I and Artaxerxes I

Darius' successor, Xerxes (486-465), was the son of Cyrus' daughter Atossa, who also happened to be the wife (and sister!) of Cambysis.   When he was 20, Darius appointed him satrap of Babylonia, the second most powerful position in the Persian Empire. Upon Darius death, Xerxes' transition to power went smoothly. Under the reign of Xerxes, however, conflicts with Greece intensified, so revenues from the empire had to be conserved to pay for military campaigns. Consequently, his religious policies substantially differed from those of his father. In addition to the dwindling revenues to support the provinces, Xerxes also destroyed temples in many of the outlying reaches of the empire. The Murashu records, cuneiform tablets from Nippur in Babylonia dating from this period, demonstrate that there were many wealthy Jews in Babylonia, but also indicate that there were hints of broader economic troubles in the empire. When Xerxes ordered the burning of Athens, it only hardened Greek resolve, intensifying these economic distractions for the Persian Empire.

While scholarly opinion varies, the book of Malachi was probably written during the reign of Xerxes. Scholars posit this date because the reduction of temple income during this time likely led to a less than enthusiastic response from the priests in the daily performance of their duties. Consequently, the general populace followed the lead of the priests. Apparently, the material prosperity predicted by Haggai never materialized. A century later, the temple was now complete, but its establishment ushered in no glorious messianic age. Judah's misfortunes were interpreted by the prophet Malachi as having been caused by the breach of the covenant, a spiritual malaise that infected God's people. Malachi reprimanded these priests for their apathy performing their duties, affirming that Yahweh still expected the best from his people. He passionately exhorts them with a portrait of their fallen state:

> What a weariness this is, you say, and you sniff at me, says the LORD of hosts. You bring what has been taken by violence or is lame or sick, and this you bring as your offering! Shall I accept that from your hand, says the LORD? Cursed be the cheat who has a male in the flock and vows to give it, and yet sacrifices to the Lord what is blemished; for I am a great King, says the LORD of hosts, and my name is reverenced among the nations. (Mal 1:13-14)

The prophet reaffirmed Yahweh's covenant love of his people, but reiterated that God demanded conduct consistent with that covenant, expecting faithfulness, honesty, and genuine worship. The message of the prophet was placed in ritual and ethical terms. The book concludes with the promise of an Elijah figure as well as a coming Day of the LORD,

> Lo, I will send you the prophet Elijah before the great and terrible day of the LORD comes. He will turn the hearts of parents to their children and the hearts of children to their parents, so that I will not come and strike the land with a curse. (Mal 4:5-6)

Malachi's message was that Israel must be properly prepared to be worthy of both of these pivotal future events.

Both Xerxes and his son Darius met untimely deaths by assassination. Xerxes was killed in a palace coup at the hands of his courtier Artabanus, who subsequently acceded to the throne. Artaxerxes, as he became called, reigned for four decades (404-358) over an empire roughly the size of his predecessor Xerxes. The economic stagnation that had begun earlier continued throughout Artaxerxes reign. Artaxerxes futilely attempted to reverse the policies of the previous administration that was unsupportive of native religious practices, but the impact of these revisions was minimal, largely due to pressing economic concerns of the empire. Protracted troubles with Greece and Egypt continued, as these countries united in sporadic revolts against the Persian Empire.

The book of Ezra-Nehemiah states that Ezra and Nehemiah both served during the reign of Artaxerxes. Ezra began in the seventh year and Nehemiah served from the twentieth to thirty-second year. Neither text, however, specifies which of Persia's three emperors named Artaxerxes is intended. Regardless, it is likely that the success of these two figures is due to a conscious imperial strategy toward Yehud. The primary purpose of such a strategy was to use Yehud to build a stable buffer between Egypt and Greece.

Dating these two important biblical figures is one of the most notoriously impenetrable problems in the Hebrew Bible. Some have argued that Ezra's reforms make more sense in light of accomplishments already made by Nehemiah's completion of the city wall. But were Ezra and Nehemiah contemporaries? In the Hebrew Bible, both Ezra and Nehemiah are said to be present at the same occasion, at the reading of the Law by Ezra (Neh 8:9, 12:36). Yet these two leaders seem to have no knowledge of one another. Oddly, the book of Ben Sira praises Nehemiah but fails even to mention Ezra (Sir 49:13). The most straightforward reading of the textual evidence in the Hebrew Bible would seem to indicate that both Ezra and Nehemiah served under Artaxerxes I, with Ezra's service beginning in 458 B.C.E. and Nehemiah following in 445-432 B.C.E. But there dating remains vexed; and no one should assume that the historical priority of Ezra is, or ever will be, definitively settled.

The book of Ezra recounts the religious reforms instituted by a priest under the civil authority of the Persian Empire who sought to teach the Law of Yahweh to the people of Yehud. The book begins with an account of Cyrus's edict for the exiles to return and rebuild the temple of Jerusalem (Ezra 1:2-4). The first six chapters of the book present an account of this rebuilding and the opposition faced by the returnees. Ezra arrived with imperial support, demonstrated by the presence of gifts from the emperor for the service of the temple. A casual reading of the biblical text conveys the impression that the land was abandoned and depopulated. He brought with him the Book of the Law (presumably, the Pentateuch) and an agenda for transforming Yehud into a purified, obedient community. This "Second Moses" was given imperial authority to appoint magistrates and judges to enforce the priestly law.

> And you, Ezra, according to the God-given wisdom you possess, appoint magistrates and judges who may judge all the people in the province Beyond the River who know the laws of your God; and you shall teach those who do not know them. All who will not obey the law of your God and the law of the king, let judgment be strictly executed on them, whether for death or for banishment or for confiscation of their goods or for imprisonment. (Ezra 7:25-26)

One of the major loci of legal enforcement was marriage, whereby Ezra attacked the problem of mixed marriages by commanding the involved parties to divorce. This penchant for legal zeal led Rabbinic tradition later to reflect that the coming of Ezra marked the historical beginning of Judaism proper.

Nehemiah's chief task was to fortify the walls of Jerusalem. Nehemiah was cupbearer to Artaxerxes the king. He was troubled over the fate of Jerusalem, particularly that the city walls still lay in ruins; so he asked the king for permission to rebuild them. The king granted his request. Nehemiah traveled under escort to Jerusalem with permission from the king to secure the necessary timber. From the outset, he encountered much opposition. Sanballat the Horonite, ancestor of the ruler of Samaria, and Tobiah the Ammonite considerably resisted Nehemiah's project. The memoirs of Nehemiah (Neh 1:1-7:5) appear in the first person, and provide a first-hand account reconstructing the city walls, as well as the opposition by Sanballat and Tobiah. Sanballat, incidentally, established a dynasty of governors over Samaria that may have endured until the time of Alexander. Discoveries at Wadi ed-Daliyeh provide evidence of numerous written contracts from around 300 B.C.E. that mention names of his family line. Other descendants are mentioned in the letters of Elephantine and the Samaritan Papyri.

Like Sheshbazzar, Zerubbabel, and Joshua, Nehemiah and Ezra appear for a time, then abruptly recede into obscurity in the biblical account. Josephus records that Ezra died at an old age and was buried in Jerusalem. The ministries of Ezra and Nehemiah, therefore, are instrumental in that they provide a glimpse of the constitution and concerns of the Jewish community of the restoration. Religious interests revolved around the Law of Moses, and in particular, the elements of temple, sacrifice, and separation of the believing community from foreign influence. Strict conformity to these stark lines of inclusion and exclusion was prerequisite to being in good standing with the legitimate community of Yahwistic faith. The paradoxical combination of universal monotheism and nationalism fueled the fires of internal diversification of the Jewish communities in the Second Temple period. Not merely the Gentiles, labeled as outsiders, but even fellow Jews were increasingly disenfranchised by their more powerful countrymen.

The Decline of the Persian Empire: Darius II to Darius III

Recurrent colonial unrest, costly and fruitless military campaigns, and internal corruption characterized the late Persian period (423-333 B.C.E.). At this point in its history, the Persian Empire was so radically different from the stable giant which preceded it that archaeologists normally refer to two separate periods, Persian I (539-450 B.C.E.), and Persian II (450-332 B.C.E.) The rulers of this last century, Darius II (423-404), Artaxerxes II (404-358), Artaxerxes III (358-338), Arses (338-336), and Darius III (336-330), struggled to maintain order in a turbulent empire facing increased tensions in its colonies. To an outside ovserver of the mid-fourth century B.C.E., the Persian Empire appeared likely to stand triumphant for centuries to come. While the prestige and power of these emperors remained strong and many rebellions of Greece and Egypt failed, yet continued colonial unrest plagued the empire and sapped its strength. Persia simply could not control the vast expanses of her domain forever. Internal conspiracies abounded as well. When Artaxerxes I died, his son Darius II assumed the throne, and piece-by-piece, the empire tragically began to disintegrate. The Greeks continued to be problematic, and he quickly lost control over Egypt in 405 B.C.E. Artaxerxes II succeeded Darius II and reigned for 45 years. By this time many of the satrapies also were beginning to revolt. Trouble fomented at home as well. Artaxerxes II's son Darius, was caught in an attempted coup and killed, and Artaxerxes II ultimately died, still grieving because of the unfortunate murder of another beloved son, Arsames. He was succeeded by Artaxerxes III, and he too was assassinated. His son, Arses, was a mere puppet king (338-336). When he died a victim of drought, his entire household was killed, and the throne was given to Darius III. He met the same fate as many of his immediate predecessors, being assassinated when the Greeks destroyed the Persian capital Persepolis in 330 B.C.E. This final blow brought about a decisive end to the great Persian Empire.

It is impossible to determine which literature of the Hebrew Bible was written during the final one hundred years of the Persian period. The stories of life during the exile recounted in the books of Daniel and Esther have settings during the Persian period, but no definitive consensus regarding a specific date when these two books were written exists. Both books, however, address a common question. How should Jews live among the seductive attractions of foreign culture? Esther risked her life in order to safeguard the future posterity of the Jews living in the Persian Empire. Daniel chose to face death rather than submit to the idolatrous practices of a foreign despot. Likewise, the apocryphal books of Tobit and Judith, short stories of devout Jews who elected to do right, even at the risk of peril and death.

The influence of Persia on early Judaism too often has been underestimated, especially when compared to that of the Greeks. It is true that during the Persian period some of the earliest Hellenistic influences were felt in Yehud. Indeed, this was the classical Greek age. It was the age of the Parthenon, of the philosophers, Socrates, Plato, and Aristotle, the poets Sophocles and Euripedes, and the historian Herodituts. Yet, this period was not lacking in Persian influence. One lasting effect of the Persians was the spread of the Aramaic language. Under Persia, Aramaic became the language of culture and diplomacy. The late Hebrew of the Bible contains numerous Aramaisms, and the Book of Ezra uses Aramaic when quoting official Persian documents. Although Hebrew did not die out altogether, Aramiac was spoken commonly throughout Yehud. The imperial protection of the Persian period shielded Yehud from outright religious persecution, a practice the Greeks would follow for at least a century.

Persia realized too late that the kingdom of Greece was a power to be reckoned with. A newcomer to the world stage became ruler of Macedon after his father Philip had been assassinated. With breathtaking speed, he crossed into Asia Minor in 334 B.C.E. with 35,000 troops and defeated the Persians in Asia Minor at the battle of Granicus. Shortly thereafter, Darius III suffered another severe defeat at the battle of Issos, and because Persia was unable to defend the Syro-Phoenician coast and Egypt, this newcomer also met little resistance there. Babylon and Susa quickly fell, ultimately bringing an end to the empire that had lasted for over 200 years, when the capital Persepolis was surrendered and destroyed in February, 330 B.C.E. Darius III was assassinated, marking the tragic end of the Achaemenid Empire founded by Cyrus. This recent arrival on the world stage would cataclysmically transform the empire and the lives of the Judean settlers for centuries to come. His name was Alexander.

Chapter 3

Alexander and the Rise of Hellenism

Alexander the Great

The pervasive and lasting influence of Greek culture on Syro-Palestine
was due primarily to the personality and brilliance of one individual--
Alexander the Great (356-323 B.C.E). While Greeks and other
Westerners had been traveling through the East as traders and
merchants for years, during the Persian period the independent city-
states of Greece united on numerous occasions to drive off the
onslaughts of the mighty Persians. Athens itself had been put to the
torch during the reign of Xerxes, but the persistent Persian occupation
would in the long run prove unsuccessful. Alexander's father, Philip,
united the fiercely independent people of Macedonia, Thrace, and Ionia
to form an uneasy alliance that would ultimately cause the Persians
great distress. Philip of Macedon was assassinated in 336 B.C.E.
leaving Alexander to assume leadership at the youthful age of 20.
Alexander's worldview extended beyond Macedonia to the Greek city-
states of the south.

At first, the Greek leaders of these city-states were skeptical of his
abilities, but in a brief period of two years, Alexander demonstrated
convincingly that he had firm control of the coalition. Two years later,
Alexander moved his armies east, defeating the Persian forces at the
river Granicus. The Battle of Issus in 333 B.C.E. marked a major
turning point in relations between Greece and Persia. The Persians
would never reverse the momentum from Alexander's overwhelming
victory here. He immediately turned southward, defeating Tyre and
Gaza in 332 after relatively short sieges. The rest of Syro-Palestine
reluctantly submitted to his suzerainty, and Egypt fell shortly

thereafter. There, Alexander founded his namesake city of Alexandria in 331 B.C.E.

Table 3.1

Major Events of the Greek Period	
333-323 B.C.E.	Alexander's Campaigns
332	Tyre and Gaza Captured
331	City of Alexandria Founded
330	Fall of Persepolis
323	Death of Alexander
323-301	Consolidation of Ptolemaic Rule over Palestine
301-198	Ptolemaic Period
198-167	Seleucid Period
167	Desecration of the Temple by Antiochus IV

Josephus records that as he passed through Palestine, Alexander sent a letter to the high priest demanding tribute and supplies for his army. The high priest, Jaddua, responded that he had given his word to Darius III not to bear arms against him and would not abandon his promise as long as Darius was alive. Angered, Alexander determined that he would make an example of Jaddua to teach the Jews a lesson. The high priest then called the people of Jerusalem to prayer for God's direction. In a dream, God revealed that he should take courage and open the gates of the city to Alexander. Obedient to this vision, the priest led a procession of his people, all clothed in white, to meet Alexander outside the city to proclaim their allegiance, after which Alexander honored the priest, entered Jerusalem, and offered a sacrifice in the temple. The priest showed Alexander the prophecy of Daniel that declared that the Greeks would destroy the empire of the Persians. Extremely pleased by what he interpreted as the divine endorsement of the Jewish deity, Alexander asked what they would desire of him. The Judean leaders requested that they be free to follow the laws of their ancestors and be excused from paying tribute on the seventh year. Alexander was more than pleased to provide such a concession.

Most authorities agree that the historicity of the above account by

Josephus is highly suspect. However, the Talmud also records a similar meeting between the high priest and Alexander. Yet even this account has its glaring inconsistencies. For example, it contains the name of a high priest, also mentioned in Nehemiah 12:11, 22, who functioned a century after the campaign of Alexander. Consequently, some meeting between the High Priest and Alexander likely took place, but presumably it was merely an opportunity for the priest to pledge allegiance as a vassal to the dominant power.

After victories over Syro-Palestine and Egypt, where Alexander was proclaimed pharaoh, he then spearheaded the campaign eastward, achieving victory at Gaugamela, Susa, and Ecbatana. Ultimately, in 330 B.C.E., Alexander conquered Persepolis, the former capital of the Persian Empire. Uncharacteristically, he burned the city, presumably out of vengeance for the burning of Athens earlier by Xerxes. By 326 B.C.E., when his army had reached as far as India, his troops absolutely refused to go any further.

To the outside observer, Alexander appeared as though he was destined to reign for a long time to come. But Alexander died in the East just seven years later at the age of 32. His legacy, which was lasting indeed, would not be because of a long and fruitful reign. Alexander's chief legacy was his gift of Greek ecumenism: Greek language, culture, and government. Possibly a result of the influence of his boyhood tutor, Aristotle, Alexander sought to unite East and West by the establishment of the Greek polis and its language in the cities of the East.

Alexander's conquests erased many of the national boundaries, so unification of language was a rapid and logical result. *Koine* or common Greek became the language of the marketplace. As people, (regardless of their native tongue) learned Greek, the literature, philosophy, and religion of Greece became accessible to the entire empire. In Alexandria, Egypt, common Greek language also became the impetus for the translation of the Hebrew Scriptures into Greek, subsequently called the Septuagint. The city had a library of over 700,000 volumes, so it is not surprising that the love of study, the arts, and literature strongly influenced the hundreds of thousands of Jews residing there.

Greek culture also permeated the rest of the occupied territories. The Greeks brought theater, logic, music, dress, and sports to the East. It was in the East, then, that cultures met and ideas metamorphosed, calling traditional Jewish values into question. In this hybrid culture of West and East, some Jews sought to become more westernized as others saw Hellenism as a threat to their very existence as God's people. The Greek city-state, or *polis*, was also a huge success. It was perhaps the most effective means by which Hellenism was propagated. Alexander habitually settled large numbers of Greek citizens at strategic places he conquered. He arranged for mass marriages between his troops and the natives of the land. In some cases these new cities began from scratch, and in others he transformed existing communities into thriving examples of the Greek cultural ecumenism he advocated. The Greeks founded about 30 of these cities in Palestine alone. Autonomy and liberty characterized these new Hellenistic communities. Citizens voted, and of course, this elaborate system provided a remarkable tax base for the empire.

The Ptolemaic Period

The death of Alexander in 323 plunged the conquered lands of Greece into decades of uncertainty. Alexander died with no legal heirs, so a council of his leading generals divided his empire among themselves. A long struggle for succession to the throne resulted. Judah's strategic location in particular made it a vortex of political and military tension. Two of these generals are important for this study: Antigonus, the governor of Asia Minor, and the Egyptian governor Ptolemy. Antigonus immediately sought to gain control of Babylonia, then governed by another general, Seleucis. Seleucis was defeated and fled to Egypt. Ptolemy, who had consolidated his power by hijacking Alexander's body in route to Macedonia and burying him in Alexandria, gave the newly arrived Seleucis an assignment as one of his leading military commanders. Antigonus turned southward, attacking a number of cities in Syro-Palestine before problems in Asia Minor caused him to return there, leaving Palestine under the authority of his son Demetrius. Taking advantage of the power vacuum, Ptolemy and Seleucis marched northward: Ptolemy gained control over Palestine and Seleucis returned to Babylon. Josephus records that in the process, Ptolemy attacked Jerusalem on the Sabbath, at first, pretending that he wanted to offer sacrifices there. When the Jews were reluctant to fight on the Sabbath, he obtained an easy victory and relocated Jerusalem's many Jews to various parts of Egypt (*Ant.* 12:3-10). Ptolemy's victory was short-lived, however. Antigonus returned less than six months later and forced Ptolemy to flee to Egypt.

Meanwhile, Seleucis organized a coalition to defeat Antigonus. Ptolemy, who was to aid him in the attack, marched into Palestine and took control of a number of cities, but never appeared to assist Seleucis in the battle. So when Antigonus was defeated at the battle of Ipsus in 302 B.C.E., Palestine officially fell under Seleucid, rather than Ptolemaic, authority. Weakened by battle with Antigonus, Seleucis' armies were not strong enough to drive Ptolemy from Palestine, a region Ptolemy and his descendants then would control for more than a century (301-199 B.C.E.). Consequently, Ptolemy and Seleucis became the bitterest of enemies.

The control of Palestine by Ptolemy brought a period of relative peace to the Jews. During the twenty years in which Antigonus and Ptolemy struggled over Palestine, armies had entered the region five times. Because Egypt now enjoyed peace, its leaders were able to divert financial resources from the military to other directions. While Seleucis laid legal claim to Palestine, Ptolemy actually possessed it. He made Alexandria the capital of Egypt in 313 B.C.E. and converted it into one of the most progressive and magnificent cities of the world.

Upon the death of Ptolemy I, however, the peace that had been established abruptly ended. From 274-198 B.C.E., during the reigns of four more Ptolemies, there were five major wars between Egypt and Syria over Palestine. The Seleucids, who laid claim to the territory, refused to relinquish these territorial claims to the Ptolemies. Though there were interludes of tentative peace, enduring peace was to prove elusive. During the reign of Ptolemy II, sources report generous treatment of the Jews. Ptolemy II, nicknamed Philadelphus, or "sister lover," because he married his full sister, promoted the spread of Hellenism, particularly the patronage of science and the arts. The Letter of Aristeus records that during Ptolemy II's reign the translation of the Hebrew Bible into Greek was authorized for the numerous Jews who lived there. His son, Ptolemy III (Euergetes) instituted a generous program of temple building, which enhanced the city of Jerusalem. It was not long, however, before the tide began to turn against the Judeans. The last two Ptolemies who ruled over Jerusalem, Philopater and Epiphanes, were weak, self- indulgent rulers. Third Maccabees 1-2 colorfully describes a growing instability, particularly related to how the Ptolemies curtailed Jewish rights during this period.

Antiochus the Great and the Seleucid Period

Ultimately, in 202 B.C.E., the Seleucid leader Antiochus III, "the Great," defeated Egypt and took possession of Syria and Palestine. Even though the Jews experienced social and economic prosperity under Egyptian rule, Palestine suffered. The numerous battles waged on her soil, particularly in the latter years of Ptolemaic hegemony, proved debilitating. In many respects the Jews welcomed the Seleucid victory, hoping that a lasting peace would provide some stability in the land. Antiochus actually reduced taxes and the Jews hoped that some degree of independence could be possible under Seleucid control.

Seleucid rule (198-167 B.C.E.) began in Palestine at roughly the same time as a new power began to rise upon the international scene. Rome had recently defeated Hannibal, and now turned its attention to Philip of Macedon, one of Hannibal's allies. Philip had negotiated a treaty with Antiochus III, who in spite of some early successes, was eventually soundly defeated by the Romans at Ephesus in 190 B.C.E. Antiochus signed a treaty with Rome in 188 B.C.E. which stipulated that his son, Antiochus IV, had to go to Rome as collateral on tribute levied of fifteen thousand talents due in twelve annual installments. Consequently, the territories under Antiochus' control became little more than sources of tax revenue for Rome. When Antiochus III tried to plunder the temple at Elam for much needed revenues, the city's enraged locals assassinated him.

Antiochus IV remained in Rome while Seleucis IV succeeded Antiochus the Great. In order to raise the impossible, but necessary tribute, Seleucis raised taxes in Syro-Palestine. He appointed Heliodorus as prime minister to oversee the collection of the revenue, a task he began promptly by plundering the temples of the Seleucid vassals. The temple in Jerusalem, inexplicably, was not pillaged until twenty years later. 2 Maccabees' sensationalistic account records that Heliodorus was prevented from being successful in this task by several supernatural beings who beat him and turned him away.

> But when he arrived at the treasury with his bodyguard, then and there
> the Sovereign of spirits and of all authority caused do great a

manifestation that all who had been so bold as to accompany him were astounded by the power of God, and became faint with terror. For there appeared to them a magnificently caparisoned horse, with a rider of frightening mien, and it rushed furiously at Heliodorus and struck at him with its front hoofs. Its rider was seen to have armor and weapons of gold. Two young men also appeared to him, remarkably strong, gloriously beautiful and splendidly dressed, who stood on each side of him and scourged him continuously, inflicting many blows on him. (2 Macc 3:24-26)

Whatever the actual circumstances might have been, Heliodorus returned from Jerusalem empty handed. He ultimately murdered Seleucis IV in 175 B.C.E.

Prior to his death, Seleucis began to fall behind in his payments of tribute to Rome. As a result, Rome insisted Seleucis send his own son, Demetrius, to Rome as a replacement for his uncle, Antiochus. Rome correctly perceived that Seleucis would be much more likely to keep current in tribute if they held his son hostage instead of his uncle. Regardless, it was not long after the release of Antiochus IV that Seleucis was murdered, providing an opportunity for Antiochus to assume the throne as its legal heir. Antiochus moved quickly, defeating Heliodorus, and acceding the Seleucid throne, as well as acquiring the nickname, Epiphanes, meaning "God manifest."

Antiochus' incarceration in Rome gave him a deep appreciation for two things: Roman organization and power. His goal, evidently, was to restore the Seleucid Empire to its former greatness by adopting the organizational practices of the Romans. Known for his highly unpredictable nature, Antiochus could be incredibly generous or fiercely tyrannical. While in Antioch, for example, after his release from Rome, he would wander the streets incognito, playing practical jokes on his friends. The Roman historian Polybius gave him the unflattering nickname, "Epimanes" (madman). For the Jews, Antiochus' instability was perplexing: he could simultaneously be strongly democratic, highly energetic, and incredibly bloodthirsty.

The unpredictable nature of Antiochus' leadership also elicited equally unpredictable responses on the part of the Jewish inhabitants of the empire. Understanding the role that internal rivalry among the Jews played in Antiochus' rule of Jerusalem, requires recognition of the role played by the Oniad and Tobiad families of Jerusalem. Josephus mentions that during the Ptolemaic period, roughly eighty years earlier, Onias II, the high priest in Jerusalem, decided to quit paying tribute to the Ptolemies (*Ant.* 12:186-236). Onias probably gambled that Seleucis II would defeat the Ptolemies. This surmise was not to be the case, however. Seleucis was defeated and Ptolemy III immediately dispatched a delegation to Jerusalem to regain tribute from Onias II. At this time, Joseph, the son of another leading family, the Tobiads, approached Ptolemy and argued that Ptolemy should make a division of powers between religious and political leaders. Ptolemy agreed and appointed Joseph as the political sovereign. This appointment effectively stripped the high priest, Onias, of his political power. An internal struggle ensued between the Oniads and the Tobiads that would continue for years to come.

The Tobiads were supporters of the Hellenists while the Oniads, secure in their roles of the high priesthood since 320 B.C.E., were anti-Hellenistic supporters of the Torah. The Tobiads wielded greater economic and political clout, and around 200 B.C.E., when they saw the locus of power shifting from the Ptolemies to the Seleucids, switched their allegiance to the Seleucids. When Antiochus Epiphanes assumed the throne in 175 B.C.E., Onias III was the reigning high priest in Jerusalem. The Tobiads had made a series of accusations against him, so he had to travel to Antioch to clear his name. While he was away, his own brother, Jason, a pro-Hellenistic Zadokite priest, offered Antiochus IV a generous increase in tribute from temple revenues if he were made high priest. Won over by Jason's bribe, Antiochus appointed him high priest in place of his brother Onias III. He served from 175-172 B.C.E. Together, Antiochus and Jason established a gymnasium and instituted a policy of Jewish and Greek syncretism whereby Jews in Jerusalem could even become citizens of the empire (2 Macc 4:7-22). It is likely that Jason had the support of the Tobiads in assuming this role. Jason soon was to be supplanted, however, by Menelaus, another pro-Hellenist who offered even more money, an additional 300 talents, to assume the high priesthood in 172 B.C.E. This, not surprisingly, was highly offensive to conservative Jews, since Menelaus was not even of priestly descent. To add insult to injury, Menelaus was forced to steal from the temple treasury to pay for the bribes. Jason, meanwhile, mistakenly heard that Antiochus had died while on a military campaign in Egypt, so he used this perceived demise as an opportunity to attack Jerusalem and besiege Menalaus in the citadel of the city (2 Macc 5:5). Antiochus, however, returned in fury to Jerusalem in 169 B.C.E., looting the temple and killing many of the city's inhabitants. This surprising return forced Jason to flee permanently to Sparta, which effectively extinguished the unrest caused by Jason's challenge to Menelaus' authority. Menelaus then served as priest until 162 B.C.E. The irony of this entire exchange is that Onias, Jason, and Menelaus, the highest-ranking religious officials in Judea, were direct political appointees of a foreigner.

Two years after Menelaus was appointed as high priest, Antiochus IV set out again to invade Egypt, defeating Ptolemy VI in 170 B.C.E. (1 Macc 1:16-19). After several stunning preliminary victories, he was met outside of Alexandria by a Roman delegation led by C. Popilius Laenas. Popilius gave Antiochus an ultimatum to stop his aggression against Egypt immediately. The Roman historian, Polybius, records that Popilius drew a circle in the sand around Antiochus and humiliated him by forcing him to make a decision before he stepped out of the circle. Antiochus relented, but on the way back through Jerusalem, evidently took his frustrations out on the city and plundered the temple on the way through Jerusalem (Dan 11:30). Some time later, Apollonius, his primary tax collector, entered Jerusalem on the Sabbath with 22,000 troops and attacked the city. Antiochus slaughtered many civilians, demolished the city wall, and enslaved many of the remaining women and children.

Antiochus' motives for such a harsh attack were a combination of many things. Surely his embarrassment and rage over his confrontation with Popilius fueled the crackdown, but there was more to it than that. Antiochus was a zealot for Hellenization of the conquered Greek territories, who saw the wide net of Hellenism as a catalyst to unite many people under his authority. His suspicion of the pro-Egyptian influences on the Jews also must have played a part in fueling his hostility.

Regardless, Antiochus quickly prohibited all Jewish rites, forced many of the Jews to eat forbidden foods, and forbade anyone from having a copy of the book of the Law. Circumcision was forbidden and in cases where women illegally had their sons circumcised, the children would be killed and hung around the necks of their horrified mothers. Antiochus also redistributed the monies of the temple treasury to Rome. The final straw was broken in 167 B.C.E. when Hellenists offered a pagan sacrifice to Zeus on the altar of the temple in Jerusalem (1 Macc 1:54, Dan 11:31, 12:11). The sanctuary was renamed the temple of the Olympian Zeus. Jews were forced to participate in a ritual honoring the Greek god Dionysus, and some may have even resorted to temple prostitution (2 Macc 6:2-7). Essentially, Antiochus made it impossible for Judeans to observe the most foundational tenets of Judaism. This "abomination of desolation" would turn out to be a mistake of epic proportion for Antiochus, leading to the Jews openly and defiantly resisting the Seleucids. This resistance is known to history as the Maccabean revolt.

Chapter 4

The Maccabean Revolt and the Hasmonean Dynasty

The Maccabean Revolt

Antiochus' policy of obliterating Yahwism proscribed most of the religious practices that defined Judaism. The Sabbath, Scriptures, sacrifice to Yahweh, circumcision, and the Jewish religious festivals were all forbidden. The temple had already been desecrated. The Jews reacted in three diverse ways to these events and policies. Some, who saw great value in Hellenism, reluctantly acquiesced; some were martyred rather than yield to the rulings of the king; and others resorted to armed resistance.

The book of 1 Maccabees recounts the story of an aged priest named Mattathais, who lived in the village of Modein, northwest of Jerusalem, with his five sons, John, Simon, Judas, Eleazar, and Jonathan. Antiochus' soldiers admonished Mattathias to offer a pagan sacrifice by presenting swine flesh to Zeus. When Mattathias refused, another citizen of the village stepped forward to offer the sacrifice. Mattathias immediately killed his fellow villager as well as the monarch's representative and defiantly pulled down the pagan altar.

This act of defiance and subsequent call to arms birthed an open revolt, and Mattathias and his family fled to the Judean wilderness for security. The Hasadim, a non-Zadokite group of pious followers of the Torah, supported this nascent resistance. Meanwhile, Syrian soldiers discovered a group of Jews illegally worshipping on the Sabbath day. When these devout Israelites refused to comply with the Syrian law that prohibited worship on the Sabbath, the Syrians slaughtered the entire party. The refusal of the Jews to fight on the Sabbath contributed to their demise, as the Jews became especially easy prey on the Sabbath. This catastrophe forced Mattathias and those who were in hiding in the Judean desert to make a controversial but necessary decision. Vastly outnumbered, Mattathias and his colleagues resolved that they would *violate* the laws of the Torah in order to *protect* the Torah. From this point on, they would fight on the Sabbath. The Hasadim, consequently, split along the lines of idealists and pragmatists, creating a division that would become more pronounced as Maccabean victories ensued.

The Hellenizers, Jews who supported the policy of the annulment of Jewish religion, were the immediate target of Mattathias and his family. Forced circumcision, destruction of Greek altars, and the murder of those who cooperated with the Syrians characterized this agenda. When Mattathias died in 166 B.C.E., his son Judas, nicknamed Maccabeus ("The Hammerer") assumed leadership of the revolt. Judas was so charismatic that his nickname would eventually be given to the entire movement. He had over 3000 soldiers at his disposal, coming primarily from rural and village areas. With them he conducted guerrilla warfare from the remote stretches of the desert against the more numerous Seleucids. Early on, the Seleucids did not appear to take the Judean threat seriously, but an alarming string of Maccabean victories eventually forced Antiochus to dispatch his prime minister, Lysias, to Palestine to track down Judas and kill him. The Syrians, however, were no match for these desperate Jewish guerillas, who were fighting on their own terrain and who were motivated by fervent religious zeal. The book of 1 Maccabees provides an account describing how Judas defeated Lysias in three separate campaigns and negotiated a settlement whereby he would cease hostilities if Antiochus would reverse his policies proscribing Judaism and grant amnesty to those involved in the previous rebellion. The Syrians reluctantly agreed to his demands. When Lysias left the country, however, Judas turned his attention to fellow Jewish Hellenistic sympathizers. He took control of Jerusalem, with exception of the citadel of the Acra, and set out on an agenda of the religious restoration of the temple. In 164, the temple was rededicated and the first sacrifice in three years was offered to Yahweh. The feast of Hanukkah, properly known as the Festival of Lights, was instituted to commemorate this rededication. Josephus states that the dedication took place exactly three years to the day from when Antiochus originally had desecrated the temple. Antiochus IV, meanwhile, died that same year while battling against the Parthians.

Taking advantage of this opportunity, Judas now laid siege to the citadel (acra) of the city in 163-2 B.C.E. The Hellenizers who occupied the citadel appealed to Antiochus Epiphanes' successor, Antiochus V, for help. He dispatched Lysias again, but now with stronger, professionally trained forces. Lysias laid siege to Jerusalem during the sabbatical year when, in keeping with the Law, no crops had been planted. Because of the shortage of produce, the citizens of Jerusalem were in no state to endure a protracted siege. Before long, however, Lysias learned of trouble at home in Antioch, so it was in the best interest of both parties to reach another agreement. If the Syrians would restore conditions in Judah as they had been prior to the accession of Antiochus IV, then the Jews would discontinue the revolt (2 Macc 11:16-21, 27-33).

Meanwhile, Demetrius, the son of Seleucis IV, was released from his custody in Rome. He immediately overthrew Antiochus V., subsequently executed Menelaus, the high priest who had purchased the office from Antiochus IV, and appointed Alcimus, a non-Zadokite of priestly descent, as the new high priest. This execution effectively removed pro-Hellenistic Jews from the political landscape, though the internal diversification of the Jewish community still persisted. While Alcimus had the support of most of the Jews, the Hasadim, that conservative Jewish political party, accused him of offering pagan sacrifices. In a horrifying and surprising turn of events, he immediately had 60 of these opponents, his own countrymen, executed.

Judas, consequently, found himself in opposition to Alcimus, who still had the support of the majority of Jews. It is possible that Judas desired the high priesthood for himself. Regardless, Judas went to war against Alchimus' supporters. The Syrians got wind of the renewed warfare, so Bacchides, the governor, sent Nicanor to spearhead the Syrian attack and to consolidate Alcimus' priesthood. Some of the local Jews joined Nicanor, but Judas ultimately won the battle. Nicanor was killed, and Judas occupied Jerusalem. The Jewish supporters of Judas declared the day a holiday called the day of Nicanor.

Ever the freedom fighter, Judas too was a quick study in the ways of international diplomacy. Judas sent an emissary to Rome to establish an alliance and negotiate a treaty (2 Macc 11:34-38). As a result of this potential alliance with their enemies, Syrian determination to eliminate Judas intensified. The Syrian governor Bacchides rapidly deployed a large army that threatened to overwhelm the much smaller Jewish forces barely exceeding 3000 men. As Bacchides approached, most of Judas' troops abandoned him, leaving only about 800 soldiers. Since religious persecution no longer existed, the followers of Judas were less likely to risk loss of life. In any regard, following a brave but futile struggle, Judas died in battle in c. 161 B.C.E.

Jonathan, Mattathais' youngest son, then succeeded his brother Judas. Jonathan, like his brother, faced considerable opposition from his own people, many of whom were happy to be under Seleucid rule, so long as their religious freedoms remained intact. Because of these pressures, Jonathan ultimately made peace with the Syrians around 155 B.C.E., bringing a period of relative stability to the region. Jerusalem remained under the Hellenist control, and Jonathan established himself at Michmash, north of the city.

Alchimus the priest died and, according to Josephus, was not replaced by the Seleucids for seven years. The situation in the Seleucid capital of Antioch can only be described as highly chaotic, with numerous rival claimants to the throne and one power struggle after another. The Syrian king, Demetrius, worried by the threat of a new claimant to the Syrian throne, Alexander Balas, was looking for support from the citizens of Judea. Balas, on the other hand, who had nothing to lose and everything to gain, wanted the support as well. Both Demetrius and Balas offered generous concessions to Jonathan. Demetrius proposed that the Jews could now legally assemble and equip an army. In addition, Jonathan would be recognized as the leader of the Jews and all hostages taken during the previous rebellions would be released. Balas, on the other hand, raised the ante. He offered everything Demetrius had promised, plus he offered to give Jonathan the prestigious title, "friend and ally of the King." But most importantly, he promised Jonathan the office of the high priesthood. The irony here must not be missed. The Maccabean revolt had in its roots, at least in part, Judean opposition to the Syrian practice of the appointment of the high priest by Antiochus Epiphanes. Now, the son of Mattathias willingly accepted appointment by an individual who claimed to be Antiochus' own son. With Jonathan's help, Balas ultimately defeated Demetrius I and became the new leader of the Seleucid Empire. Jonathan was present at Alexander Balas' wedding to Cleopatra where his high priesthood was reconfirmed and he was given the governorship of Judea.

Jonathan was of priestly descent, but was not a Zadokite. For some of the Jews, his geneaology was a serious problem. The Damascus Document from the Dead Sea Scrolls, for example, portrays a non-Zadokite "wicked priest" whose questionable status compelled the community to withdraw from the established temple cult to the Judean desert. This struggle of the legitimate priestly line was a controversial issue for most of the Second Temple period. Jonathan supplied the troops as promised and began to expand his territory. Alexander Balas reigned only a short while (150-145 B.C.E.) until Demetrius II replaced him. Jonathan eventually was killed by another claimant to the Seleucid throne, the disreputable Tryphon, in 143 B.C.E.

Jewish Independence and the Hasmonean Dynasty

Jonathan's brother Simon became the new leader of the Maccabean resistance movement. He was the last surviving son of Mattathias. In many ways, Simon seems to have adopted some of the best leadership qualities from his two brothers; the military acumen of Judas, and the diplomatic abilities of Jonathan. Due to the strength of the movement and Simon's diplomatic negotiations with Demetrius II, he secured political freedom from the Seleucids in 142 B.C.E. (1 Macc 13:41-42). Simon had gained what his father and brothers before him had merely dreamed of, Jewish political independence. Simon abolished the Seleucid calendar, adopted a Jewish calendar in its place, and boldly began dating documents from the beginning of his reign as high priest over the new nation. The next year he expelled foreign troops from the citadel in Jerusalem and renewed alliances with Rome. For the first time in 34 years, the Jews were able to select their own high priest. The choice of Simon surprised no one, but since Simon was a non-Zadokite, the Jews reached a compromise that he should only remain priest until a proper priest could be appointed (1 Macc 14:41). Like a royal monarch, he wore a purple robe and a gold clasp, but carefully avoided the politically dangerous title of king. History, then, refers to Simon and his successors as the Hasmoneans, since one of Mattathias' ancestors was named Hashmonay. The Hasmoneans controlled Judea from 142-63 B.C.E.

Table 4.1

Hasmonean Rulers of Judea (142-37 B.C.E)	
Simon	142-134 C.E.
John Hyrcanus	143-104
Aristobulus I	104-103
Alexander Jannaeus	103-76
Salome Alexandra	76-67
Aristobulus II	67-63
John Hyrcanus II	63-40
Mattathias Antigonus	40-37

About this time, the Parthians captured the Seleucid monarch, Demetrius II. The next leader of the Seleucid throne, Antiochus VII, demanded the return of all the territory Simon claimed as his own, particularly the Acra, Gaza, Joppa, and all other fortified cities (1 Macc 15:2-9, 26-35). Naturally, Simon refused, so Antiochus invaded Judah, laying siege to Jerusalem. Now advanced in age, Simon appointed his two sons John and Judas to be his military commanders. The initial defeat of the Hasmoneans was resounding. To make matters worse, Simon was assassinated, due to the treachery of his son in law, Ptolemy. Ptolemy had been governor of the city of Jericho and presumably had aspirations of usurping the high priesthood. He hosted a banquet for Simon and two of his sons, Judas and Matthias. After the wine flowed freely and the guests were sufficiently drunk, he signaled for his supporters to assassinate Simon, and to capture Simon's widow.

Simon's son, John Hyrcanus, was not present at the banquet. After strengthening alliances with the Romans, he assumed the throne, and his first order of business was to punish Ptolemy. Josephus reports that John Hyrcanus attacked the fortress where Ptolemy resided, who promptly responded by torturing John's mother at the top of the citadel in full view of her son (*Ant* 13:230-235). In an attempt to capitalize on John Hyrcanus' distractions, Antiochus VII used the opportunity to resume his attack against Judea, besieging Hyrcanus in Jerusalem. Feeling the pressure of the siege and unsure of Roman military support, John Hyrcanus negotiated an agreement whereby all the territory outside Judea gained by Judas and Jonathan was given up and tribute was restored. Although Antiochus VII destroyed the walls of Jerusalem, he permitted temple worship to continue. His victory, however, was merely temporary. The Parthians killed Antiochus in 129 B.C.E., effectively ending forever the dominion of the Seleucids.

John Hyrcanus took advantage of the chaos that so characterized the Seleucid Empire during the last half of the second century B.C.E. He reestablished Jewish independence and nurtured his alliance with the Romans, using mercenary armies to build Judea into an important military power. He laid siege to the city of Samaria and demolished it. He destroyed the temple on Mt. Gerazim built by the Samaritans, extended his territory to Samaria and Idumea, and forced circumcision upon his defeated foes. Revenues for these military exploits came mainly from temple taxes. He also was known as a grave robber, who primarily plundered the wealth of foreign kings in their tombs, but also the tomb of King David. He even minted his own coins.

In spite of these successes, Hyrcanus' popularity at home was always in question. Much of the populace admired him, for he brought international notoriety to Judah, made numerous conquests, and established several alliances with major powers. But others strongly resisted his aggression. Josephus reports that John Hyrcanus had once been close allies with the Pharisees but a falling out occurred that resulted in mutual hostility when he shifted support to the Sadducees (*Ant* 13:299-292). The Pharisees had challenged the legitimacy of his lineage, since his mother had been a prisoner of the Seleucids. He was not a Zadokite and his violation of the tomb of King David created great hostility from the more conservative parties of Judaism.

Hyrcanus ruled from 134-104 and was succeeded by his son, Judas Aristobulus I, who reigned only one year. Prior to his death, Hyrcanus had made provisions for Aristobulus to assume the high priesthood and for his widow to assume leadership over the government. Aristobulus, however, promptly put his own mother in prison, killed one brother, and cast two others in prison. His mother eventually starved to death in captivity. Even though he was not a descendant of David, Aristobulus took for himself the title of king, perhaps the first Hasmonean to do so. He expanded the kingdom north to Iturea and the northern part of the Galilee, forcing males in his kingdom to be circumcised. Aristobulus I died of a mysterious disease, and his widow Salome Alexandria immediately freed the brothers he had imprisoned. She then married one of them, Alexander Jannaeus, in accordance with the biblical practice of levirate marriage, where a brother was commanded to marry a childless sister-in-law. She then decreed him to be the new ruler and high priest. She and Alexander undertook their marriage in order to consolidate the throne, knowing full well it was prohibited for those in the priesthood.

Alexander Jannaeus then assumed the throne, continuing the military expansion of the kingdom including the Transjordan and the Philistine plain. While he was a formidable ruler internationally, his reign was a disaster at home. In addition to his questionable marriage, he demonstrated utter contempt for his office as high priest. On one occasion during the Feast of Tabernacles in 95 B.C.E., he poured the holy water on the ground instead of the altar. The enraged worshippers at the temple promptly pelted him with citrons and caused such a stir that he retaliated by killing thousands of his countrymen (*Ant.* 13: 13.5). Later, following an unsuccessful military campaign in Arabia, he returned to outright civil war at home. His own subjects had invited the Seleucid monarch Demetrius III, to lead the attack against the Hasmonean ruler. After a long struggle, Alexander checked the insurrection. He then crucified 800 Jews who had fought alongside Demetrius as punishment, first forcing them to witness the massacre of their own wives and children. Ironically, some of the most violent actions of the Second Temple period against the Jewish people did not come from foreign oppressors, but instead were instigated by an individual who was both a Jewish monarch, and a high priest.

Alexander Jannaeus was in ill health for the last years of his reign. Prior to his death, he named his wife Salome Alexandra, who had been married to Aristobulus, his successor. Oddly, Josephus does not explain why his wife was awarded the throne and not his son. Since many of her opponents were of the party of the Pharisees, Salome diffused tensions by naming some of the Pharisees as her advisors. Since as a woman she could not serve as high priest, Salome appointed her son John Hyrcanus II to the office. While Hyrcanus II served as high priest, her other son, Aristobulus II, was busy building up an army and fortifying the land. Upon her death in 67 B.C.E., Hyrcanus II, supported by the Pharisees, struggled with Aristobulus II, who had the military advantage and was supported by the Sadducees. Due to this military advantage, a compromise of sorts was reached whereby John Hyrcanus II would retain considerable wealth, but would seek neither the high priesthood nor the monarchy, and Aristobulus would become both king and high priest. Whether Rome preferred Hyrcanus is uncertain, but nevertheless, it interpreted these actions as hostile. Hyrcanus was persuaded to back out on his part of the agreement and join the Idumean ruler Antipater in marching against Aristobulus. Both sides appealed to the Roman general Pompey for support. This internal rivalry would ultimately lead to the demise of the Hasmonean dynasty. Aristobulus would be the last king of an independent Israel, as Israel's hegemony would last less than a century.

In spite of all its chaos and bloodshed, the Hasmonean dynasty was not without its successes. These priest-kings transformed Judea from a small isolated Persian sub-province to a much more formidable geographic entity. Simon conquered Gezer (1 Macc 13:43-48) and John Hyrcanus annexed territories east of the Jordan. Aristobulus I extended territory northward to southern Lebanon. Alexander Jannaeus conquered several sites, including Gaza, Dor, the Golan Heights, and the Gilead. The charisma of the Maccabean family and their tenacity in relentlessly pursuing political goals led to unexpected, albeit short-lived, success. The Hasmoneans' combination of political power and religious ideology forced entire populations to be converted to Judaism. John Hyrcanus, for example, converted the Idumeans while Aristobulus I did the same to the Itureans. The historical record seems to suggest that such blatant proselytism may have backfired, as some of the earliest examples of anti-semitism were reactions against Hasmonean purges against those perceived as collaborating with paganism.

Strangely, some of the shining successes of the Hasmonean revolt were what originally attracted the attentions of Rome. Rome had been steadily growing in power and had been historical allies of the Judeans. This alliance, however, was not destined to endure. Pompey, was charged with the task of leading the campaign in Syro-Palestine. A party of Jews, presumably led by the Pharisees, approached Pompey, and asked him to abolish the Hasmonean dynasty. It is ironic that the Romans originally entered Judean politics by invitation. In 63 B.C.E., Pompey marched into Jerusalem and laid siege to the temple, where Aristobulus had fled for protection. Some of Aristobulus' supporters refused to surrender, and had taken refuge in the temple. After a three-month stalemate, Pompey entered the temple, including the Holy of Holies. He carried Aristobulus and many Jews captive to Rome to be displayed among other spoils of battle.   At a single stroke, this act toppled the Hasmonean dynasty.   When the Roman monarch, Herod the Great, assumed the throne in 38 B.C.E., he eventually killed every member of the Hasmonean line, extinguishing the dynasty forever.

Chapter 5

The Roman Domination of Judea

The Early Years of Roman Domination

After the conquest of Jerusalem, Pompey returned to Rome. For the next forty years, the Roman Empire experienced one of its greatest periods of internal upheaval. As a newly annexed territory of the Roman province of Syria, Judah--or Judea as it now was called by Rome--was no longer as strategically located as it had been in the past. It lay on the eastern border of the Roman Empire. While its geographic proximity to Egypt in terms of trade with Asia Minor heightened Palestine's strategic value, Rome's ongoing battles with the Parthians, who now controlled Mesopotamia, sharply reduced the possibility of added income for the empire due to stable trade between Mesopotamia and Egypt. As a new vassal state, the Judeans began to pay tribute to Rome. In order to bridge the culture gap between West and East, the Romans typically used vassal kings who could understand the peculiar ways of Eastern cultures that were less hellenized than those of the West.

Initially, the triumvirate of Julius Caesar, Pompey, and Crassus ruled Rome. Crassus, who ruled over Syria, was also responsible for the territory of Judea. Crassus promptly plundered the temple treasuries under his control, including the temple in Jerusalem, to finance his bloody war with the Parthians. In 51 B.C.E., he was killed in battle with this powerful foe. Meanwhile, civil war broke out in Rome between Julius Caesar and Pompey. Pompey was defeated, and fled to Egypt for protection, only to be assassinated by Ptolemy XIII shortly after his arrival in Egypt. Julius, who had been pursuing Pompey, entered Egypt in 48 B.C.E. Perhaps he should have been

grateful for Ptolemy's intervention, but because of conflicts between
Ptolemy XIII and Caesar's sister, Cleopatra, he chose to align with
Cleopatra, besieged Alexandria, and killed Ptolemy XIII.

Table 5.1

Major Events of the Roman Period	
63 B.C.E.	Pompey Invades Jerusalem
40-37	Parthian Invasion of Rome
37-4	Herod the Great Reigns over Palestine
20	Reconstruction of the Temple Begins
6-4	Birth of Jesus of Nazareth
4 B.C.E.-6 C.E.	Archelaus Reigns over Judea
4 B.C.E.-39 C.E.	Herod Antipas Rules over Galilee
6 C.E.	Coponius becomes First Roman Procurator
18-36	Caiaphas as High Priest
26-36	Pilate Serves as Procurator
30	Crucifixion of Jesus
40-44	Herod Agrippa Rules Palestine
66-70	First Jewish Revolt
70	Destruction of Jerusalem Temple by Titus
74	Fall of Masada
95	Rabbi Gamaliel II appointed Patriarch by Rome
132-135	Second Jewish Revolt

After his resounding victory over Pompey and Egypt, Julius Caesar
returned to Rome, which was rife with political unrest. The escalation
of internal national strife resulted in his murder by Cassius and Brutus
on March 15, 44 B.C.E. His murder further fueled the ongoing civil
war that would not end until Octavian became the sole ruler of Rome
and the Syrian provinces in 31 B.C.E. In the interim, this internal
unrest caused Rome to loose its focus on Syria and Palestine. Taking
advantage of the internal preoccupations of Rome, the Parthians seized
Syria and Judea. This territory would not be regained until 37 B.C.E.
when the Roman Senate appointed Herod King of the Jews, recaptured
Jerusalem.

The Judean political climate was equally turbulent during the period from Pompey's conquest of the city in 63 B.C.E. to the ascension of Herod the Great. Antipater, the Roman procurator, had appointed Hyrcanus II as high priest, though virtually everyone knew that Antipater was the power behind the office. The Jews absolutely detested Antipater. Although his mother was a Jew, his father was an Idumean, descending from the biblical Edomites, thus historically one of the Jews' most menacing enemies. Antipater supported Rome without wavering. When emperors changed, he had the political acumen to convince these newly established leaders of his unwavering support. He was not nearly so careful to cultivate compatible relationships with the Jews, which went from bad to worse. Between 56 and 53 B.C.E., several revolts by remnant forces of the Hasmoneans resulted in disaster for the Jews. These revolts cost the lives of over fifty thousand Jewish insurrectionists. True to form, in the civil conflict between Julius Caesar and Pompey, Antipater originally sided with Pompey, but immediately transferred his allegiance to Julius Caesar after Pompey's defeat by sending massive amounts of aid to Caesar in Egypt. Upon Caesar's return through Judea, the grateful emperor confirmed Antipater's selection of Hyrcanus II as high priest, and proclaimed Judaism a lawful religion in the empire. Rome exempted the Jews from military service, withdrew many Roman troops from Judea, and remitted taxes already paid to the empire. This Roman clemency, however, did not prevent Antipater from levying his own taxes on the Jews, which did little to bolster what meager support he had from the local populace.

Herod the Great

When the senate murdered Julius Caesar in 44 B.C.E., Antipater the Idumean took advantage of the unstable situation by appointing his two sons as governors. His oldest son, Phasael, became governor of Judea, and he named his twenty-five year old son, Herod, governor of Galilee. The appointment in Judea went unchallenged, but the independent-minded, nationalistic Jews of Galilee resisted Herod's appointment. Herod quickly dealt with the situation by capturing and killing Hezekiah, a Zealot who instigated the resistance. Tensions continued to escalate to the extent that in 41 B.C.E. a Jewish delegation met with the new emperor, Mark Antony, to impeach Herod and Phasael. Herod, master politician that he was, so impressed Antony that the Roman leader made both he and his brother tetrarchs.

Antipater, Herod's father and former procurator, had been fatally poisoned less than a year after the assassination of Julius Caesar. The Parthians once again saw these occurrences as opportunities to take advantage of the internal preoccupations of Rome. They invaded Syria and Judea, and appointed Antigonus as high priest of Judea and Galilee. Antigonus, in turn, captured Phasael, tetrarch of Galilee, and Hyrcanus II, the former high priest. Herod fled to Rome, and by means of suitable bribes eventually gained appointment as King of the Jews. Shortly thereafter, in 39 B.C.E., Rome responded to the Parthians by dispatching Herod, who subsequently captured the two pivotal fortresses of Joppa along the coast and Masada on the Dead Sea. The Parthians finally were defeated by Rome a year later and in 37 B.C.E., Herod laid siege to Jerusalem and reconquered the city in a bloody battle. He carried Antigonus to Antioch, and had him beheaded. Consequently, Herod began a reign that would last 30 years.

Herod was an enigma as a ruler. On one hand, he was a remarkable success. Despite opposition from the Jews, from the stubborn remnants from the Hasmonean dynasty, and even from his own family, he was able to fashion a kingdom of considerable import and establish stability as a ruler. On the other hand, he was one of the most despicable Hellenistic monarchs Judea would ever know, maintaining his reign by fear, intimidation, and oppression. The Jews detested Herod just as they had his father, both because he was an Idumean and because of his Hellenistic leanings.

Early on, Herod earnestly endeavored to win the favor of the Jewish people. To appease Hasmonean factions from the period of Israel's independence, he sought for and secured the release of the former Hasmonean high priest Hyrcanus II from the Parthians. He allowed Hyrcanus a place of honor in his own court. He also entered into a marriage alliance with Mariamne, a Hasmonean princess and granddaughter of Aristobulus II. The problem, however, was that in order to establish this alliance, he first had to divorce his own wife, Doris. Not surprisingly, this political maneuver did little to win favor among the conservative Jews. He initially refused to have his own image inscribed on his coinage, and even appointed Hananel as high priest and successor to Hyrcanus II rather than assume the role himself, as would have been his rightful privilege as a Roman monarch. He further reduced taxes on two occasions, once when Judea was experiencing a severe famine.

Perhaps his most magnanimous effort to win favor among the Jews was the rebuilding of the temple in Jerusalem. Herod had entered into a large number of massive building projects, including the port city of Caesarea on the Mediterranean coast. He named it Caesarea Maritima in honor of Octavian, now celebrated as Caesar Augustus. Caesarea became the capital of Roman government in Palestine for the next six hundred years. Recent excavations have revealed an immense harbor, as well as palaces and other public buildings, a hippodrome, theater, an advanced sewer system, and an aqueduct. He rebuilt Samaria and gave it a new name, Sebaste. At Jericho, he built a magnificent winter palace, and he established a network of fortresses at Masada, Herodium, Caesarea, Alexandrium, Hyrcania, and Macherus. All in all, he built or rebuilt nearly 15 cities during his reign.

The temple, however, was his most ambitious project of all. The second temple was now 500 years old, and had been damaged many times in some of the nearly 200 battles that took place in Jerusalem between its restoration and the time of Herod. In order not to violate Jewish Law, he had all the stones quarried outside the city, and even trained 3000 priests to do all of the construction work. The builders pulled down the old structure and within a year and a half, the new temple proper was completed, but on a raised platform which made it one of the highest parts of the city. It took another eight years to complete the outlying courts and enclosures. So ambitious was this project that the temple was not fully completed until 64 C.E., long after Herod's death. Built in Hellenistic style, the Herodian temple was so richly embellished that its white marble glistened, appearing like a snow-capped peak from a distance. One of the great ironies of Herod's life is that the individual the Jews most hated left the most indelible mark on the face of Israel. The spectacular temple and the network of fortresses including Masada and Herodium are some of the most impressive constructions in the Near East.

The New Testament portrays Herod as the jealous king, who upon receiving the report that the king of the Jews had been born in Bethlehem, massacred all the baby boys under age two in the town who resided there. While his infanticide is unknown outside the New Testament, such an action would not be out of character with Herod.

For instance, he had his Jewish wife Mariamne and her mother Alexandra executed for alleged treason.   He executed any insurrectionists who challenged his authority--even two of his own sons.   Violent activities such as these led Augustus to quip, "I would rather be Herod's pig (*hys*) than his son (*huios*)." In Herod's final years, he was gravely ill, and had given up hope of ever winning the favor of the Jews. He began to allow the practice of inscribing an eagle, the Roman symbol, on his coinage, and hung a gilded eagle on the gate of the Temple.   Premature news of his death led two leaders of the Pharisees, Judas and Matthais, to call for the destruction of the image at the Temple.   Herod retaliated by burning these two leaders, along with many of their followers at the stake.   The next night, there was an eclipse of the moon, interpreted by the Pharisees as God's displeasure over the death of these two martyrs.   Aware of Jewish hatred, Herod commanded his sister, Salome, that upon his death, many Jewish leaders should be gathered to his palace at Jericho and killed, so that the other Jews would mourn at Herod's death. It was a command, however, that Salome wisely did not obey.   Nevertheless, upon Herod's death in 4 B.C.E., riots did indeed break out in Jerusalem that led to the deaths of roughly three thousand Jews.   Evidently, the accumulated frustrations kept in check by Herod's brutality were released when he died. Many of the leaders of the rising unrest had very diverse goals, which did little to strengthen a unifying opposition or to establish any lasting rebellion.

The New Testament Era

After his death, Herod's kingdom was divided among his three sons: Antipas in Galilee and Perea; Philip in the Golan Heights; and Archelaus in Judea, Samaria, and Idumea.   Before Herod's successors could even be considered, a rebellion broke out in Judea, which Archaelaus, brought the revolt to a bloody conclusion.   Of all of Herod's sons, Archaelaus gained the worst reputation.   He scandalized the Jews by marrying his brother's widow and eventually was deposed by the Roman emperor and banished to Gaul.

Philip was the only one of the brothers who enjoyed a long and peaceful reign.   There seems to have never been a single complaint of harsh judgment against him by the people.   He named its capital

Caesarea, in honor of the emperor. In order to distinguish it from his father's Caesarea Maratima, it was designated Caesarea Philippi. The population of the region was primarily Gentile, so when he had the image of Caesar imprinted on his coinage, hardly a protest was uttered. When Jesus and his disciples needed to escape the pressures and controversies of Judea and Galilee, they often retreated to the area of Philip's domain. Recent archaeological excavations at Sepphoris, for example have demonstrated that the city was a thoroughly Roman polis, though with a sizeable Jewish population.

Antipas, more than any of his brothers, followed in the footsteps of his father Herod. He was a tyrannical leader, a prolific builder, and a stable ruler who endured the tenures of several emperors. It is Antipas who is mentioned in the Gospels as receiving the rebuke of John the Baptist because he divorced his first wife, daughter of the Nabatean king, and married his brother's wife, Herodias. Following the infamous dance of Salome, Herodias' daughter, Antipas promised Herodias anything at his disposal. Already seething over John's condemnation of their relationship, Herodias demanded the Baptist's head, which Antipas promptly if reluctantly provided. His conniving nature is evident as Jesus referred to him as "that fox" (Luke 13:32). The Gospels further record that Jesus had a face-to-face encounter with Antipas. Herod happened to be in Jerusalem for the feast of Passover when Jesus was arrested and brought before the Roman procurator Pilate. The New Testament indicates that Herod had heard of some of Jesus' miracles and was possibly hoping to see some of them. Whether Pilate hoped to avoid the messy issue of condemning Jesus, or if he was paying Antipas the professional courtesy of giving him the opportunity to pass sentence on Jesus is not known. In any regard, Antipas returned Jesus to Pilate without taking any action.

From 6 to 66 C.E., a series of less than able military governors ruled Judea. These governors ruled in Caesarea, had Roman troops at their disposal, and had as their purpose collecting taxes and keeping the peace for the empire. The first of these rulers, Copernius, ordered a census under the direction of Quirinius, governor of Syria, which may be the census referred to in Luke 2:2. If so is poses one of the more difficult problems in dating Jesus' birth. Regardless, Jews reacted with hostility to the census, possibly because of the prohibition of David's census in the book of Kings. A riot broke out under the instigation of two Zealots, Zadok and Judas of Gamala, who were immediately executed by Rome. Although the revolt was crushed, its ideals lived on throughout the movement of the Zealots. This revolt is mentioned in Gamaliel's speech in the book of Acts (Acts 5:34).

After two relatively unknown procurators, Augustus then appointed the first Judean procurator, Valerius Gratus. He significantly increased taxes because the residents of Judea lodged an appeal to Tiberius against his appointment. The results of the appeal are not known. Valerius Gratus appointed four high priests during his reign (15-26 C.E.). Two of these, Annas and Caiaphas, are mentioned in the New Testament. The relative frequency of the appointments highly suggests that Valerius Gratus was taking bribes to place key people in the high priesthood.

The next procurator, Pontius Pilate (26-36 C.E.), also is mentioned in the New Testament. His sensitivity to Jewish culture was less than noteworthy. Early in his reign, he entered Jerusalem with his troops bearing Roman standards with the image of the emperor, immediately offending Jewish sensibilities. He initially agreed to meet with the offended crowds of Jews, but instead surrounded the crowd with his soldiers and ordered them to disperse. The Jews stubbornly refused, even to the point of baring their necks and offering to die rather than live under the emperor's image. Disappointed, Pilate retreated from the confrontation.

Josephus relates the brutal side of Pilate is related in several accounts. On another occasion, Pilate wanted to build an aqueduct into Jerusalem, so he callously confiscated temple treasuries to do so. When mobs protested, he ordered his soldiers to infiltrate the crowd incognito. At the appropriate signal his soldiers turned upon the instigators of the protest, slaughtering the multitudes. Pilate also ruthlessly silenced a group of Samaritans when crowds appeared on Mt. Gerazim to listen to a prophet who claimed to have found the lost vessels of the temple. The statement in Luke 13:1, "Galileans whose blood Pilate had mingled with their sacrifices," fits appropriately with Pilate's violent reputation. It was Pilate who gave the order for the crucifixion of Jesus. His decision to keep the inscription, "the King of the Jews," over the protests of the Jewish leaders points to these same combative traits. Pilate's harsh treatment of his subjects, and the altercation with the Samaritans in particular, led to an imperial summons before Tiberius to consider accusations against him. Tiberius died, however, before Pilate arrived in Rome. A number of legends exist regarding the fate of Pilate, but nothing of his demise is known.

After the death of Tiberius, Caligula became emperor. Prior to the reign of Caligula, the Romans permitted Jewish citizens to be exempt from taking part in pagan rituals. The Jews, however, presented a difficult dilemma for Rome. The Jews were unlike most other native religions of the empire, they refused to worship any other god but theirs, denied the divinity of the emperor, and prohibited images in public places. Caligula resolved to reverse this policy. Riots erupted in Alexandria, Egypt, pitting Jews against gentiles, and ended in much bloodshed. He even commanded his subordinates to erect a statue of the emperor in the temple in Jerusalem. The Roman governor of Syria, Publius Petronius, delayed the implementation of Caligula's command long enough for Agrippa II, a personal friend of the emperor, to rescind his edict. Herod Agrippa I, grandson of Herod the Great, and son of Aristobulus, had spent a great deal of time in Rome and was a close friend to Caligula, so he received the tetrarchy vacated upon the death of Philip, as well as the title, "King." This appointment aroused the jealousy of his sister Herodius, who persuaded her husband Antipas to ask for royal status, too. Agrippa beat Antipas to the punch, sending a delegation with accusations against his rival, which lead to Herod Antipas' banishment to Rome. Consequently, Caligula added Galilee, Perea, and eventually Samaria, Judea, and Idumea to Herod Agrippa's territory.

Table 5.2

The Roman Emperors	
Augustus	27 B.C.E.-14 C.E.
Tiberius	14 –37 C.E.
Caligula	37-41
Claudius	41-54
Nero	54-68
Four Emperors	68-69
Vespasian	69-79
Titus	79-81
Domitian	81-96
Nera	96-98
Trajan	98-117
Hadrian	117-138

Herod Agrippa had rather warm relations with the Jews. Agrippa's intercession with Rome led to the delivery of the Jews. When his daughter wanted to marry a Gentile, he required that his future son-in-law be circumcised according to Jewish Law. Agrippa is mentioned in Acts 12:1-3 as the person, eager to please the Jews, who was responsible for the death of the early Christian leader, James, son of Zebedee. The book of Acts tells with satisfaction of Agrippa's death (Acts 12:20-23).

The new emperor, Claudius, returned Judea to the authority of a procurator, again located in Caesarea. The Book of Acts mentions two of these, Antonius Felix (52-60), and Porcius Festus (60-62), as procurators to whom Paul appeared after his arrest. The corruption and despotism of these and others nourished anti-Roman sentiment, which was already running high. Such resentment would eventually erupt into open revolt under the leadership of the Zealots and various other revolutionary parties.

In an effort to conciliate the Jews, Rome appointed Herod Agrippa II as sovereign and religious leader of the Jews. Rome failed to realize, however, that his scandalous personal life led the Jews to hate him, much like they detested the Roman procurators who preceded him. It is this Herod before whom Paul appeared, after his arrest in Acts 26.

The Jewish Revolt and the Destruction of Jerusalem

It is difficult to fully delineate the exact circumstances leading up to the First Jewish Revolt of 66-74 CE. A series of incompetent Roman administrators, combined with the social tensions between the rich and the poor, and between urban and rural constituencies, and then summed with the diverse array of messianic expectations exacerbated the tense climate already present. Jewish unrest in Caesarea was one of the leading causes of the revolt. Nero's policies had relegated Jews there to second-class status, but the sacrifice of a bird in front of the Caesarean synagogue prompted the Jews to send a delegation to the procurator Florus, along with a sizeable contribution. Florus gratefully received their bribe but did nothing to help their plight. Furthermore, Florus pilfered the temple of 17 talents, ostensibly as a gift to Rome. Completely outraged, the Jews took up a mock public offering for the procurator, to which he responded by sending his troops to loot and kill many in the city. The Jews' resistance was a surprisingly strong demonstration of force, and as a result, Florus' troops withdrew.

Meanwhile, Eleazar, the son of the high priest and captain of the temple guard, persuaded the priests to accept no offerings from aliens. This refusal ultimately resulted in the abolition of the daily sacrifice on behalf of Caesar, an act tantamount to a declaration of war. Concurrently, the Zealots attacked and captured Masada, killing all the occupying Roman troops. They also burned the palace of Agrippa II and the high priest, and drove the Romans from the fortress of Antonia and from Jerusalem.

In response to uprisings in Galilee, Cestus Gallus, governor of Syria, marched on Judea, assuming he could easily quash the rebellion. When he entered Jerusalem, he immediately became convinced that he could not be victorious, and was forced to withdraw, abandoning much of his equipment. In the north, the Sanhedrin elected Flavius Josephus as commander of the Jewish troops in Galilee, but he squandered nearly half a year feuding with the local populace. The Zealots were very suspicious of Josephus, thinking he maintained concealed loyalties to Rome. One such zealot, John of Gischala, failed in an attempt to assassinate Josephus.

Word of the continuing problems in Palestine finally reached the emperor, so Nero ordered Vespasian to restore order in Palestine. Two legions joined with the legion of Vespasian's son, Titus, then withdrawn from Egypt to besiege Jotapata in 67 C.E. In spite of an oath of suicide taken by the Jewish troops under Josephus' command, Josephus recognized his plight, and fled to surrender to Vespasian. Later, in Rome, Josephus predicted that Vespasian would be the next emperor. The Roman army quickly overran Galilee, and John of Gischala fled to Jerusalem.

In 68 C.E., as Vespasian neared Jerusalem, Nero committed suicide in Rome. Vespasian suspended his siege to return to Rome and claim the throne, and the Jews saw the suspension as divine deliverance. This two-year hiatus should have allowed time for the revolutionaries to reorganize themselves, establish provisions, and build lasting fortifications. Instead, the rebels devoured one another in militant infighting, and various revolutionary factions battled bitterly. With Vespasian on the throne, Vespasian's son Titus assumed command of the rekindled attack and shortly thereafter Jerusalem fell (in August of

70 C.E.) to his legions. To commemorate this victory, two arches were erected in Rome. One was destroyed in the 14th-15th century. The other still stands today, as the Arch of Titus. Josephus states that Titus wanted to preserve the temple as a monument to the generosity of Rome, but his soldiers acted against his orders and set the Holy of Holies on fire. While it is true that the Romans typically didn't destroy the temples of conquered peoples, most historians raise doubts about the account of Josephus regarding the destruction of the temple. Regardless of who or what actually precipitated the fire, the temple was destroyed, and much of Jerusalem with it. In one last defiant expression of power, immediately after the destruction of 70 C.E., the Romans mandated that the half-shekel tax originally sent to the temple treasury in Jerusalem would now go to the temple of Jupiter in Rome.

The last zealot outpost of the Jewish revolt was Masada. Herod had fortified this military outpost by adding a casemate wall, defense towers, cisterns, barrack, and palaces. Josephus recounts the story of the Zealots last stand against Rome. In 72 C.E., Flavius Silva, the Roman Governor, marched with the 10th legion to begin an extended two-year siege. Eleazar ben Ya'ir commanded the Zealot outpost on Masada's pinnacle. Over the course of the siege and in spite of innumerable difficulties, Silva built a massive ramp and battering ram, and finally breached the wall. What he did not realize was that on the night before the Romans broke through the wall, the Jewish insurrectionists had taken a vow of suicide, unwilling to afford Rome any victory. Josephus reports that each male killed his family. Ten remaining individuals were chosen by lot to kill the others. One remaining survivor was to set fire to the place and then kill himself. When Silva breached the wall and entered the fortress, he found over 960 dead Zealots, and all the supplies, foodstuffs, and valuables burned.

The basic elements of Josephus' story of Masada are confirmed by archaeology, including the Roman camps, siege works, and the ramp. Yigael Yadin, the excavator of Masada, even discovered eleven lots with names inscribed. Whether these names were the eleven mentioned in Josephus narrative cannot be determined. Other details, however, do not match up with the account of Josephus. Josephus indicates the zealots took all their possessions and built one large fire, thus leaving the Romans with nothing to show for their victory. Archaeological evidence indicates, however, that there were actually many fires, as might be expected when a conqueror destroys a city. Instead of the foodstuffs being burned, a relatively large supply of food and supplies were excavated. Additionally, skeletons were excavated in caves, indicating that some of the survivors may have hidden there to escape the fate of their countrymen.

The Second Revolt

Unrest in Palestine subsided for nearly sixty years. What scholarship commonly calls the Second Jewish Revolt began in 132 C.E. when the emperor Hadrian made public his plans to rebuild the city of Jerusalem as a gentile city and give it a new name, Aelia Capitolina. An integral part of Hadrian's plans was to prohibit particular elements of the Jewish religion, especially male circumcision. The Jews responded by defiantly declaring their independence, and following a new leader, Shimon bar Kosiba, who was given the punning nickname, "Bar Kochba," or "son of the star." This designation derived from the messianic Balaam prophecy that a star would proceed from Jacob and rule over Israel (Num 24:17-18). The goal of the Jewish revolt was nothing less than expelling Rome and recreating an independent Jewish kingdom. Rabbi Akiba, one of the forerunners of Rabbinic Judaism, went so far as to proclaim Shimon bar Kosiba the Messiah. For a short time Bar Kosiba's forces regained Jerusalem and restored sacrifices at the site of temple ruins. Unlike the First Revolt, the Second Revolt was completely messianic in nature. The Jews even minted coins with the inscription, "year one of the restoration of Israel."

Hadrian ordered Senerus to put down the revolt by means of massive punitive measures. He succeeded, but at tremendous cost. Over 850,000 lives, including many of the Roman forces, were lost in the rebellion. Bar Kochba and Rabbi Akiba also were killed. Josephus reports that so many Jews were sold into slavery that prices plummeted to only slightly more than what one might pay for a horse. Hadrian rebuilt the city as he had promised, renaming it Aelia Capitolina. Jews, in fact, were forbidden to enter the city at all. Both circumcision and Sabbath worship also were forbidden. Where the temple once stood, an altar to Jupiter, the chief god of the Roman religion, was erected. The city that once touted the capital of Israel and home of Yahweh's temple was now a gentile bastion for the Roman Empire. Rome succeeded in the destruction of an economic and political center, depopulated the homeland of the Jews, and left Jews in the Diaspora in disarray. From this time on, Jerusalem ceased to be a significant source of trouble to the empire. Both Jews and gentiles interpreted the outcome of the Second Revolt as an utter failure. Hindsight being what it is, later Rabbinic literature would be much more reluctant to adopt such a lofty title for the leader of the failed second revolt, bar Kosiba, and so instead bequeathed the dubious epithet, Bar Kozeba, meaning, "Son of the Lie."

Bibliography

Part One: History of the Second Temple Period

Ackroyd, Peter. *Exile and Restoration*. Philadelphia: Westminster: 1968.

Berquist, Jon. *Judaism in Persia's Shadow: A Social and Historical Approach*. Minneapolis: Fortress Press, 1995.

Briant, Pierre. *From Cyrus to Alexander: A History of the Persian Empire*. (2 vols.) Winona Lake, IN: Eisenbrauns, 1998.

Carter, Charles E. *The Emergence of Yehud in the Persian Period: A Social and Demographic Study*. Journal for the Study of the Old Testament Supplement 294. Sheffield: Sheffield Academic Press, 1999.

Cohen, Shaye J.D. *From the Maccabees to the Mishnah*. Philadelphia: Westminster Press, 1987.

Dandamaev, Muhammad A. *A Political History of the Achaemenid Empire*. Leiden: E.J. Brill, 1989.

Davies, W.D. and Louis Finkelstein, eds. *The Cambridge History of Judaism*. Cambridge: Cambridge University Press, 1984.

Feldman, Louis H. and Reinhold Meyer. *Jewish Life and Thought Among Greeks and Romans: Primary Readings*. Minneapolis: Fortress Press, 1996.

Grabbe, Lester L. *Judaism from Cyrus to Hadrian*. (2 vols.) Minneapolis: Fortress Press, 1992.

Jagersma, Henk. *A History of Israel from Alexander the Great to Bar Kochba*. Philadelphia: Fortress Press, 1986.

Luker, Lamontte M., ed. *Passion, Vitality, Foment: The Dynamics of Second Temple Judaism*. Harrisburg, PA: Trinity Press International, 2001.

Modrzejewski, Joseph Mélèze. *The Jews of Egypt: From Rameses II to Emperor Hadrian*. Princeton: Princeton University. Press, 1995.
Peters, F.E. *The Harvest of Hellenism: A History of the Ancient Near East from Alexander the Great to the Triumph of Christianity*. New York: Simon and Schuster, 1970.
Russell, D.S. *Between the Testaments*. Philadelphia: Fortress Press, 1960.
Smith, Daniel L. *The Religion of the Landless: The Social Context of the Babylonian Exile*. Bloomington, IN: Meyer-Stone, 1989.
Vanderkam, James C. *An Introduction to Early Judaism*. Grand Rapids, MI: Wm. B. Eerdmans, 2001.
Yamauchi, Edwin M. *Persia and the Bible*. Grand Rapids, MI: Baker, 1990.

Part Two

Pluralism and the Jewish Communities

Chapter 6

The Breakdown of Consensus: Protosectarianism and the Babylonian Returnees

Before the Exile: Roots of Sectarianism

Social and religious sectarianism characterized Second Temple Judaism, particularly in the Hellenistic and Roman periods. This pronounced sectarianism, however, had its roots in tensions from much earlier times, chiefly in the Persian period, but also earlier, during the monarchy. Even for classical Israel, the Bible preserves traces of rival factions between north and south, priest and Levite, city and rural dwellers. These factions engaged in ideological struggles over who would prove to be the legitimate representation of God's people in the world. These rivalries were kept in check by the powerful institution of the monarchy, so when the monarchy dissolved in the post-exilic period, tensions almost immediately escalated.

As early as the reign of King Solomon in the tenth century B.C.E., the northern tribes chafed as they were forced to provide tax support and manual labor for many projects located disproportionately in the south. The historical texts of 1 Kings 4 speaks of twelve officials throughout Israel who provided food for the king and his household:

> Solomon also had forty thousand stalls of horses for his chariots, and twelve thousand horsemen. And those officers supplied provisions for King Solomon, and for all who came to King Solomon's table, each one in his month; they let nothing be lacking. Barley also and straw for the horses and swift steeds they brought to the place where it was required, each according to his charge. (1 Kgs 4:26-28)

This text stresses that the demands of the king and his court were exceedingly weighty, as his pretensions outran his means. In addition to providing support for the monarchy, the temple priesthood also had to be provisioned. Therefore, to provide a vehicle for collecting revenue, Solomon designed twelve new administrative districts to serve as a means of collecting taxes from the country. These twelve districts also may have been designed to destroy old tribal allegiances from earlier periods. That 1 Kings records no appointed official for collecting revenue in Judah is striking. Evidently, Judah was not required to serve among the state drafted labor pool. This southern preference led to an obvious tension between north and south, which came to a head shortly after the death of Solomon.

Prior to his death, Solomon had appointed his son, Rehoboam, as the royal successor. Rehoboam met his first major resistance almost immediately in the form of a coalition of northern tribes led by Jeroboam. Solomon previously had exiled Jeroboam to Egypt; he wisely recognized the death of this monarch as a fresh opportunity to unite the northern tribes against Judah. Jeroboam and the coalition approached Rehoboam and demanded that he reverse his father's harsh policy of oppression against the north. While the elders who had served with his father recommended that Rehoboam bow to Jeroboam's demands, Rehoboam, instead, listened to the shortsighted advise of his young peers. Cast in powerful Near Eastern imagery, the fateful retort by Rehoboam was, "My father made your yoke very heavy, but I will add to your yoke; my father chastised you with whips, but I will chastise you with scorpions" (1 Kings 12:14b). Consequently, the ten tribes of the north went their own way, and civil war resulted. "What portion have we in David?" they queried. "We have no inheritance in the son of Jesse. To your tents, O Israel! Look now to your own house, David" (1 Kings 12:16b).

The tribes of the north, henceforth called Israel, elected Jeroboam as their own king, built their own capital at Tirzah, and even constructed shrines of worship that rivaled the temple located in the southern kingdom of Judah. These two kingdoms rubbed together against one another at the boundary of the tribe of Benjamin, ten miles north of Jerusalem. Although an uneasy alliance between Israel and Judah developed in later years, civil war rocked the nation for a generation after the division.

The Kingdom of Israel was much larger, more internationally involved, and consequently, a bigger threat to neighboring nations. Israel eventually would fall to Assyria in 722 B.C.E, when they destroyed its relocated capital, Samaria. After the Northern Kingdom's demise, the Assyrian empire assimilated most of its people and territory. The smaller Kingdom of Judah was left alone as the sole heir of classical Israelite heritage. The inhabitants of the Southern Kingdom, Judah, were deported to Babylon over a century later. There they preserved the traditions of ancient Israel, and eventually returned to the land of promise after exile. Since it was the southerners who perpetuated the traditions of Israel, the animosity against the north is replete in the historical literature of the Hebrew Scriptures. The historians of the Deuteronomistic History do not grant a single king in the North a passing grade. These historians even interpreted Israel's close contact with other foreign cultures as a leading cause of her demise. This animosity may have been at the root of later rejection of Samarians by the returnees. If recent trends of dating much of the historical material in the Hebrew Scriptures as late as the Second Temple period are correct, the rampant hostility toward the North may reflect more of the climate during the time of the composition, or at least the final redaction, of these materials, than that of the actual period of the monarchy itself.

Nevertheless, in all likelihood the monarchy checked the natural tendency to disintegrate into disparate factions. Needless to say, even in the pre-exilic period, there were stresses over the legitimacy of the monarchy itself. Strong anti-monarchic sentiments appear in 1 Samuel 8:4-28, 10:17-18, and 1 Kings 12:1-4. Additionally, the book of Deuteronomy grants only grudging concession to the monarchy:

> When you come to the land which the LORD your God gives you, and you possess it and dwell in it, and then say, 'I will set a king over me, like all the nations that are round about me': you may indeed set as king over you him whom the LORD your God will choose. One from among your brethren you shall set as king over you; you may not put a foreigner over you, who is not your brother. Only he must not multiply horses for himself, or cause the people to return to Egypt in order to multiply horses, since the LORD has said to you, 'You shall never return that way again.' And he shall not multiply wives for himself, lest his heart turn away; nor shall he greatly multiply for himself silver and gold. (Deut 17:14-17)

Elsewhere, the historical literature portrays the monarchy in a more positive light as the prophets of God anointed the first three leaders of the nation, Saul, David, and Solomon. With very few exceptions, the monarchs of the divided kingdoms of Israel and Judah did little to increase confidence in the institution of the monarchy. For the most part, they acted like most other ancient Near-Eastern despots, selfishly enhancing their kingdoms, often at the expense of their subjects. The institution of the monarchy, however, kept disparate factions from exerting undue influence, as all institutions and religious movements were ultimately subject to its suzerainty.

Pressures also existed in the pre-exilic period over the legitimacy of the priesthood and worship. These pressures may have provided the given impetus to later concerns over temple, priesthood, and calendar in the Second Temple period. Jeroboam's introduction of illicit shrines and high places is condemned unequivocally in the literature of the Hebrew Bible. The biblical writers interpreted his appointment of an alternative priesthood as an illicit abuse of the power of the monarchy. Earlier, Solomon had banished Abiathar, David's high priest, in favor of Zadok.   The reason for this expulsion was that Abiathar had supported David's other son, Adonijah, as heir to the throne of David. This appointment of a new high priest led to lasting tensions between the descendants of Zadok, who went on to attain the lion's share of priestly power, and other priests, who eventually would be relegated to a lower status as Levites or disenfranchised priests.   Even the Pentateuch presents a mixed picture of the Aaronic priesthood, as it depicts Aaron in both positive and negative lights.   The pre-exilic prophets challenged the authority of priests who were not faithful in calling Israel back to the covenant and warned against syncretism in any form, which was interpreted as a breach of the covenant.

There were also long-standing competing traditions regarding the location of the sacred shrines essential to Israel's faithful worship of Yahweh. Shechem is one city of major importance. In the 17th-16th centuries B.C.E., a large Canaanite temple stood there. In the early days of Israel, the tribes conducted worship at that site (Josh 24, Deut 27).   Moses had commanded that the blessings and curses of the covenant commands of Deuteronomy be uttered on Mt. Gerazim and Mt. Ebal (Deut 27). Indeed, the early narratives of the patriarchal history of Abraham and Jacob also are linked geographically to the area around Shechem (Gen 12:6-7, Gen 33:18-20). The book of Deuteronomy was not originally a Jerusalem-oriented document; rather it focuses on the Levites in the countryside. While it does emphasize worship at a central shrine, it never explicitly stipulates that the central shrine will be Jerusalem, only "the place where I will cause my name to dwell" (Deut 12:11). In fact, the only center of worship explicitly stated in the book is in the rural countryside near Mt. Gerazim at Shechem--not Jerusalem. It is also important to note that after the division of the kingdom, Jeroboam I began his reign at Shechem, and only later moved the capital of Israel to Tirzah (1 Kgs 14:17; 15:21,33).

On the other hand, the Deuteronomistic History and Chronicles are strongly Jerusalemistic. This tension between worship in Jerusalem and Shechem that had origins in earlier periods was a key ingredient in the struggles between the Samaritans and the Jerusalem establishment during the Second Temple period.

Jeroboam also made adjustments to the sacred calendar by moving the autumn feast to the fifteenth day of the eighth month, making it one month out of sequence (1 Kgs 8:2). The Deuteronomistic History resolutely condemned this change, and provides evidence that quarrels over calendar preceded and even anticipated the obsession with the sacred calendar that characterized later periods.

Late in Judah's history, Josiah instituted reforms designed to bring Judah back in line with the commandments of the Law that had long since been neglected or forgotten. The book of Kings mentions that as Josiah refurbished the temple, his workers came across an ancient law book, interpreted by most to be the book or portions of the book of Deuteronomy (2 Kgs 22-23). The reforms enacted follow the commands of Deuteronomy to the letter. Josiah slaughtered the illicit priests at Bethel, had their bones burned, and prohibited worship at the high places (1 Kgs 13:1-2). Josiah's remedy was the centralization of worship in Jerusalem, as Passovers were to be only celebrated there.

After the Exile: The Emergence of Sectarianism

After the exile, much of the heart of the struggle was between those who had returned (or were eventually to return from Babylon) and those who had remained in the land of Judah. While in Babylon, intense theological ferment characterized the mindset of the displaced

Judean exiles. These exiles previously had been the upper crust of the society of Judah: the well educated, the wealthy, the religious and political leaders of the southern kingdom. While in Babylon, they reflected on the centuries of existence under the monarchy, recorded their observations, and edited materials written before the exile. As they returned to their homeland, they expected automatically to resume their rightful place as leaders of the reconstruction. Indeed, not everyone in Babylon was interested in returning to the homeland. In the forty years since the destruction of Jerusalem, those deported to Babylon had settled in, had begun new enterprises and gained new wealth. The Hebrew Bible indicates that while many of the Babylonian returnees had considerable wealth the local populace of Judah remained rather poor, existing mainly as farmers and peasants (Ezra 2:18-19, 8:26-7, Zech 6:9-11),. The struggle that ensued between the returnees and the local populace was not merely geographical but economic as well. The Babylonian returnees viewed the people of the land of Judah and Samarian Yahwists with utter contempt. Alternately, the new nation of Israel is denoted within the book of Ezra with the expressions, "exiles," "the exile," or "the congregation of exiles."

Historians point to three examples that demonstrate that the Babylonian returnees sought to restrict who would inherit the right to define and control the social mores and religious beliefs of the restoration: the restriction of those who would assist in the rebuilding of the temple and city walls; the theology of the empty land; and the prohibition against mixed marriages.

Opposition to Rebulding the Temple

The local populace's opposition to the rebuilding of the temple in Ezra's account portrays the Babylonian returnees at odds with the native Israelite population. Ezra records three such examples of tension. The first is found in Ezra 4:

> When the adversaries of Judah and Benjamin heard that the returned exiles were building a temple to the LORD, the God of Israel, they approached Zerubbabel and the heads of the families and said to them, 'Let us build with you, for we worship your God as you do, and we have been sacrificing to him ever since the days of King Esar-haddon of Assyria who brought us here.' But Zerubbabel, Jeshua, and the rest of the heads of families in Israel said to them, 'You shall have no part with

us in building a house to our God; but we alone will build to the LORD, the God of Israel, as King Cyrus of Persia has commanded us.' Then the people of the land discouraged the people of Judah, and made them afraid to build, and they bribed officials to frustrate their plan throughout the reign of King Cyrus of Persia and until the reign of King Darius of Persia. (Ezra 4:1-5)

Exactly who are these "adversaries?" Josephus identifies them as the Samaritans, but that identification is probably anachronistic. Possibly the designation, "adversaries" is a polemical term referring to fellow Judeans who were not foreigners at all, but who had been ethnically disqualified to participate in the rebuilding because they were not part of the elite group who had returned from Babylon. Whoever they may have been, they obviously felt they had a legitimate right to participate in the rebuilding. In fact, these "adversaries" may have felt that theirs was the strongest nationalistic claim, since they had remained in the land of promise. When the returnees refused their offer of assistance, they used whatever political power they had in the province to thwart the construction. Evidently their initial challenges were successful, since the book of Ezra records that the temple rebuilding project came to a halt. Ezra 4 mentions two very different groups: the "people of the land" are distinguished from the "people of Judah." Oddly enough, the reference to the "people of Judah" depicts the Babylonian returnees, not those who had actually inhabited Judah during the exile. Ironically, those who might have lived for the last forty years in what had once been the kingdom of Judah where not designated as the people of Judah by Ezra-Nehemiah.

A second account in Ezra 4:6-24 tells of how the officials of Samaria wrote a letter to the Persian king, accusing the Jews of conspiring to revolt against the Persians by rebuilding the city walls. The letter reads as follows:

To Artaxerxes the king: Your servants, the men of the province Beyond the River, send greeting. And now may it be known to the king the Jews who came up from you to us have gone to Jerusalem. They are rebuilding that rebellious and wicked city; they are finishing the walls and repairing the foundations. Now be it known to the king that if this city is rebuilt and the walls finished, they will not pay tribute, custom, or toll, and the royal revenue will be impaired. Now because we eat the salt of the palace and it is not fitting for us to witness the king's dishonor, therefore we send and inform the king, in order that search

> may be made in the book of the records of your fathers. You will find in the book of the records and learn that this city is a rebellious city, hurtful to kings and provinces, and that sedition was stirred up in it from of old. That is why the city was laid waste. We make known to the king that, if this city is rebuilt and its walls finished, you will then have no possession in the province Beyond the River. (Ezra 4:11-16)

As a result of the intervention of provincial authorities, the emperor, Artaxerxes I, ordered the Jews to stop building the city walls.

A similar letter is found in Ezra 5:7-17, an account of opposition decades later when Haggai and Zechariah encouraged the Judeans to resume completion of the temple. Tattenai the governor wrote to Darius to verify that the Jews had indeed received permission from Cyrus years earlier to rebuild the temple. Darius searched the archives of Persia and discovered that Cyrus had indeed ordered the building of the temple. Darius further decreed that the Jews be allowed to complete work on the temple with the following declaration:

> Now therefore, Tattenai, governor of the province Beyond the River, Shetharbozenai, and your associates the governors who are in the province Beyond the River, keep away; let the work on this house of God alone; let the governor of the Jews and the elders of the Jews rebuild this house of God on this site. Moreover I make a decree regarding what you shall do for these elders of the Jews for the rebuilding of this house of God; the cost is to be paid to these men in full and without delay from the royal revenue, the tribute of the province Beyond the River. (Ezra 6:6-8).

Consequently the ability to participate in the rebuilding the temple and city walls became an indicator of a community's good standing with the returnees. As construction began, both physical and metaphoric walls were erected. As the walls of the city separated the holy city from the profane peoples around it, social walls of exclusion prevented other groups from being considered as legitimate members of the community of faith. Other groups that challenged the exiles may not have been recorded in the Hebrew Scriptures. Evidence exists, for example, of a possible rival temple in Lachish during this period. Lachish was clearly a governmental center in the Persian Period. A solar shrine was erected on the summit of the mound along with a limestone altar 27x17 meters in size. Among archaeological finds there were bronze lamps and small stone incense altars. The settlement came to an end at the beginning of the Greek period, so the extent of the influence of this site is not known.

Theology of the Empty Land

The books of Jeremiah and Ezekiel indicate that after Jerusalem's destruction the land of Judah was utterly depopulated and abandoned by God and his people. Jeremiah 44:2-3 states:

> You yourselves have seen all the disaster that I have brought on Jerusalem and on all the towns of Judah. Look at them; today they are a desolation, without an inhabitant in them, because of the wickedness that they committed, provoking me to anger, in that they went to make offerings and serve other gods that they had not known, neither they, nor you, nor your ancestors.

This "empty land" theology asserts that Judah had been left without a remnant, except for those who remained in Babylon. Ezekiel 11 depicts a similar state of affairs for the land of Judah. When the glory of the Lord departed the temple, God's glory also left Jerusalem, giving the impression that God had joined the exiles in a foreign land, and only returned after the land of Judah was cleansed from her sins:

> Thus says the Lord God: though I removed them far away among the nations, and though I scattered them among the countries, yet I have been a sanctuary to them for a little while in the countries where they have gone. Therefore say: Thus says the Lord God: I will gather you from the peoples and assemble you out of the countries where you have been scattered, and I will give you the land of Israel. When they come there they will remove from it all its detestable things and al its abominations. (Ezek 11:16-17).

The Vision of the Two Figs in Jeremiah 24 portrays the exiles deported to Babylon as "good figs" while those who remained in Judah and those who dwelled in the land of Egypt are "bad figs." These bad figs are reputed to be "a horror to all the kingdoms of the earth, to be a reproach, a byword, a taunt, and a curse in all the places where I shall drive them" (Jer 24:9). The implications of this text are far-reaching. It furthers the claims of the Babylonian Diaspora to be the only true remnant of Israel. Only through this group will legitimate renewal and restoration be possible.

Jeremiah predicts the same fate for those who fled to Egypt after the destruction of Jerusalem. In Jeremiah 42-44, the Judeans who fled to Egypt are portrayed as pagan worshippers of foreign gods. Yahweh states, "My name shall no more be invoked by the mouth of any man of Judah in all the land of Egypt saying, 'As the Lord God lives'" (44:26). By the simple process of elimination, only the Babylonian community is left to be the exclusive possessor of hope for Israel's future restoration. Both groups, those who remained in Judah and those who fled to Egypt, are anathema. There is literally no one left in the land of Judah and those who fled to Egypt are under a horrific curse. Common sense and careful reading of these and other exilic texts indicate that Judah was anything but without habitation. Jeremiah 41:4-5, for example, presents an account of 80 worshippers from Shiloh and Samaria coming to present offerings at the temple after its destruction. The Elephantine Papyri also include numerous Yahwistic names associated with the city of Samaria. The effect of such a strongly ideological presentation of Judah, is that those who had remained in the land must obviously be imposters and outsiders in the eyes of those returning from Babylon. The books of Ezra and Nehemiah depict the same scenario: those who remained in the land are decidedly outsiders, while the only true representatives of the former nation of Judah are the exiles.

The Problem of Exogamy in the Postexilic Period

One problematic bit of evidence of the tensions between the returnees and the inhabitants of their former homeland occurs over the contested subject of mixed marriages. The roots of the prohibition against outmarrying are clearly pre-exilic, or at the very least are portrayed as pre-exilic in the literature of the Hebrew Bible. The patriarchal narratives condemn marriage outside of Abraham's clan though the Moabitess Ruth is cited as a righteous gentile who accepted the God of Israel as her own. When the northern kingdom of Israel was destroyed in 722 B.C.E., the book of Kings records that the Assyrians settled peoples from other nations in place of the original inhabitants. Obviously, some Israelites eventually intermarried with the foreign populace. After the exile, both Ezra and Nehemiah reflect great distress that the former inhabitants of Israel had intermarried with Gentiles relocated there by these foreign powers. Ezra and Nehemiah both take strong steps to resolve this problem; and go to the extreme of demanding that the Jews divorce their foreign wives (Ezra 10:18, 10:15). Ezra admonishes the Jews of that they:

> have trespassed and married foreign women, and so increased the guilt of Israel. Now then make confession to the LORD the God of your fathers, and do his will; separate yourselves from the peoples of the land and from the foreign wives. (Ezra 10:10-11)

Ezra expelled 113 foreign wives and children. Why he ignored marriages between Israelite women and foreign men is uncertain.

Nehemiah even resorted to physical violence to assure that the proper marriage boundaries were adhered to,

> In those days also I saw the Jews who had married women of Ashdod, Ammon, and Moab; and half of their children spoke the language of Ashdod, as they could not speak the language of Judah, but the language of each people. And I contended with them and cursed them and beat some of them and pulled out their hair; and I made them take oath in the name of God, saying, 'You shall not give your daughters to their sons, or take their daughters for your sons or for yourselves.' (Neh 13:23-25)

These strong prohibitions against these mixed marriages defined boundaries of Israelite ethnicity. As distinctions between Jew and non-Jew were more strictly defined, boundaries between Jew and Jew also came under severe scrutiny. It was no longer acceptable to be merely a Jew; but Jewish groups began to turn on one another with the same critical eye, often viewed yet other Jewish groups as "outsiders."

The writings of the Chronicler, which date from the same time as Ezra and Nehemiah, oddly do not share this same distaste for mixed marriages. A more inclusive attitude appears on the part of the writer of 1 and 2 Chronicles (2 Chr 30:5-11, 18; 34).

In the Hasmonean period, all forms of intermarriage were anathema. For example, the Qumran text, 4QFlorelegium, states that no Ammonite, Moabite, foreigner, or proselyte will be able to enter the temple in the future messianic age. The book of Jubilees contains a tirade on Genesis 34's narrative of Shechem's rape of Dinah:

> And if there is any man in Israel who wishes to give his daughter or his sister to any man who is from the seed of the gentiles, let him surely

die, and let him be stoned because he has caused shame in Israel. And
also the woman will be burned with fire because she has defiled the
name of her father's house and so she will be uprooted from Israel....
And it is a reproach to Israel, to those who give and those who take any
of the daughters of the gentile nations because it is defilement and it is
contemptible to Israel. And Israel will not be cleansed from this
defilement if there is in it a woman from the daughters of gentiles or
one who has given any of his daughters to a man who is from any of the
gentiles. For there will be plague upon plague and curse upon curse,
and every judgment, and plague, and curse will come. (*Jub.* 30:7-9, 13-
15a.)

These texts in the Hebrew Bible are in opposition with others that
provide a very different perspective. The book of Jonah, for example,
beautifully depicts Yahweh's love for the foreign city of Ninevah. The
rebel prophet Jonah is commanded to preach to this hated city. He
refuses, not because he fears the Assyrians, but because he is keenly
aware of the mercy of God, who will abound in love and will forgive
even these pagan foreigners. Similarly, the book of Malachi gives
gentiles credit for genuine worship of God while God's own people are
not faithful in performing their duties to God. Some biblical scholars
have pointed to texts in Isaiah 55-66, Ezekiel 38-39, Isaiah 24-27, and
Zechariah 9-14 as containing allusions to internal Jewish protest against
the ruling establishment set in place by the returnees.

Throughout the Hebrew Bible, a number of gentiles embraced the
Israelite religion. While there is no idea in the Hebrew Bible of non-
Israelites becoming Israelites, there are intimations and adumbrations
of such, as gentiles could bless God, sacrifice, and acknowledge their
faith in Yahweh. While no mechanism existed to allow outsiders to
become insiders, the model of the reverent gentile is evidenced by the
lives of Jethro (Exod 12:10-11), Hiram (2 Chr 2:11, 1 Kgs 5:21),
Nebuchadnezzar, Cyrus, and Artaxerxes (Dan 2:47, 3:26, 4:34-37).
Other foreigners such as the "mixed multitude" of the Exodus, Doeg
the Edomite, Ittai of Gath, Uriah the Hittite, and others are mentioned
in a positive light in the Hebrew Scriptures. Even the resident alien is a
potential victim of abuse, and so is protected in the Torah.

Conclusion

These cited examples demonstrate historical precedents for the rampant sectarianism characteristic of Judaism in the late Second Temple period. Struggles between the northern and southern tribes, between city dwellers and rural peasants, between Babylonian returnees and native Israelites challenged established definitions of Jewish identity. Social boundaries based on geography and ethnicity began to drive wedges between Jewish communities. Most of these examples suggest a rising hostility between groups that laid claim to the land of their ancestors. The monarchy's collapse created a vacuum whereby these incipient tensions escalated.

Chapter 7

Issues that Divided the Jewish Communities

Jewish beliefs in the Second Temple period were anything but uniform. The Judaisms that arose during this time envisioned themselves to be existing in a post-classical age. In this post-classical age, the concept of Israel drastically changed. The Exile and Diaspora forced a new evolving sense of identity. Socio-religious groups such as the Hasadim, Pharisees, Sadducees, Essenes, Zealots, Samaritans, Therapeutae, Enoch groups, and even early Christianity and nascent Rabbinic Judaism, all sought to define themselves in light of the tragedy of the exile, the loss of political autonomy and the loss of the Davidic line, and the new cosmopolitan setting particularly characteristic of the Greek and Roman periods. Scholarship has produced no thoroughgoing consensus regarding the religious nature of post-classical Jewish society. This lack of consensus, among other things, revolved around alternative responses to four crucial questions: Who would be the legitimate believing community of Judaism? Around what would this community be organized? How would the community and its traditions be preserved? What would characterize its cult? The divergent responses to these four crucial issues were the heart and soul of deep-seated tensions over the legitimacy of temple, priesthood, Hellenism, Torah, and calendar. In light of the lasting tensions over these issues, each of these questions merits a full discussion.

Who would now become the legitimate believing community of Judaism to justly carry on the traditions of ancient Israel in a post-classical age? Disagreements over this issue largely revolved around matters of geography and genealogy. The Jewish communities during the Second Temple period resided largely in three locals: Palestine,

Babylon, and Egypt.   In one way or another, all three communities claimed superiority based on geography.   Palestinian Jewry possessed the land of promise; the returnees from Babylon derived their status from the upper echelon of the pre-exilic Israelites transported to Babylon; and Egyptian Jewry boasted a Jewish community of over 200,000 in Alexandria alone.   As these communities came in contact with the gentiles, issues of genealogy came into play.   Could a gentile convert to Judaism?   Could a Jew intermarry with those of gentile descent?   Was it even appropriate to marry those from outside one's community?

The second question was equally crucial: Around what would this new community be organized?   During the Second Temple period, the Davidic Kingship, the Jerusalem temple, and the Promised Land were no longer viable options for many in the Diaspora, or for that matter, the inhabitants of Judah itself.   Three new political points of reference came to replace these former institutions as the center of the community: the priesthood, the Second Temple, and Torah.   During this period, the question of legitimate priesthood was a matter of heated debate, particularly in light of the fact that for much of the Hellenistic and Roman periods, the high priesthood was an appointment of the gentile ruling powers.   Such appointments were subject to bribes and other external influences.   In addition to the priesthood, the temple in Jerusalem was also a pivotal icon for Judaism, both inside and outside Palestine.   To be sure, not all Jewry endorsed the religious establishment of the Jerusalem temple.   At least three other Jewish temples in Palestine and Egypt flourished.   At Qumran, the covenant community felt that the Jerusalem priesthood and temple practices were hopelessly corrupt, while the Samaritans argued that the Jerusalem temple was illegitimate from its very inception.   The former opted for no temple at all, longing for a future time when their community could erect a new purified temple, while the latter built a rival temple on Mt. Gerazim near Shechem.

A third crucial issue was how these communities could preserve their religious traditions and cultural identity.   The importance of maintaining religious purity in light of the pressures of other cultures was always divisive.   Hellenistic influence on Palestinian and Diaspora Judaism cannot be overestimated.   Such exposure to this foreign culture raised fresh questions with important consequences.   To what extent should the faithful make compromises with the rapidly changing social environment of Greco-Roman society? Concerns regarding preservation of the community also raised issues of the text and canon of the Hebrew Bible. Should they make translations into other tongues in order the preserve the communities residing in the Diaspora? Which books were religiously authoritative and which were not? How could one account for the diverse textual traditions in the Hebrew Bible? Would these disparate textual traditions need to be standardized?

A final critical question concerns what practices would characterize the cult of the believing community. Whereas Christian sectarian debates of the early centuries of the Common Era centered around theological issues such as the nature of God, Jesus Christ, and the atonement, the cutting edge of Jewish "theology" resided in the Torah and the relation of the community to the Torah. Marriage, Sabbath, festivals, and calendar were all crucial issues to Palestinian and Diaspora Judaism during the Second Temple period. Consequently, the Law became the focal point for that community, particularly because of the precarious nature of the temple and the priesthood. Since physical appearance, clothing, speech, and occupations did not always render Jews distinctive, these communities erected other boundaries to protect and maintain their identity as followers of the covenant. During the Maccabean period, circumcision became perhaps the defining marker of Judaism in Judea, but this may not have been the case in the Diaspora. Even so, common sense would indicate that the immediate determination of who was and was not circumcised was next to impossible. Thus, while a sense of solidarity, common origins, and a distinctive history determined one's "Jewishness," religious leadership did not always clearly define the lines between whether one was considered a faithful Jew or not. These sticking points of temple, priesthood, Hellenism, Torah, and calendar were points of unresolved turmoil. Consequently, many of these groups either knowingly or unknowingly enhanced the dichotomy between members and outsiders, with outsiders often defined as fellow Jews.

The Temple

The temple was perhaps the dominant communal institution of early Judaism. In many ways, it gained a centrality the first temple never had. Yet in other ways, it was inferior to Solomon's temple in several

respects.   Shortly after the return from Babylon in 539 B.C.E.,
Sheshbazzar and the returnees laid the foundation of the second temple.
However, due to controversies with the Palestinian community over
who had the authority to rebuild the structure, the project languished.
The Judeans, who had remained in the land for several generations,
resented the unilateral actions of the returnees. The traditional Jewish
perspective assumed that the Samaritans had also offered to assist in the
temple reconstruction, an offer spurned by the Babylonian returnees.
Those who had returned from Babylon felt the Samaritans had
outmarried with the gentile population, corrupting their divinely
ordained heritage. The Samaritans, on the contrary, argued they alone
had faithfully adhered to their Mosaic heritage by leaving their sacred
shrine exactly where the Torah had commanded that it be located—at
Mt. Gerazim. This hostility eventually led to building a rival temple on
Mt. Gerazim, near Shechem.   Then Sheshbazzar and other early
returnees mysteriously vanished from the historical record, and the
reconstruction of the Jerusalem temple came to an abrupt halt.

Work on the temple resumed in 520 B.C.E. through the leadership
of two prophets: Haggai and Zechariah. Haggai daringly predicted the
completion of the temple would usher in a messianic age, where the
treasures of the nations would be brought into the temple. The prophet
Zechariah expressed the same hope for the rise of the Jewish state that
revolved around a prosperous temple cult.   In spite of Syrian and
Samarian opposition recorded in the book of Ezra, the temple was
finally completed in 515 B.C.E.

In most respects, the Hebrew Bible records that the second temple
as an edifice was but a pale reflection of its grand predecessor built by
Solomon. It had no supernatural commissioning, and its architectural
beauty did not rival the artistry of the first temple. Perhaps even more
disappointing, Haggai's hope of the messianic kingdom did not
immediately materialize with the completion of the temple.   Why this
hope did not quickly come to fulfillment is a matter that is still open for
discussion.   Much later, the rabbinic tradition held a cryptic
interpretation of the seeming failure of the second temple. The first
temple, according to the rabbis, possessed several things that the second
temple lacked: the sacred fire, the ark, the Urim and Thummim, and
the Holy Spirit (*Ta'an* 2.1 [65a]).

In spite of these visible shortcomings, the second temple enjoyed a
centrality for Jewry unequaled by its predecessor.   Josephus stated it

succinctly—"one temple for the one God." The temple provided a visible and psychological rallying point for people whose political and religious autonomy was endlessly uncertain. The half-shekel temple tax, roughly two days wages paid by devout Jews in Palestine and the Diaspora, was a binding force for the centrality of the temple. Jews in Palestine and the Diaspora endeavored to make a pilgrimage to the Jerusalem temple for Passover at least once in their lifetime. Four times every seven years the faithful were to spend their tithe in Jerusalem, in addition to the half-shekel tax.

The historical record readily demonstrates the religious and cultural centrality of the temple. The book of 2 Maccabees, for example, begins and ends with the theme of the temple's purity. Love for temple and Torah motivates the faithful martyrs to give their very lives, rather than succumb to the evils of Hellenism. Likewise, 1 Maccabees recounts that a single act, the desecration of this temple by Antiochus IV, evoked such hostility that it solidified a broad resistance of the Jewish people, ultimately leading to national independence. The Judeans were willing to fight and shed blood to protect this sacred shrine. Josephus provides a wealth of information about the construction of the Second Temple while under Persian domination and subsequent renovations in the Hasmonean and Roman periods. During the Hasmonean period John Hyrcanus remodeled the temple significantly. Later, after the conquest by Rome, Herod the Great completely demolished this temple and entirely rebuilt it into a splendid Hellenistic structure. Set on a raised platform with a Greek facade and beautiful white marble, Herod enlarged the temple platform, and built a number of gates and courts covering roughly twenty-six acres. It was truly one of the wonders of the ancient world, providing a spiritual link to heaven, and a visible link to Israel's national past.

The design of the temple speaks volumes about the "in-group" and "out-group" issues that preoccupied Second Temple Judaism. The structural design of the temple consisted of a series of courts with several series of ascending steps that, like concentric circles, limited contact with the temple cult. At the center of the edifice was the Holy of Holies, where only the high priest could enter once a year on the Day of Atonement. This perfect cube was thirty-six feet square, set apart by an embroidered curtain. In the first temple of Solomon, the Holy of Holies contained the Ark of the Covenant, but during the Second Temple period, the Holy of Holies sat empty. Outside of the Holy of

Holies lay The Holy Place, where other priests performed their daily duties. The Holy Place contained the menorah, the altar of incense, and the table of gold with the twelve loaves of shewbread that the priests changed every Sabbath eve. Fifteen steps down, the Court of Israel surrounded the Holy Place and the religious leaders permitted only Jewish males access. A wall roughly one-meter high separated the non-levitical men from the priests. Outside the Court of Israel was the Court of Women--and still further removed, the Court of the Gentiles. Naturally enough, the structure of the temple provoked great curiosity among the non-Jews, who the priests prohibited from participating fully in certain aspects of temple service. Gentiles could purchase a goat or a lamb to be offered by a priest, but signs in Greek and Latin prohibited them from entering into the Court of Israel upon punishment of death.

At the heart of the temple service were the daily sacrifices offered every morning and evening. These sacrifices are carefully described in the Torah. The *Tamid* Offering was made twice a day, at dawn and dusk. A lamb was first bound, then slaughtered and offered as a whole burnt offering. The sacrifice ended with an offering of wine on the altar, followed by the priestly blessing for the day or evening. The priests offered double sacrifices on the Sabbath and feast days. Priests also offered many additional sacrifices on the feast days, and private offerings by individuals were added to the daily sacrifices. Like spokes of a wheel converging on the center, Jews from the Diaspora and gentiles alike flocked to Jerusalem to participate in these cultic activities and also to celebrate the three major annual festivals of Passover (*Pesah*), Pentecost (*Shavuot*), and Tabernacles (*Sukkot*). The offering during these periods included a sacrifice and a communal meal of celebration.

In spite of the Jerusalem temple cult's enormous popularity, at least three other Jewish temples erected during the Second Temple period flourished. Presumably, some were built because of geographical necessity. Scholars know relatively little about the Jewish communities they served. Two of these were located in Egypt, in Leontopolis and Elephantine, respectively. One religious leader of the Egyptian community, Onias III, built the temple of Leontopolis on the justification that Isaiah had prophesied that one day there would be an altar to Yahweh in the heart of Egypt (Isa 19:19). We do not know when the Jewish community at Elephantine built the temple there, but it was destroyed in 410 B.C.E., and officials at Elephantine sent letters to

Jerusalem to obtain approval to rebuild it. After a delay of three years, the Jerusalem priestly establishment reluctantly gave approval, as long as no sacrifices were made. In Palestine, the Samaritans erected their own temple at Mt. Gerazim, a response due in part to increasing hostility with the Jerusalem priesthood.

For some Jewish groups, the temple was a concrete reality. For others it became a metaphor of an idealized hope for the future. At Qumran, for example, the temple was a prominent symbol. The organization of the community approximated that of the temple in Jerusalem and the rules for the priesthood applied to every member of the commune. These faithful followers of the sect had retreated into the desert village of Qumran in the second century B.C.E., in part because they denied the legitimacy of the high priesthood and the temple cult in Jerusalem. One highly influential document from Qumran, *The Temple Scroll*, was this community's elaborate reconstruction of how the temple should be designed and how its daily activities should be conducted. According to this important document, after an eschatological battle between the Sons of Light and the Sons of Darkness, the victors would build a new purified temple. No evidence exists that the Qumran covenant community actually tried to build their own temple during their roughly two hundred years of existence, probably because they did not have the resources to do so, or more likely because they perceived their daily devotion to the community was the spiritual equivalent of the proper observances of the temple cult.

Similarly, the gospels of early Christianity strongly criticized the temple cult. Instead, for the early Christian church, the temple became a metaphor for the believers in Jesus, the body of Christ. The book of Hebrews speaks typologically about the temple and the apostle Paul argues that each believer is the temple of the Holy Spirit who now dwells in the individual spirit rather than in stone buildings. Such a perspective is not unlike other Jewish perspectives that reinterpreted the form and function of the temple. For instance, the Jewish philosopher Philo also allegorized the temple cult within a neo-Platonic framework. This fusion of Judaism and Hellenism proposed that as humans ascended through the spheres, they moved beyond mere matter, ultimately completing the spiritual transition to pure form. Consequently, Philo questioned the necessity of a physical temple.

In addition to the temple, other centers of national life developed during the Second Temple period. One of these was the synagogue. Synagogues were common in the late Second Temple period, both in the Diaspora and in the homeland. The word "synagogue" derives from the Greek, meaning "house of assembly." Scholars used to suggest that the synagogue emerged during the exile in Babylon, but such origins cannot with confidence be confirmed. The earliest undisputed reference comes from Egypt in the third century B.C.E, and denotes a *proseuche*, or house of prayer. Such a reference is a far cry from the synagogue rituals and buildings depicted in Rabbinic Judaism. Today, most scholars agree that no single line of development of the synagogue exists, and that the synagogue of the rabbinic period may have been the historical result of a convergence of several institutions, from places of prayer, to schools, meeting halls, and places of study. This diversity also is evident in the archeological record. Of more than fifty synagogue ruins in Israel discovered in the 20th century, no two are alike.

Most of the knowledge of synagogue worship comes after the Second Temple period, as late as the fourth century C.E. Worship in the synagogue was probably independent of the sacrificial center of the temple, and was an important institution in Jewish life, not only in the Diaspora, but also in Palestine. Yet it was not competitive but complimentary with the temple establishment. Here Torah study conveniently replaced temple service as the focus of religious activity.

Another important institution of Judaism was the home. With the loss of the first physical temple in 586 B.C.E., no sacrificial system existed for the inhabitants of the land. The exiles in Babylon and the inhabitants of Judah compensated for this loss by sanctifying the smallest ideas of life. The home itself was an effective ritual center in its own right, comparable to a temple. One common identifier of a Jewish dwelling in antiquity was the *mezuzah*, an amulet fastened to the right front doorpost of the home. These amulets typically contained verses from the Mosaic Torah, such as Deuteronomy 6:4-9, which exhorts:

> Hear, O Israel: The LORD our God is one Lord; and you shall love the LORD your God with all your heart, and with all your soul, and with all your might. And these words which I command you this day shall be upon your heart; and you shall teach them diligently to your children, and shall talk of them when you sit in your house, and when you walk

by the way, and when you lie down, and when you rise. And you shall bind them as a sign upon your hand, and they shall be as frontlets between your eyes. And you shall write them on the doorposts of your house and on your gates.

These *mezuzot* (plural) are mentioned as early as some of the texts from Qumran and the influential Letter of Aristeas. Other activities of the home evolved into ritual performances, as the temple reasserted itself as a dominant image of holiness and sanctification. Even preparing foods as proper or kosher, like removing blood from meat, became an opportunity for sanctification. With the loss of the Jerusalem temple, the home, like the synagogue, became a holy place where Jews could effectively observe the requirements of Torah in daily life.

The Priesthood

The history of the early priesthood in ancient Israel is one of the great complexities in the study of the Hebrew Bible. When the first temple flourished, power in Israel was divided among three types of leaders, each functioning primarily in their own unique settings. The king controlled the palace and political connections with other nations, the priests administered the temple sacrificial system, and the prophets ministered in the marketplace. All this changed, however, with the rebuilding of the temple in the Persian period. The roles of the king and prophet disappeared and the priests assumed the primary position of both religious and political leadership. Without a functioning monarchy in the Second Temple period, the office of the priesthood made an enormous leap in importance and power.

A clear, three-fold hierarchy of the priesthood emerged: high priest, priests, and Levites. Persons who served in these offices had to be individuals of impeccable lineage. Leviticus requires every priest to be a descendant of Aaron. Disagreements arose, however, over the lineage of the two surviving sons of Aaron: Eleazar and Ithamar. Solomon exiled Ithamar's descendant Abiathar, who had been high priest during the reign of David, and awarded Eleazar's descendant Zadok the high priestly office. Tensions escalated during the Second Temple period over whether only Zadokites could hold the high priestly office or whether all Aaronides could possess the position. By the latter part of the Second Temple period the Zadokites held the lion's share of priestly power, while the rest of Aaron's descendants largely served a secondary and decidedly subservient role.

Jerusalem's high priesthood was the indigenous office of authority for Jews during the Second Temple period. The dissolution of the monarchy in Judah had created a vacuum eventually filled by the influential office of the high priest. In 520 B.C.E. the political and religious power seemed to be shared by Zerubbabel, the prince and descendent of David, and Joshua the High Priest. Later in the period, however, the roles of the high priest and king coalesced and overlapped, as the high priest became the undisputed head of the Jewish state. The power of the high priesthood reached its climax in the Hasmonean period where the high priest held such political clout that he even presided over the Jewish senate (1 Macc 12:6). Not only did the High Priest represent authority over religious tradition and sacrificial rites, but also he supervised routine affairs of government. Not surprisingly, this surge of power in the office of the high priesthood led to abuse by those who longed for the authority inherent in the office. Jason, for example, bought out the office from Antiochus Epiphanes. Menalaus, an individual who had no priestly credentials at all, later successfully outbid Jason for the position. When Herod the Great became king a century later, he appointed and deposed high priests at his arbitrary pleasure, and later Roman officials appointed new high priests so often that it was almost an annual affair.

These high priests visibly shaped the religious landscape. One primary religious function of the high priestly office was the annual sacrifice during the Day of Atonement. On that day, *Yom Kippur,* the high priest entered the Holy of Holies to sprinkle the blood of the sacrifice on the horns of the altar. The entire Jewish priesthood assisted in the important cultic practice of sacrifice. The High Priest divided other priests into 24 groups, 16 from the lineage of Eleazar (Zadokites) and 8 from Itamar's lineage (1 Chr 24:4-19). The priests assigned levites to each of the 24 priestly groups to assist in the priestly duties, as well as a portion of the Judean population. Each group served two weeks per year plus the three major festival weeks. Their primary duties involved offering each day's morning and evening sacrifices, care of the vessels of the sanctuary, and perhaps even administration of justice. The various duties of the priests were assigned by lot on a daily basis.

The Levites assisted the priests and served the congregation as porters, gatekeepers, treasurers and musicians. Some evidence indicates that they also may have had a teaching role during the Second Temple period. Regardless, the Levites clearly performed a subservient role in comparison to the priests, as described in post-exilic biblical literature. The book of Ezra records that 428 priests joined in the return from Babylon with Ezra which only 74 Levites. Perhaps the Levites had little incentive to make the arduous journey to Jerusalem only to perform menial tasks. The book of Ezekiel proposes an exclusively Zadokite priesthood, arguing that the Levites were guilty of idolatry and thus relegated to menial jobs (Ezek 44:6-31).

In the first century C.E., the priestly class received enough revenue to be considered one of the wealthiest parties in Jewish society. Josephus and the New Testament record the numerous and obvious power struggles for priestly control of the Jerusalem temple. Whoever controlled the temple controlled much more than mere religious ritual, but wielded great financial, political, and social power. Financial revenue came from three main sources: the first fruit offerings; the sacrificial dues received from the offerings; and the tithe. The ½-shekel tax that male Jews over the age of 20 paid also supported the temple and priesthood. With the enormous revenues generated by these four sources, the priesthood held a monopoly of sorts on the cult in Jerusalem. These powerful priests controlled access to the temple by defining and determining the holiness of the worshippers and their sacrifices. In turn, they controlled access to God. The priests, in no small measure, determined who was Jewish and who was eligible to take part in the sacrifices. Obviously, some felt the priests were abusing their authority. These opponents could either retreat in passive resistance to the status quo, as did the community at Qumran; they could debate with the priests on their own turf, as Jesus did; or they could openly rebel, as many of the Zealots did, particularly in the middle of the first century C.E.

Hellenism

The blitzkrieg arrival of Alexander the Great on the international scene brought with it a host of Hellenistic influences on Palestinian and Diaspora Judaism. Alexander and his followers were Greco-chauvinist missionaries of Hellenistic culture. They established Hellenistic cities and left behind Greek troops to intermarry with the local populace. Greek institutions and culture spread to the remotest regions of the empire. Hellenistic influences included language and literature, customs and dress, architecture and the arts, as well as religious and philosophical beliefs. These pervasive influences were vibrant, dynamic, and alien to Jewish culture. Exposure to Hellenism was a centuries-long process that no one escaped. Greek citizens enjoyed special rights and privileges that often made Hellenism popular with native culture. Even those who despised Hellenism knew that to be successful nationalists they needed to know well the culture of the imperialists. This knowledge was clearly a matter of survival. Judah had been inundated with foreign merchants, government officials, and soldiers. Yet this condition presented a double-edged sword. The advent of Hellenism in the East not only produced a change in indigenous culture, but to a lesser extent, the orientalization of the Greeks themselves. Thus, Judaism, like Hellenism, also became a portable culture. Greeks could--and did--embrace Judaism. The practice of observing the Sabbath is but one example of Greek adaptation of Jewish culture.

Jews reacted to the infusion of Hellenism in many of the same ways as other indigenous cultures. Consequently, scholars have debated the degree of Hellenization among Judeans. There appear to be numerous examples of those who felt little conflict between Judaism and the new cultural context. The famous Jewish philosopher, Philo, for example, lived in Alexandria, Egypt, a Greek *polis*. He wrote and expressed his thoughts in Greek yet evidently remained a devout Jew. The Letter of Aristeus also conveys the attitude that Jews could be a part of Hellenistic society without sacrificing their Judaism. Similarly, in the book of Tobit, Tobias gave his son a Greek education, yet remained loyal to the Torah. One of the best examples of external influence comes from coins minted during the Hasmonean period. Written in both Greek and Hebrew, they use Hellenistic titles and names, as well as their Jewish counterparts. Even the symbols on the coins are Hellenistic. But perhaps the most telling evidence of Hellenistic influence of the Jewish people was the translation of the Hebrew Scriptures into Greek, called the Septuagint. The Septuagint is the only oriental book translated into Greek in antiquity; furthermore it is the first translation of any civilization's sacred scripture into another tongue. The Torah was translated in the early third century B.C.E., and was followed later by the translation of other books of the Hebrew Bible by different individuals in subsequent decades. Consequently, the Hebrew Bible then was made available to those Jews in Alexandria who did not have the ability to read the Hebrew language.

Reaction to Greek cultural symbols often was interpreted as a means of expressing loyalty to Judaism. Pressure to adopt the ways of the Greeks appears to be less pronounced in the Ptolemaic period than under the Seleucids, yet many Jews were never fully at home in the hellenized world. The exalted emphasis on the human body and the capricious nature of the gods of Greek religion were particularly troubling to many Jews. Yet, at the same time individuals could not escape the trappings of Hellenistic culture if they were to trade, be educated, or live in the larger cities. On the other hand, many Jews saw Hellenism as an alarming threat that could extinguish the very existence of Judaism. The books of 1 and 2 Maccabees portray Jewish supporters of Hellenism as little less than apostates who betrayed their place as loyal followers of Yahweh. The suppression of Jewish worship by the Seleucid ruler Antiochus was a watershed event that solidified strong resistance against the Hellenistic Seleucid establishment and the cultural values it espoused. Those who compromised orthodoxy by associating with these pagans, such as the high priest Jason, appear in the surviving literature as treacherous infidels. Many Jews became suspicious of any semblance of unorthodoxy. Consequently, Jewish communities often turned inwardly upon each other, accusing each other of infidelity, and worrying that their entire religious heritage was at stake.

A final analysis reveals the Jews had no simple homogenized response to the rise of Hellenism. To speak glibly of a simply dichotomy between Judaism and Hellenism is to oversimplify a highly nuanced cultural phenomenon. Even modern interpretations of Hellenism are often colored by the views of the interpreter. Some evaluate the contributions of Hellenism to Judaism positively, in that the Jewish response to Hellenism brought about a recognizable faith that was able to deal effectively with the struggles of a changing culture. Others offer a more negative view that Judaism and Hellenism represented a clash between two divergent and totally distinct cultures. Some even have argued that the day-to-day lifestyle of the average rural Jew barely was affected by Greek culture. This, however, is difficult to imagine. The newly minted ideas of the Greeks built a legacy for all cultures of their empire, and the Jews were no exception. A devotion to learning, the Greek language and literary genres, and even Greek architecture were qualities many Jews eagerly adopted.

The Torah

One of the oddities of the beginnings of the Maccabean revolt highlights the importance of the Torah to Second Temple Judaism. When Antiochus desecrated the temple in 167 B.C.E. by offering a pagan sacrifice to Zeus, the Jews rallied in defense of the faith of their ancestors. The specific rallying point mentioned in the book of 1 Maccabees, however, was not at all the temple, but rather the Torah. Mattathias issued a defiant challenge, "Arrogance and scorn have now become strong; it is a time of ruin and furious anger. Now my children, show zeal for the *law*, and give your lives for the covenant of our ancestors" (1 Macc. 1:49-50). The Seleucids correctly perceived devotion to the Law as a serious threat, and consequently burned many of the copies of the Torah (1 Macc. 1:56-7).

The Israelite concept of Torah is defined more as revelation than legislation. The Hebrew word *torah* translates into the Greek language as "law." Referring to the first five books of the Hebrew Bible, the Torah not only contained legal materials, but also narratives, poetry, songs, blessings, genealogies and many other literary genres. The Torah was essentially the national constitution of the Jewish people. The Torah conveyed all ethical instruction, cultic regulation, civil and criminal law. The distillation of that Law carefully was passed down from one generation to the next. Observance of Torah had always been a unifying force in Israel, but was even more so due to the demise of the monarchy and the precarious nature of the second temple. Jews could observe obligations to the Torah no matter where they lived in the empire. The Law even sanctified the smallest details of life, from ceremonial preparation of foods to daily prayers.

Of course, no written law could hope to presuppose every eventual contingency. As historical and cultural circumstances changed or when contradictions in the Law became evident, further supplementation became necessary. The Hebrew Bible itself attests to such a problem as judges and priests assumed authority in matters related to the interpretation of the Law. In the Second Temple period, respected Jewish teachers debated the application and interpretation of Torah commands. Consequently a corpus of oral arguments served to clarify and articulate Israel's obligations to the Law. Thus, this Oral Law became a fence around the Torah to preserve its commands in a changing culture. The Hebrew term, *halakah* refers to moral and ethical instruction while *haggadah* denotes doctrinal teaching of this oral tradition. Those customs or beliefs, as associated with recognized authority, were accepted by a majority of teachers, and functioned as an Oral Law so long as they did not contradict the Pentateuch. Around 200 C.E., the Jews would write down this Oral Law as the Mishnah. The Mishnah would eventually become the core of the Talmud three centuries later. As might be expected, the authority of this Oral Law was questioned by some and rejected outright by others.   The Sadducees and Samaritans rejected the Oral Law in its entirety, affirming the sole authority of the Mosaic Law. Early Christianity appealed to the legalism of the Pharisees as an example of the abuses inherent in these oral traditions. Christians claimed that the death of Jesus the Messiah freed them from the constraints of the Old Covenant, the Torah. This newly discovered freedom for the early Christians did not mean outright rejection of the Law, but adherence to a new covenant. This new covenant embraced some traditions of Israel, yet rejected others. Similar to the Oral Law that reinterpreted the Torah for new generations, Christians adhered to a law written in the human heart.

The Calendar

No part of the Hebrew Bible presents a full accounting of the cultic calendar. The portions of the calendar that are documented can only be gleaned from incidental references. It appears that, as with much of the Ancient Near East, the Israelites followed a lunisolar calendar.

Table 7.1

	Hebrew Calendar	
Babylonian Name	**Hebrew Name**	**Time Frame**
1. Nisanu	1. Nisan, *Abib (Neh 2:1, Esth 3:7)	March/April
2. Aiaru	2. [Iyyar], *Ziv (1 Kgs 6:1, 37)	April/May
3. Simanu	3. Sivan (Esth 8:9)	May/June
4. Duzu	4. [Tammuz]	June/July
5. Abu	5. [Ab]	July/August
6. Ululu	6. Elul (Neh 6:15)	August/September
7. Tashritu	7. *Ethanim [Tishri] (1 Kgs 8:2)	September/October
8. Arahsamnu	8. *Bul [Marcheshran] (I Kgs 6:38)	October/November
9. Kislimu	9. Chislev (Neh 1:1, Zech 7:1)	November/Dec.
10. Tebutu	10. Tebet (Esth 2:16)	December/January
11. Shabatu	11. Shebet (Zech 1:7)	January/February
12. Addaru	12. Adar (Ez 6:15; Esth 3:7,13; 8:12; 9:1, 15, 17, 19,21)	February/March
13.	13. [Adar Sheni] (Second Adar)	

*refers to Canaanite month names
[ ] denotes months the Hebrew Bible does not explicitly mention

The moon determined the months, while the seasons dictated the years. Of course, 12 lunar months do not divide the solar year evenly, and solar days do not divide each month into equal parts. The lunar calendar fell behind by 11 days per year. Scholars do not know how the Jews in the biblical period corrected this shortage, but they do know that by 380 B.C.E., the Jews implemented the practice of intercalcation whereby a month was added roughly every three years.

The Hebrew Bible presents three different methods for naming of months. In some instances, it uses Canaanite names for the months; in other instances, it employs Babylonian, and in still others, it refers to months simply by ordinal numbers, such as the expression, "the seventh month.

During the Second Temple period the sacred calendar became an important concern and a magnet for controversy. Years earlier, Ezekiel had elaborated a specific cultic calendar, and the priestly portions of the Pentateuch likewise are preoccupied with calendric concerns. The first Jewish document with a complete rendering of the calendar is *1 Enoch*. In this account, the angel Uriel reveals the sacred calendar to Enoch (*1 En.* 72-82). This calendar, however, was not based on a lunar model, but a solar model of 364 days, 52 weeks of seven days. In this system each month begins on a Wednesday and has 31 days. The four remaining days are seasonal markers dividing summer, fall, winter, and spring. This solar calendar had much to commend it to many Jewish communities in the period. With the regularity of this calendar, every festival began on the same day of the week each year rather than changing each year as they did under a lunar calendar.

But the issue became much more than a preferential concern. *Jubilees* is an excellent example of this preoccupation, defending the solar calendar against a corrupt lunar alternative followed by the Hasmonean priests. The fallacy of the lunar calendar, according to the book of Jubilees, was that the important sacred mandates of the faith were invalidated if performed on the incorrect dates. Sectarian literature from the community of Qumran indicates that their community followed the same solar calendar. The *Habbakuk Commentary* from Qumran presents an interesting account of the Wicked Priest who appears to the community on the Day of Atonement. If this reference is indeed historical, and the Wicked Priest was part of the Jerusalem cult, quite unlikely, then, would he journey to Qumran on the most sacred day of the cultic year? But if two distinctly different calendars are being followed, such confusion is resolved. Thus, the solar calendar became another way of criticizing the Hasmonean regime. Such calendric concerns even may have foreshadowed changes that Early Christianity implemented by moving the day of worship from Saturday to Sunday.

Conclusion

In the Second Temple period, any consensus that might have existed over the issues of temple, priesthood, Hellenism, Torah, and calendar evaporated. The breakdown of this consensus led to many divergent Judaisms. Controversies over what would constitute the people of God in this generation were revived. The sticking points of temple, priesthood, Hellenism, Torah, and calendar proved irreconcilable between these varied constituencies of Judaism. The New Testament and Rabbinic literature mention some of these communities, and ignore others. But they all played a crucial role in the socio-religious setting of the period. Thus, comprehending the basics of these diverse groups is essential to understanding Second Temple Judaism.

Chapter 8

Schisms and Heterogeneity: Judaisms of the Second Temple Period

For most of the Second Temple period the Jews existed as a colony of one of the dominant powers of the age: Persia, Greece, or Rome. Their lack of political autonomy accentuated the need for clear socio-religious boundaries within Palestinian and Diaspora Judaism. Language, land, ideology, and political loyalties separated the Jews of this period. Formerly, they were a nation with fixed borders; now they were an amorphous cluster of constituencies with no defined center. Such diversity resulted in many expressions of Judaism competing as normative models of classical Hebraic faith. Earlier scholarly reconstructions of this period regarded the Pharisees and Rabbinic Judaism alone as the normative representation of Judaism, but all other expressions of Judaism as sects. Such a distinction is problematic. Sociologists use he term, "sect" is used to refer to a community that exists in opposition to a central institution. Such a condition in Jewry around the turn of the Common Era is difficult to document. Recently, students of this period have recognized that the Pharisees, like other socio-religious communities, represent a burgeoning diversity among the Jewish communities during the Second Temple period.

Josephus claimed that there were 24 Jewish sects in the first century C.E. The actual religious picture was undoubtedly more complex than that. Each faith community sought in its own way to find its place in a tumultuous cultural context. Conformist models of community sought to adapt to the changing cultural setting by cooperating with and being assimilated by that culture. Revolutionist perspectives sought to change the social world, engaging in social and political activities that hoped to confront this hostile culture and change it from outside. Eschatological models were content to wait for the destruction of the present evil order by divine forces. Introversionist perspectives withdrew from the world into purified communities. Lastly, utopian leanings sought to reconstruct the world from within according to divine principles, without the need for external revolution. The extent to which student of the Bible can define which specific groups fit these models is extremely difficult and highly nuanced. Some communities, for example, became more revolutionist as political situations changed. But one element is common to all of the various parties of Judaism. They were all "intentional" societies of like-minded people who had made self-conscious decisions to join a group that they believed offered a form of Jewish identity superior to others.

Sketchy and even contradictory sources have led to most of the problems in examining the parties of Judaism during the Second Temple period. All written sources available to date were politically and ideologically motivated. As outsiders, scholars look upon these disparate groups as sects or parties of a larger amorphous Judaism, but the self-understanding of these communities was quite different. The truth is that most of these movements simply referred to themselves by the title "Israel" since they understood their community to be nothing less than the oppressed successors of ancient Israel, though of course under foreign rule. This self-definition provided an enhanced status as the remnant, the elect of Israel. Likewise, this self-understanding of their community as God's holy nation impacted the way they related to other Jewish parties. The boundaries between these communities were not equally crossable. Some were closed to outsiders; others were more open. To some, outsiders were merely non-Israelites, but to others an outsider was anyone who was not a part of their own   narrow community. So, outlining the more crucial parties proves essential to grasping this period.

Hasidim

The origins and nature of the Hasidim or "Hasideans" has been the subject of much speculation. Some scholars have interpreted this group as the forerunners of the Essenes or Pharisees, as authors of apocalyptic literature, or as the source behind the biblical book of Daniel. None of these views, however, have enough specific evidence to convince wider scholarship. More likely, the Hasidim may have been part of the popular revolt surrounding the Maccabees during the third century B.C.E. They seem to have been a definite, coherent entity, but the extent to which they were an organized community is debatable. The designation may simply refer to a somewhat loosely knit faction of pious Jews, possibly scribes, who associated themselves in support of the revolt of Mattathias and Judas. Scholars of an earlier generation speculated that the Hasidim were a pacifist group, but the historical record indicates otherwise: at the very least they willingly cooperated with the initial stages of the Maccabean revolt.

The first book of Maccabees (2:42) describes this group as mighty warriors who offered themselves willingly in support of the Maccabees. The high priest Alchimus, himself a Hellenizer, recognized their association with Judas Maccabeus and accused them of stirring up sedition and warfare (1 Macc 7:13). At some point in the conflict, however, the tables turned, and members of the Hasidim deserted Judas' cause. This turnabout apparently was rooted in their faith in the empty promises of the Syrian emissaries, Baccides and Alchimus, that peace could be brought through cooperation. The Hasidim were among the first to seek peace. Alchimus, however, double-crossed the Hasidim, killing over sixty of their followers (1 Macc 7:13). The first book of Maccabees does not record why Alchimus turned on the cooperating party, but scholars assume their past opposition to the Seleucid faction prompted him to neutralize any possible threat of future uprisings. The Hasidim quickly disappeared from the historical record, and are not mentioned in the literature of the late Second Temple period.

Samaritans

Nowhere is the issue of contradictory and ideological sources more problematic than with the Samaritans. Whether the uniqueness of this group is due primarily to geographic, ethnic, or doctrinal differences is not clear, nor is how much interaction existed between Samaritans and other Judaisms of the Second Temple period. Jewish sources describing the Samaritans are incredibly hostile while Samaritan documents are extremely late. Both are worth a critical examination.

Samaritan history is difficult to trace, though about 300 still live today in Nablus near Shechem. Two radically different versions of the origins of this important community appear during the Second Temple period. The Samaritans refer to themselves as the only authentic Israelites, descendants of the northern tribes of Ephraim and Manasseh. Samaritan documents argue that the wicked priest Eli established an illegitimate priesthood when he moved the sanctuary from Shechem to Shiloh. These documents reason that the book of Deuteronomy indicates clearly that Mt. Gerazim is the only place where Yahweh promised to cause his name to dwell--never Shiloh, and certainly never Jerusalem. The Samaritan traditions of their own origins are not without merit. The term that the Old Testament uses to speak of the Samaritans (*šōmrōnîm*) is found only in 2 Kings 17:29. Samaritan sources use this same term, but only to refer to the inhabitants of the city of Samaria, not the members of the Samaritan religious order. The Samaritans instead preferred the term "*šōmer,*" which means, "to keep," a clear self-designation as keepers of the law. From this insight, sufficient doubt arises as to whether the passage in 2 Kings 17 refers to the Samaritans at all. Given the polemical nature of the passage, 2 Kings 17 is no longer widely regarded as an account of the origins of the Samaritans as a religious group, but instead is to refer only to the inhabitants of the city of Samaria. Some recent translations even use the term "Samarians" rather than "Samaritans" in verse 29. Perhaps the biggest problem with Samaritan accounts of their own origins is that all the sources that describe these early beginnings date from the Middle Ages or later. There are simply no sources from the Second Temple period that confirm this account.

The Jewish perspective of the origins of the Samaritan community is qualitatively different. Samaritans are described in 2 Kings 17 as descendants of colonists, brought into the region by the Assyrians when they conquered the Northern Kingdom of Israel in 722 B.C.E. This group retained only a thin veneer of genuine Israelite religion. Whatever knowledge of biblical monotheism they possessed was both syncretized and superficial. Most of 2 Kings 17 is a theological reflection of the underlying reasons behind the fall of Samaria and Israel. The context implies that the Assyrians deported all residents of Samaria and replaced them by a number of settlers from Babylon,

Cuthah, Avvah, Hamath, and elsewhere. Ultimately, this geographic exchange resulted in years of intermarriage between the colonists and the resident population of Israel.

Ezra 4 mentions that the "enemies of Judah and Benjamin" wanted to assist with the temple project, but the Babylonian returnees rejected them. Consequently, they then opposed the construction of the temple. Ezra 3 indicates that the "people of the land" opposed the project from the outset. Until recently, the normative assumption was that these two groups refer to the Samaritans. This view, however, can no longer be held with certainty. If the Samaritan accounts of their own origins are taken into consideration, the last thing they would have wanted to do was erect a temple *in Jerusalem*, since Mt. Gerazim was the only legitimate site for the location of the temple. Most likely the "enemies of Judah" and Benjamin were northerners of some sort, and the "people of the land" were the Palestinian-born populace who felt that the ruling powers would perceive the existence of the temple as an attempt to assert independence. Since neither of the accounts in 2 Kings and Ezra 3-4 unequivocally refer to the Samaritans, the view that the Samaritans were a mixed culture of Jews and gentiles who broke from Judaism over the building of the Second Temple remains questionable.

References to the Samaritans in apocryphal and pseudepigraphical literature are much more explicitly hostile. The apocryphal book of Ben Sira states, "My whole being loathes two nations (*gôyim*), the third is not even a people (*'ām*); those who live in Seir (Edom) and Philistia, and the degenerates (*nābāl*) who dwell in Shechem" (Sir 50:25). Dating from the second century B.C.E., this is the first clear reference to the Samaritans as a coherent group in Jewish literature. The book of Second Maccabees 6:1-2 implies that the Samaritans actually welcomed the hellenizing practices of Antiochus IV, an implication Josephus makes explicit. *The Testament of Levi* mentions a number of evils done by the Shechemites, evils that elicit the punishment, "from this day Shechem shall be called a city of imbeciles" (*T. Levi* 5:2). The books of Jubilees and Judith also attest to anti-Samaritan hostilities.

Josephus mentions a Samaritan temple erected in the time of Alexander the Great on Mt. Gerazim. He speaks of a Jewish high priest named Manasseh who married the daughter of Sanballat, the Cuthian governor of Samaria. Manasseh renounced his allegiance to the Persian emperor Darius, and transferred his loyalty to the Greeks and Alexander. Sanballat rewarded him by allowing him to build a temple at Mt. Gerazim. Josephus provides an account of the process of building, but his account sounds suspiciously like his other stories of temple building, so some scholars assume he borrowed elements from these parallel sources. Archaeological evidence is vague and Samaritan sources seldom mention the temple, so the exact origins of the Samaritan temple are in dispute. Clearly, however, John Hyrcanus destroyed the Samaritan temple in 128 B.C.E.

The Samaritans themselves were not a monolithic religious system. In fact, several complex sects existed within Samaritanism, most notably, the Dositheans. However, the faith of these Samaritan communities revolved around five cardinal distinctives. First, radical monotheism characterized this party. So radical was their faith in Yahweh that when the Hebrew Pentateuch refers to God as "Elohim" (plural), the Samaritan Pentateuch changed the name to a singular form. Second, it views Moses as the only inspired prophet. In the Middle Ages, Samaritan literature depicts Moses as the pre-existent primordial light who illuminated the world, so the future restorer of the new age ultimately would be like Moses. Third, the Torah is the only Scripture for the Samaritans. The Samaritan Pentateuch is unique, written in Hebrew, but with an archaizing script. There are numerous variations between the Masoretic Text of the Hebrew Bible and the Samaritan Pentateuch. One of the most significant differences between the Samaritan Pentateuch and the Hebrew Bible is in the Decalogue. The Samaritan Pentateuch combines the first two commands and adds a tenth, advocating Mt. Gerazim as the only legitimate place of worship (which in turn is the fourth distinctive of Samaritan faith). As the religious navel of the world, Gerazim is where, according to Samaritan tradition, Abel built the first altar. Later, the priest Eli mistakenly moved the shrine to Shiloh, and David ultimately transferred it to Jerusalem. The Samaritans offered sacrifices regularly at Mt. Gerazim. In fact, Samaritans today still sacrifice at Mt. Gerazim during the Passover. They reject the feasts of Purim and Hanukkah and adhere to a slightly different calendar. The final distinctive teaching of the Samaritans is that their teaching regularly refers to an apocalyptic Day of Vengeance. The evil priest Eli instituted the Period of Disfavor that will continue until the Messiah initiates the new age of grace. On the Day of Vengeance, Samaritans will be vindicated and a Moses-like Messiah will lead the community to glory.

The case of the Samaritans shows how partisan depictions separated groups of this nature. To outsiders, the Samaritans behaved as Jews. They were monotheists, followed the Sabbath, circumcision, and the dietary laws of the Torah. But they did not associate with Jews in any way, nor did other Judaisms associate with them. They identified themselves as ethnic Israelites, but not Jews. The social borders between the two groups were airtight. In fact, Jews and Samaritans regarded one another as foreigners. They worshipped at their own holy sites, had their own calendar, and lived completely independent of one another.

Two instances from the life of Jesus in the New Testament highlight the extent of the animosity between Jews and Samaritans. In John's gospel, he relates a conversation between Jesus and the woman at the well (John 4). Jesus' disciples were stunned to find that Jesus had entered into a spiritual conversation with the woman. On another occasion, in the parable of the Good Samaritan, Jesus uses a Samaritan as an example of how people ought to treat one another. Whereas religious Jews avoided contact with the injured traveler, in the narrative the Samaritan ironically proves to be the only person to come to his aid. The point of Jesus' parable illustrates, among other things, just how despised the Samaritans had become to other Jewish communities.

Pharisees

Most students of the Bible think they know more about the Pharisees than they actually do. Again, the problem is one of available sources. The data is limited, late, contradictory, and tendentious. The Pharisees had no writings of their own, at least none that have been clearly identified from this period. Thus, reaching firm conclusions about their origins, beliefs, and influence remains vexing. Three main ancient sources speak explicitly of the Pharisees: Josephus, the New Testament, and the Rabbinic Writings. The fragmentary nature of the primary sources has led to oversimplified harmonizations of these accounts and often-romantic speculations about the history, political outlook, and the characteristics of this group. Recent research has made these issues even more obscure, as the primary sources of Josephus and Rabbinic Literature only relatively recently have been subject to historical-critical analysis. The New Testament is equally ideological, as it consistently depicts Pharisees as hypocrites. Of the three sources, the New Testament and the Rabbinic Literature are most similar in their descriptions of the group. While the New Testament primarily portrays the Pharisees as the chief nemesis of Jesus, it sides with Rabbinic Literature by presenting them as a lay movement of individuals devoted to ritual purity, the Sabbath, and tithing. These lay leaders seem to have been educated, but they held subordinate positions in society. Scholarly reconstructions in the last several decades have portrayed the Pharisees primarily as a table fellowship sect that made the home a miniature version of the temple. Thus, the Pharisee was analogous to the priest, the hearth of the home to the altar, and the house to the temple itself. Aspects of domestic life--such as food, sex, and marriage--lay at the heart of the Pharisees' concerns. The name "Pharisee" may revert to the Hebrew *pārāš*, which means, "to stand apart." Surprisingly, while the New Testament and Rabbinic Literature speak of the ancestral traditions of the Pharisees, they do not specifically connect the Pharisees with the Oral Torah, a doctrine that clearly characterized Rabbinic Judaism.

Josephus presents a picture of the Pharisees that complicates the one offered in the New Testament and Rabbinic Literature (*Ant.* 18:12-17). Even his own writings often contradict themselves. While Josephus mentions the Pharisees less than 20 times in his writings, he describes the group as the leading sect of Judaism. He asserts that he himself aligned with all three of the major Jewish sects--Sadducees, Essenes, and Pharisees--only to ultimately identify himself as a Pharisee. Realistically, for Josephus to unite with each of these groups, given his own chronology showing he would have had to accomplish this before age 19, would be nearly impossible.

Josephus states the Pharisees were the most accurate of all groups in interpreting Hebrew Law; thus, they were not only distinctive, but also decisive. They believed in the immortality of the soul and in the concept of divine fate, and held a mediating position between the extreme predestinarianism of the Essenes and the free will of the Sadducees. Josephus portrays the Pharisees as having so much influence with the people that even kings and high priests were subject to their powerful wishes. His descriptions of the authority of the Pharisees are exaggerated, since his own historical narratives seem to be fairly neutral to the Pharisees, indicating that they may have not had the political clout that he assigns them elsewhere.

Josephus did not discuss the origins of the Pharisees, but they seem to have flourished from the Hasmonean period to the destruction of the temple in 70 C.E. He mentioned that John Hyrcanus broke with the Pharisees when they criticized the priestly offices he held. Considerable opposition of the group to Alexander Janneus is also evidenced. Josephus records that on Janneus deathbed, Janneus instructed his wife, Alexandra Salome, to make peace with the Pharisees. During her reign the Pharisees probably had a great deal of influence with the governing class. This clout evidently diminished greatly under Herod, however, as he had a number killed and thousands more fined for refusing an oath of loyalty. Recent analysis, therefore, indicates that Josephus' superficial portraiture has led to the depiction of the Pharisees as an all-powerful legalistic leader of "consensus Judaism" which in turn is patently incorrect.

The New Testament consistently portrays the Pharisees as stereotypical opponent of Jesus. They challenged his credentials and were often the unwilling recipients of some of Jesus' more polemical teachings. All four gospels link the Pharisees with the Scribes. From this linkage, at least some of the Pharisees were scribes. Matthew's gospel pairs the Pharisees and Sadducees in challenging the authority of Jesus, while Matthew and John pair them with the chief priests. In spite of their adversarial presentation in the gospels, the teachings of Jesus often are similar to the Pharisees. Belief in the concept of resurrection, acknowledgement of angels and demons, and openness to the reinterpretation of the Law are all traits that Jesus' teachings shared with the Pharisees. In fact, Josephus, the New Testament, and the Rabbinic Literature are all unanimous in supporting the Pharisees' belief in the afterlife.

The question also is open regarding the relationship of the Pharisees to the rabbinic movement, which rose out of the catastrophe of the destruction of Jerusalem in 70 C.E. Until recent decades, the Pharisees were thought to be the forerunners of Rabbinic Judaism. The Rabbinic Literature, however, does not make this association, and it remains silent on the Pharisees actually cited by name in Josephus and the New Testament. In addition, love of the study of Torah and the importance of Oral Torah as chief cornerstones of the Rabbinic Movement are not mentioned in association with the Pharisees in the Mishnah. It is also remarkable that the Rabbinic traditions say nothing about their political agenda. Most rabbinic literature focuses on ceremonial issues of purity, washing, eating, tithing, and the Sabbath. Any attempt to draw a line of continuity between the Pharisees and Rabbinic Judaism must, at least as this point, be speculative. Therefore, that all aspects of Rabbinic life originated with Pharasaic traditions seems unlikely.

Essenes and the Community at Qumran

Pliny the Elder, Philo, and Josephus, describe the Essenes, but they are not mentioned in the Hebrew Bible, the New Testament, or the Apocrypha. Pliny's now infamous account tells how,

> Lying on the west of Asphaltites, and sufficiently distant to escape its noxious exhalations, are the Esseni, a people that live apart from the world, and marvelous beyond all others throughout the whole earth, for they have no women among them; to sexual desire they are strangers; money they have none; the palm trees are their only companions.   Day after day, however, their numbers are fully recruited by multitudes of strangers that resort to them, driven thither to adopt their usages by the tempests of fortune, and wearied with the miseries of life.   Thus it is, that through thousands of ages, incredible to relate, this people eternally prolongs its existence, without a single birth taking place there; so fruitful a source of population so it is that weariness to life which is felt by others (*Nat* V.17).

Philo's account is remarkably similar, stating that the Essenes lived in villages, and shunned property, sacrifice, the taking of slaves, marriage, and the taking of oaths. He notes they were devoted to the study of the Law and doing good works; furthermore they strictly observed the Sabbath. Philo also mentions 4000 Essenes were in Palestine. Josephus echoes the above observations, stating that the Essenes were one of three primary sects in Judaism, along with the Pharisees and Sadducees.   Given the Essenes' elaborate initiation process, Josephus' claim that he himself personally experimented with all three sects shrinks even further from the truth.

The Essenes appear to have been spread throughout Palestine. Their uncertain origins probably date around 200 B.C.E., and they seem to disappear with the destruction of Jerusalem in 70 C.E.   They had elaborate   procedures   for   admission   and   equally   elaborate preoccupations with the cohesion of that community.   They took their meals in common, and held ritual purity a prerequisite for every aspect of the community.

One of the more lively debates in Dead Sea Scroll studies is over the relationship, if any, the Essenes had with the community at Qumran. There is an uneasy consensus that the community at Qumran was some type of Essene commune, although this consensus has faced a strong challenge in recent decades. The location of Qumran is roughly equivalent to Pliny's description of the Essenes, and the process of admission, communal property, celibacy, and dissent with Jerusalem temple ritual, where the life of the community serves as a substitute for sacrifice, are all common to both Essenism and Qumran. The Qumran community was obsessed with the priesthood, however, which is missing in descriptions of Essenism, as is the dualistic light and darkness motif is also absent.

Archaeological and literary evidence indicates that there may have been three different periods of occupation at the site of Qumran. The earliest archaeological stratum (Period 1a) appears to originate during the time of John Hyrcanus at the latest (134-104 B.C.E), and perhaps earlier. The initial phases of the community must have preceded the actual settlement at Qumran. *The Damascus Document*, for example, refers to two important individuals: the Wicked Priest, and the Teacher of Righteousness. Most interpreters assume that the Wicked Priest was probably a Hasmonean who was not a Zadokite. Many scholars concur that this was most likely Jonathan the Maccabee. If this identification is accurate, then the community was probably founded between 150-140 B.C.E. The group absolutely rejected the non-Zadokite priesthood of Jonathan and the Hasmoneans. The Damascus Document refers to a "flight to Damascus," which may have been a cryptic reference to a self-imposed exile to Qumran. The persecution of the Pharisees by John Hyrcanus may have caused other disenfranchised groups like them to flee to other locations. During this period designated by the archaeological record as 1b, (135-104) there was extensive enlargement of the site, indicating an influx of inhabitants. Early in the first century, B.C.E., there is evidence of an earthquake and fire, followed by a period when the site was unoccupied. Qumran was rebuilt during the reign of Herod's son Archelaus and destroyed in 68 C.E. during the Roman occupation of Judea.

The covenanters of Qumran held rigorous admission standards as a community completely committed to a total life reorientation toward

the new life of the community that they called the *yāhād*. The borders
of the yahad were not easy to cross. A potential member would first be
examined by the priest, followed by a one-year probationary period. If
after a year the individual successfully completed a rigorous
reexamination, he would be admitted to "the purity of the many," and
could partake in the common meal. After another trial year the
successful applicant would be admitted to the "drink of the many,"
property would be turned over to the commune and the applicant could
speak in the assembly. Everything was submitted to the will of the
congregation, from sexual relations to meals, careless talk, dress, and
washings. Even natural bodily functions were subject to the regulations
of the community. There was a long list of punishments for offenders
and punishment was strictly maintained. For example, individuals
could be expelled from the community for misuse of the divine name,
informing against the sect, or complaining about the teachings of the
community. Temporary censure and limitation of food rations could be
caused by speaking angrily against a member, gossiping, using
insulting language, lying about money, or bearing a grudge. Food
rations could also be reduced for offenses such as missing a vote,
falling asleep during the assembly, laughing loud and foolishly,
exposing one's genitals, or even gesticulating with one's left hand.

The central event of the community was the common meal, and the
site of Qumran contains several large reservoirs for ritual washings.
They observed a solar calendar of 12 thirty-day months plus one day
each quarter. With this calendar, holy days fell on the same day of the
week each year. This rigid structure of calendar, communal life, and
admission requirements provided order for the community.

The community of Qumran envisioned itself as an eschatological
community. Referring to themselves by the self-designation, "Israel,"
or "the remnant left to Israel," they felt that God had called them out of
the world. The commune was highly structured into categories of
priests and laity, and further distinguished into figurative units of
thousands, hundreds, fifties, and tens. Messianism played a key role in
the foundation of the community. The *telos* of the community was
rooted in an eschatological idea of a battle between the "sons of light"
and the "sons of darkness," whereby the sons of light would emerge
victorious. There are definite similarities to the Samaritans in that a
final day of reckoning is projected; yet one key difference lies in the
way these two communities perceived themselves as eschatological

socio-religious groups. While the Samaritans saw themselves as the *original* Israelites, the covenanters at Qumran envisioned themselves as the *last* Israelites.

The re-establishment of the Zadokite priestly line was of utmost importance to Qumran. One of their most popular self-designations, "sons of Zadok," was a euphemism for the entire community, not just the priests. The group interpreted the law strictly. One of the documents present among the Dead Sea Scrolls was the Temple Scroll. A typical hermeneutic in the Temple Scroll, for example, was to take legal texts from Leviticus and Deuteronomy, combine them, and heighten them to raise the standards of the Law. In doing so, the community may have viewed the Temple Scroll as Scripture and equal in authority to the Pentateuch. Their hyper-nomistic stance demonstrated their perception of themselves as the Torah community.

It is also possible to link the origins of the covenanters at Qumran with the Sadducees. Recent publications of what is known as the Halahkic Letter (4Q394-399) have added new insights about the origins of the Qumran community. It is speculated that the earliest members of the community were Sadducees who refused to support the new hierarchy in Jerusalem after the Maccabees gained independence from the Seleucids. The new Hasmonean leaders replaced Zadokite priests with their own, non-Zadokite priesthood. Evidently some of their Sadducean brethren continued to serve in the temple under the new regime. This compromise was unacceptable to those who separated themselves from the Jerusalem establishment and fled to "Damascus," a metaphor for their new home near the Dead Sea.

There are also parallels between the Qumran community and early Christianity. Early Christian emphasis on baptism and the celebration of the communal meal all have strong parallels to Qumran. Another parallel is John the Baptist's ministry of baptism in the remote desert of Judea, and his monastic brand of breaking with the Jerusalem establishment. Jesus' comments about being children of light also echo eschatological themes of Qumran regarding the Sons of Light and the Sons of Darkness. Others are quick to point out the major differences between the early Christian community and the yahad at Qumran. While these parallels are intriguing, there has still been no definitive proof of a direct connection between Qumran and the Jesus Movement or early Christianity.

Enoch Groups/Enochic Judaism

An inordinate amount of literature in the Second Temple period centers on the mysterious figure of Enoch, an individual mentioned in the Hebrew Bible for only seven verses, but who commanded a great deal of attention in later literature. Genesis 5:24 states, "Enoch walked with God; then he was no more, because God took him away." The books of 1 Enoch, Jubilees, the Temple Scroll, the Damascus Document, the Proto Epistle of Enoch, the Similitudes of Enoch, and the Testament of the Twelve Patriarchs all render significant witness to a non-conformist priestly tradition that was different from the Zadokite priestly establishment, each exhibiting a fascination with Enoch. There is no evidence of a schismatic party of Enochians, but there is extensive literary evidence of a religious tradition quite different from that espoused by the Zakokites.

This literature is characterized primarily by the concept of the origin of evil through a group of rebellious angels responsible for the spread of sin and rebellion. The Zadokite status quo maintained that in creation, God transformed primeval chaos into order. As a result, sin and evil were limited by precise boundaries. The Jerusalem temple was the visual earthly symbol of that order, and the priests faithfully kept the sacred spiritual regularity that God had inaugurated at creation. Enochic Judaism, on the other hand, held that original sin had corrupted the world. Primordial beings crossed over God's sacred boundaries, resulting in the physical union between evil angels and human women, their offspring thus wreaking havoc in the world (*1 En.* 15:8-10). In this sense, the human race is a victim of evil, yet still responsible for it. Restoration of this corrupted world order would not come through the temple, but through some future cosmic crisis. The Elect One would reign in glory and judge the evil in the world (*1 En* 55:4).

Historically, the origins of this tradition may have roots in the Maccabean period, and evidence in the Damascus Document indicates that this may have even been a parent movement to the community of Qumran. The preponderance of literary evidence would indicate that Enochic Judaism was extremely popular in the late Second Temple period. Beliefs in the super-human origins of evil, the freedom of these and all beings to rebel, and the freedom of God to deliver the world from such rebellion were the philosophical pillars of this alternative way of thinking.

Scrbes

The scribes of the Second Temple period were probably not a unified social organization. This scribal office seemed to entail a variety of roles, but predominantly the term refers to individuals who were experts in Jewish law. Scribes appear in 1 Maccabees in association with the Hasidim against the reforms of Antiochus IV and as those seeking peace with Alchimus and Bacchides, yet the precise relationship with the Hasidim is unknown. Josephus does not appear to use the term as an organized social group, but they do appear to be community officials with somewhat unrestricted access to the king. As such, these scribes were responsible for supervising the observance of the Law. One early description of the scribe appears in the apocryphal book of Ben Sira. Here the scribe is portrayed as an individual of wisdom and discipline in the study of the Torah, one whose piety and prayerfulness are recognized not only in Israel, but among the gentiles as well.

> On the other hand he who devotes himself to the study of the law of the Most High will seek out the wisdom of all the ancients, and will be concerned with prophecies; he will preserve the discourse of notable men and penetrate the subtleties of parables; he will seek out the hidden meanings of proverbs and be at home with the obscurities of parables. He will serve among great men and appear before rulers; her will travel through the lands of foreign nations, for he tests the good and evil among men. He will set his heart to rise early to seek the Lord who made him, and will make supplication before the Most High; he will open his mouth in prayer and make supplication for his sins.
> If the great Lord is willing he will be filled with the spirit of understanding; he will pour forth words of wisdom and give thanks to the Lord in prayer. He will direct his counsel and knowledge aright, and mediate on his secrets. He will reveal instruction in his teaching and will glory in the law of the Lord's covenant. Many will praise his understanding, and it will never be blotted out; his memory will not disappear, and his name will live through all generations. Nations will declare his wisdom and the congregation will proclaim his praise; if he

lives long, he will leave a name greater than a thousand, and if he goes to rest, it is enough for him (Sir 39:1-11).

This statement from Ben Sira demonstrates, at least to some extent, the level of respect the scribes held.

If it were not for the New Testament, there would be no reason to categorize the Scribes as a religious group. In the New Testament, the terms lawyer, scribe, and teacher appear to be roughly synonymous. The gospels present these individuals in close association with the Pharisees. All four gospels link the Pharisees and Scribes as the most visible opponents of Jesus, for they questioned his lack of concern for observance of the ceremonial law. Eating with defiled hands and healing on the Sabbath were two of their chief sources of hostility, but Jesus' associations with sinners also troubled these leaders. If the late pericope of John 8 is a reliable witness, it was the Pharisees and Scribes who brought Jesus the woman who had been caught in the act of adultery, and it was they who questioned the practice of Jesus eating with known sinners. The Scribes interpreted the Law and delivered judicial pronouncements on cases brought to them. It is conceivable that many of the pluralistic religious parties of the Second Temple period had scribes.

Sadducees

The Sadducees suffered much of the bad press that characterized other religious groups of the Second Temple period. Josephus, the New Testament, and rabbinic sources all refer to this priestly group, but they are equally unsympathetic. Josephus, for example, states that they persuaded none but the wealthy, so obviously they themselves were individuals of a significant degree of wealth. Unlike the Pharisees, the Sadducees disappeared after 70 C.E. As there are no extant documents produced by the group itself, an objective accounting of the origins and characteristics of the group is difficult. The community likely originated in the Hasmonean period. Josephus is the first to mention the Sadducees, and does so in connection with John Hyrcanus, when the Hasmonean high priesthood broke with the Pharisees. Later, Salome Alexandra broke political ties with the Sadducees and transferred her support to the Pharisees.

The word "Sadducee" may have derived from the Hebrew word "*zādôk*," which means "righteous." Whether they were named after the priest Zadok is unclear. They seemed to be affluent priests who were closely associated with the temple in Jerusalem. The temple cult provided a power base and source of wealth for the Sadducees. This would account for their sudden disappearance after the temple was destroyed in 70 C.E. It is now becoming apparent that the Sadducees were not a single, coherent group at all, but represented at least three different traditions: one established near 150 B.C.E. at the temple in Leontopolis under the Ptolemies, another that withdrew into the Judean wilderness, and a third that remained in Jerusalem, forming an alliance with the Hasmonean rulers John Hyrcanus and Alexander Jannaeus.

Aristocratic religion is usually traditional and conservative. This seems to have been true for the Sadducees, who strictly adhered to the Law, rejecting oral tradition and defended priestly prerogatives. This does not mean that they had no oral interpretation of the Torah, but that they did not ascribe divine authority to their Halakah. Some have speculated that the Sadducees, like the Samaritans, limited their biblical canon to the first five books. The New Testament indicates that they rejected late developments such as a belief in resurrection, immortality of the soul, divine foreordination, and angels and demons. The Talmud and Josephus both report that in later days, public opinion forced the Sadducees to yield to Pharisaic pressures.

The New Testament depicts the high priest as a Sadducee and leader in the Sanhedrin. As leader of the Sanhedrin, he undoubtedly had close contact with the Romans. Consequently, they were often unwitting tools of the Romans, or risked the loss of their prestigious position. This is perhaps one reason for their negative portrayal in the New Testament and Josephus. After 70 C.E., the Sadducees no longer played an important role in Jewish life. Logically, the destruction of the temple meant the loss of their base of power and authority among the Jews.

Therapeutae

The only written source on this unusual monastic group was Philo's *On the Contemplation of Life*. Philo describes the Therapeutae as a group of ascetics who lived near Alexandria, Egypt, during the first century C.E.   Consisting of both men and women, they divested themselves of their possessions, owned no slaves, abandoned all ties with blood relations, and emphasized celibacy and cultic purity. Similarities to Essenes are remarkable, so the suggestion that the Therapeutae may have been a branch of the Essenes is not out of the question.   Their name derived from the Greek, meaning, "to heal," but the reason for the designation is not clear.   Presumably, the title Therapeutae became popular because they had a reputation for being adept in the art of healing either the human body or the spiritual soul. Their emphasis on the symbolism of numbers was also unique to this group.   They revered the numbers of seven and fifty as sacred, assembling together, as Philo states, after seven sets of seven days. They also observed dietary restrictions, such as abstaining from wine and meat.   Philo describes their practice of a sacred banquet in which many specific orders were followed, succeeded by the singing of sacred hymns to God.   Philo explains their worship at the banquet as follows:

> Such are the preliminaries. But when the guests have lain themselves down arranged in rows, as I have described, and the attendants have taken their stand with everything in order ready for their ministry, the President of the company, when a general silence is established- here it may be asked when is there no silence- well, at this point there is silence even more than before so that no one ventures to make a sound or breathe with more force than usual – amid this silence, I say, he discusses some question arising in the Holy Scriptures or solves on that has been propounded by someone else. In doing, this he has no thought of making a display, for he has no ambition to get a reputation for clever oratory but desires to gain a closer insight into some particular matters, and having gained it not to withhold it selfishly from those who, if not so clear-sighted as he, have at least a similar desire to learn (*Contempl. Life* 10.75, 11.83-84, 11.90).

There is no mention of the Therapeutae in the New Testament and their influence in Palestine appears rather limited.   Philo appears to be quite impressed with the group as he describes them as both a model of mutual love for God and an attraction to the pursuit of philosophy. Elsewhere, Philo's view of women is quite dismal, unsuited for intellectual pursuits, so it is hard to imagine that he would have fabricated the contention that both men and women shared equally in the study of philosophy.   The Therapeutae evidently left no trace on

Jewish life, but they may have influenced Christian monasticism, particularly in Egypt.

Zealots, Fourth Philosophy, Sicarii and other Revolutionaries

Josephus is the only source of information about these volatile first-century revolutionary groups. However, Josephus had a rather heated history of personal conflict with revolutionaries, so his evidence must be taken with the utmost caution. He mentions at least five such revolutionary parties or individuals: the Sicarii, Zealots, John of Gischala, Simon bar Giora, and the Idumeans, but he does not draw tight distinctions between these movements. Rather than representing a single, homogeneous body, the term "zealot" probably serves as a collective title for the numerous rebel groups that revolted against Rome.

One of the premier examples given in Josephus was Judas of Galilee, an insurrectionist and founder of what Josephus calls "The Fourth Philosophy." Josephus used this designation to distinguish it from three other socio-religious groups of the period: Pharisees, Sadducees, and Essenes. Judas informed his countrymen that they were cowards and infidels if they continued to pay taxes to Caesar,

Table 8.1

	Jewish Revolutionary Movements
40 B.C.E.	Hezekiah, the Chief Brigand killed by Herod
20	Pollio and Samaias refuse oath to Herod
10	6,000 Pharisees refuse oath to Caesar
4	Eagle Incident, Judas and Matthias
	Herod kills the babies of Bethlehem
	Passover Revolt, suppressed by Archelaus
	Revolt of Judas, son of Hezekiah, 2000 killed
	Messianic movements of Simon and Anthronges
	Feast of Pentecost revolt
6 C.E.	Census riots led by Judas the Galilean
26-36	Incidents under Pilate: mass protests after Pilate brings Roman standards into Jerusalem; uses temple revenue to build aqueduct, crushes resistance; crucifixion of Jesus, suppressed popular revolt in Samaria
	Suppressed popular revolt in Samaria
c. 40s	Tholomaeus and Theudas executed
46-48	Jacob and Simon crucified by Tiberius Alexander
c. 50	Passover riot under Procurator Cumanus. 20,000 Jews killed
52-60	Procurator Felix purges revolutionaries
60	Egyptian Jew stirs thousands in revolt, Romans suppress
66-73	The Jewish War: John of Gischala, Menahem (descendant of Judas of Galilee) lead revolt. Masada suicide
133-135	Second Jewish Revolt under Simeon ben Kosiba. Hadrian decimates city. Jerusalem becomes a Roman city

since taxation, in his mind, equated to slavery. His stubborn resistance to Rome, in his mind, was tantamount to a spiritual battle against paganism.

The death of Judas is recorded in the New Testament book of Acts (5:37) as one in a long line of revolutionaries whose movements lost their impetus for continuity. Revolutionary activity against Rome followed Judas' death for the next sixty years. Many of these revolutionary groups perceived any cooperation with Caesar as a violation of the first commandment of the Decalogue. With ideals and dedication similar to the Maccabees, these zealots waged war with anyone who disagreed with them. The fickle and cruel Roman leadership certainly did not help matters. Successive procurators were heavy-handed in their management of the Jews, which, in turn, incited more revolt. In Pilate's procuratorship alone (26-36 C.E.), there were over a half a dozen such incidents. Two of the sons of Judas the Galilean, Jacob and Simon, were crucified under the procuratorship of Tiberius Alexander (46-48 C.E.), and later revolts under his successor, Cumanus, led to the deaths of over 20,000 Jews. Josephus designates Judas' descendants by the term Siccarii or "daggermen." These assassins would infiltrate a crowd and kill Roman officials hand-to-hand with daggers hidden in their clothing.

Recent scholarship has recognized the heterogeneity of revolutionary groups, particularly in the first century of the Common Era. There was a broad resistance to Roman expansion, particularly in Palestinian Judaism. As often happens in these cases, many groups turned inwardly upon one another.

The Am Ha-aretz

Pre-exilic religion in Israel focused on the community, but expressions of faith in the Second Temple period placed more emphasis on the individual. Each person sanctified his or her life through daily rituals. Every moment was an opportunity to observe the Law of Moses. Larger rituals, such as Sabbath, circumcision, and the prohibition of foods, were also paramount. Sources from that period show that popular piety included the study of Scripture, worship in the synagogue, dietary prohibitions separation from pagans and paganism, and pilgrimages to the Temple for the major festivals.

The pluralistic nature of the religious situation in Palestine during the Second Temple period is demonstrated by an examination of the major socio-religious groups in Palestine. There is simply no single normative expression of Judaism. There is no such thing as *the Jewish perspective* on many religious issues. Evidence for popular religion in Israel and the Diaspora is quite meager. At the same time, it must not be affirmed that Jewish identity was impossible to determine. All of the major socio-religious parties of Judaism held to monotheism, identification with the religious history of the Israelites, a rejection of images in worship, the Torah, and circumcision. Yet it should not be missed that the vast majority of Jews living in Palestine were not members of any of the parties mentioned above. The later rabbis referred to this group as the *am ha-aretz* or "people of the land." Pious in their own way, the *am ha-aretz* couldn't afford the luxury of devoting all their time and energies to the rigid demands of many of these communities. Religion was in a constant state of flux. Teachers and religious authorities came and went. Some arose from grass roots, while others were appointed by Rome. Religious parties began, flourished, withered, and died-but life for these common people went on. Second Temple Judaism is an example of the metamorphosis of faith whereby religious institutions adapted to their changing environment. Only a few survived the traumatic events of the destruction of the temple and Roman domination of Judea. Those who did underwent radical changes to their belief systems, ritual, and self-understanding.

After the destruction of Jerusalem, a radical change occurred in Jewish sectarianism. Many of the major parties discussed above were replaced by a homogeneity equally as peculiar and thoroughgoing as the heterogeneity that characterized the Second Temple period. Christianity eventually went its own way from Judaism, while the rabbis assisted in developing a new order. Ironically, the destruction of the Temple marked another new beginning for Judaism which turned out to be much more homogeneous in nearly every respect.

Chapter 9

Hillel and Jesus: Forerunners to Rabbinic Judaism and Early Christianity

Both early Christianity and Rabbinic Judaism emerged from the milieu of Second Temple Judaism. Rabbinic Judaism evolved during the nascent age of Christianity, and early Christians were originally all Jewish Christians. For this reason, formative Christianity demands to be studied in the context of early Judaism, and visa versa. Hillel and Jesus were perhaps two of the most influential figures in Judaism from the time of Ezra to the destruction of Jerusalem in 70 C.E. These two forerunners of Rabbinic Judaism and early Christianity, respectively, often are studied with little reference to one another. When they are examined, it is often through the powerful lens of confessional ideology. However, the relationship, if any, between these two important figures deserves investigation.

Hillel and Jesus were both born in a pivotal time in the Ancient Near East. Rome was solidly in power in Palestine and the Jews of that land explored ways to exist with some degree of limited autonomy under Roman Rule. Hillel (60 B.C.E. to 20 C.E.) preceded Jesus (6 B.C.E. to 30 C.E.) by five or six decades, so few conclude that Jesus attached himself to Hillel in any official way. Hillel, in fact, already had died before Jesus reached adulthood. Nevertheless, as a youth, Jesus may have met Hillel among the sages of the temple, and even if he did not, he possibly may have had some knowledge of this great rabbi's teaching. There are remarkable parallels between these two first-century figures. Both Hillel and Jesus summarized the Torah succinctly, attracted disciples, taught in the temple, and rejected the revolutionary tendencies of the Jewish Zealots. Neither recorded their own autobiographical information, but their followers passed down details about their lives and teachings to subsequent generations. But what more is known of these two remarkable individuals?

The Problem of Sources

Common depictions of Hillel and Jesus often are built uncritically on later written sources. The Rabbinic portraits of Hillel in the Mishnah originate no earlier than the second century C.E. Likewise, the Gospels of the New Testament date to the last quarter of the first century C.E., decades after Jesus' death and resurrection. While the search for the historical Jesus has always consumed the minds and talents of modern Christian scholarship, in relatively recent years the desire for a historical reconstruction of the events and teachings of Hillel has, in some respects, become the Jewish equivalent to the Christian search for the historical Jesus. When critics speak of the historical Hillel or the historical Jesus, they refer to the individual who can be reconstructed or recaptured with scientific tools of modern historical research. The lateness of these collections, and the unique perspectives of both the Mishnah and the New Testament present challenging problems for such an important task.

The nature of these sources also radically varies. Talmudic literature speaking of Hillel differs notably from any of the Gospels. No talmudic gospels of any of the rabbis survive. In fact, the greatest rabbinic authorities do not stand as authorities on their own right, but always are viewed in the context of spirited disputation, with one rabbi challenging another's viewpoint. Hillel most frequently is quoted in the *Pirqe Avot,* or *The Ethics of the Fathers,* a second-century collection of practical teaching on conducting one's life. The later rabbinic writings of the Mishnah and Talmud likewise adopt Hillel as their spokesperson and make him their own. Literally nothing in any of the rabbinic corpus overtly opposes Hillel. These anecdotal sources delight in depicting Hillel as the ideal scribe, making objective historical reconstruction difficult. Only relatively recently have historical critics systematically reflected on the historicity of the sources related to the life of the Hillel.

Likewise, the stories related to the life of Jesus were first passed down orally through the teaching and preaching of the Jesus Movement and early Christianity. Scholars have debated for several centuries exactly how this transpired. The Gospels also present problems examining of the life of the historical Jesus. All four of the Gospels vary in some detail about the events, message, and activities in the life of Jesus. Matthew, Mark, and Luke--the Synoptic gospels--record most of Jesus' ministry as taking place in the northern region of Palestine in the Galilee, with only one recorded Passover. The Gospel of John, however, records three or four Passovers and places the majority of Jesus' ministry in Judea. These Synoptics portray Jesus as a miracle-working proclaimer of parables, while John records extensive discourses and relatively few miracles. Readers find some sayings of Jesus in one gospel and not others, and numerous differences exist in these sayings, even when they are shared by more than one gospel.

The aim of all of the gospels is a decidedly spiritual one: to strengthen faith in Jesus Christ. These gospels do not even closely resemble complete narratives or historical summaries of the life of Jesus. While Luke's account specifically mentions that his gospel seeks to present an orderly account of events in the life of Jesus based on actual eyewitnesses, all of the gospels clearly arrange their materials along thematic lines. Matthew, for example, divides his account into five major blocks, each with alternating sections of narrative and discourse. Mark groups certain miracle stories together into collections of healing miracles and nature miracles, and places all of Jesus' parables together in a single unit. John's gospel organizes itself around seven miracles or signs, separated by lengthy discourses, with almost no interest in the parables of Jesus.

Other external sources provide scant assistance. The Roman historians--at least the few who mention Jesus at all--perceive him as little more than a historical curiosity. Josephus says more about the figure of John the Baptist than he does Jesus. What Josephus does record about Jesus almost certainly has been the object of Christian interpolation from later periods, particularly his surprisingly confessional statement that Jesus was the Christ. The discovery of the Nag Hammadi documents in Egypt in 1945 led to another important extra-biblical source emerging for the life of Jesus, the Gospel of Thomas. This important document has generated considerable popularity and debate, being not a narrative at all, but rather a collection of 114 sayings of Jesus, many of which directly parallel teachings in the Gospels. Some have argued that the Gospel of Thomas reflects individual traditions as early or earlier than the canonical gospels. Others, however, counter that the Gospel of Thomas has been awarded too high a place of importance, chiefly because scholars so yearn for more material on the life of Jesus. They argue that the gospel reflects a later Gnostic element within the Jesus Movement. Other extra-canonical gospels are of little or no value for a historical reconstruction of the life of Jesus. Scholarship widely affirms that late sources such as the Gospel of Peter have no pre-synoptic traditions of Jesus.

Consequently, for readers to more objectively examine the lives of Hillel and Jesus, they must be aware of some of the problems with the historicity of the available sources. Since neither Jesus nor Hillel left behind any kind of autobiographical materials, and their followers failed to record teachings and insights while these influential rabbis were still alive, these problems likely will remain unsolved. While absolute objectivity is not reachable, one need not wallow in complete relativism. In spite of the challenges that the sources provide, readers can still recover a logically coherent picture of Hillel and Jesus from these sources.

Hillel

The rabbinic sources indicate that Hillel was born to relatively poor parents in Babylon, and that he later migrated to Palestine. While there, he developed an astounding reputation as a scholar and teacher of Judaism. He purportedly studied under the early sages Shemaiah and Abtalyon. Due to his uncanny ability to interpret the traditions of Judaism, the rabbinic sources proclaim that he was elevated to the role of Nasi and was president of the Sanhedrin for over 40 years. He was married and had children, for his offspring and their descendants followed and preserved his teachings. Most notable of these spiritual descendants were Johannon ben Zakkai, Simeon ben Gamaliel II, and perhaps the most famous of the early rabbis, Judah the Patriarch. Hillel, therefore, successfully gathered committed disciples who obviously felt impressed to pass on his teachings to future generations of the faithful.

The rabbinic literature delights in repeating the contrast between the proverbial patience of Hillel and the irascibility of another infamous rabbi, Shammai. Hillelites, obviously responsible for the entire corpus of stories about these two great figures, consistently demonstrate the superiority of Hillel. Shammai, on the other hand, receives a decidedly unfavorable presentation. Perhaps the most celebrated interaction between these two leaders revolved around the meaning of the Torah:

> On another occasion it happened that a certain heathen came before Shammai and said to him, "Make me a proselyte, on condition that you teach me the whole Torah while I stand on one foot." Thereupon he repulsed him with the builder's cubit that was in his hand. When he went before Hillel he converted him. He said to him, "What is hateful to you, do not do to your neighbor. That is the whole Torah, while the rest is commentary thereof; go and learn it." (*b. Sabb* 30b-31a)

Anecdotes such as this prompted the rabbis to render the following comparisons:

> 'A man should always be gentle like Hillel, and not impatient like Shammai,' and 'Shammai's impatience sought to drive us from the world, but Hillel's gentleness brought us under the wings of the Shekhinah.' (*b. Sabb.* 30b-31a)

Portrayed as a model of virtue and an example of the ideal sage, stories about Hillel are more often didactic than historical. He is most famous for creating the earliest known list of principles for interpreting the Torah. Not only was he known for developing a method of exegeting existing Torah commands, but also he made significant changes in the Law. The foremost example of this was the ordination of the *prozbul*. The Torah taught that every seventh year all debts were to be forgiven. Consequently, people refused to lend money to the needy for fear they would not get it back. The *prozbul* created a legal way out of this dilemma. According to Hillel, the lender could provide a certificate, called the *prozbul,* which kept certain debts from being annulled. While rabbis have argued that Hillel made this change based on sound exegesis of the levitical law. Actually, Hillel's immense power and authority in the early Rabbinic period account for his exegesis becoming authoritative.

More than any of the other rabbinic sages, Hillel is known for his wise sayings. His subjects were wide-ranging and his compassion notable:

Be the disciples of Aaron; love peace and pursue peace, love humanity, and bring them near to the Torah. (*m. Ab.* 1:12)

The more flesh, the more worms; the more possessions, the more care; the more women, the more witchcraft; the more slave women, the more thieving; the more Torah, the more life; the more schooling, the more wisdom; the more counsel, the more understanding; the more righteousness, the more peace. If a man has gained a good name he has gained it for himself; if he has gained for himself words of Torah, he has gained for himself life in the world to come. (*m.. Ab.* 2:5-7)

If I am not for myself, who is for me? But if I am only for myself, what am I? And if not now, when? (*m. Ab.* 1.14)

Hillel is unquestionably the dominant figure in the rabbinical traditions about the Pharisees. Because his followers presumably assumed leadership of Pharasiac Judaism, the traditions about Hillel and his teachings controlled legal decisions and greatly influenced later rabbinic interpreters. Of his successors, rabbis considered only Yohanan ben Zakkai and Rabbi Akiba as his equals.

Jesus

Scholarly consensus allows a rough outline of the life and ministry of Jesus of Nazareth. Jesus was born around 6 B.C.E., when Herod the Great ruled Palestine and Caesar Augustus was emperor in Rome. He grew up in the town of Nazareth in Galilee. The gospels portray Galilee as a bucolic backwater, yet Nazareth was a mere four miles from a major urban center, the thriving city of Sepphoris. Recent archaeological research has revealed that Sepphoris was a sophisticated Roman city and that Galilee was a hotbed of political activity. This new evidence questions some of the popular assumptions about the gospels that present Jesus as a humble carpenter, ministering and teaching, far away from the political scene in Jerusalem.

The presumed son of Joseph and Mary, Jesus had a number of siblings, one of whom grew up to become a dominant leader in early Christianity. We know next to nothing about the childhood of Jesus. As an adult, he entered public ministry after baptism by John the Baptist in the Jordan River. Jesus and John both preached a message of repentance, shared disciples for a time, and had overlapping ministries. When he entered his own public ministry, Jesus gathered his followers from the common men and women of Galilee. He led these disciples from village to village, preaching, teaching, and healing large crowds of curious onlookers. This public ministry probably lasted for three years. He commanded authority to reinterpret the Torah, heal the sick, even to forgive sin. His primary message was submission to God's rule of the human heart, which he called the Kingdom of God.

Jesus' popularity aroused the suspicions of both the Jewish and the Roman leadership. Tensions rose as confrontations with the religious leadership intensified. The Synoptic gospels record one climactic journey to Jerusalem, where Jesus expected to suffer and even to die. As relationships with the Jewish authorities deteriorated, the High Priest arrested and interrogated Jesus, delivered him to the Roman governor, and charged him with treason against the Roman Empire. After administering the customary flogging, Pontius Pilate ordered Jesus to be crucified shortly before Passover. A sign on the cross, "Jesus of Nazareth, King of the Jews" identified the political crime of treason against Rome. Jesus died, and he was buried in a borrowed grave.

All four gospels report that a few days after his burial, Jesus triumphantly rose from the grave, although Mark's original ending closes with the frightened first witnesses of the empty tomb scattering in terror. Jesus appeared to his followers on a number of occasions, ascending to heaven shortly thereafter. These witnesses of the resurrection were convinced unequivocally that Jesus was no longer dead. The belief in the resurrection of Jesus motivated his followers to become valiant witnesses of Jesus' life and ministry. In spite of persecution, the Jesus Movement grew and spread from Jerusalem, heading north to Antioch and Asia Minor. Second generation converts carried the message of Christianity to Rome and Egypt as this new religion matured.

The gospel sources in the New Testament for the life of Jesus have been subject to historical-critical reflection for over two centuries. Beginning in Germany, scholars--such as Hermann Reimarus in the eighteenth century and David Strauss in the nineteenth century--began to question the historical reliability of the gospels. These and other scholars grew skeptical of the gospels as historical accounts of the life of Jesus; instead, they claimed the gospels were mere inventions, created by the early Christian community to justify their existence as a religious faith. In 1906, Albert Schweitzer published *The Quest for the Historical Jesus*, a milestone examination of the history of Jesus scholarship from the previous two centuries. Schweitzer argued that the historical Jesus was an eschatological prophet whose historicity was just as elusive as ever. He contended that it was the spiritual Christ, not the historical Jesus, who had made himself known to followers over the centuries.

This "first quest" deeply divided the Jesus of History from the Christ of Faith. Succeeding scholars like Rudolph Bultmann contended that the gospel material originated in the early church, not in the historically verifiable life of Jesus. Bultmann's goal was to demythologize the gospels in order to recapture the message of the early church. In the 1950s, however, one of Bultmann's students, Earnst Käsemann, questioned such a position, claiming that one simply could not divorce early church doctrine from its historical roots. His influential study led to a succession of scholars in the 60's and 70s who once again critically addressed the historically verifiable materials related to the life of Jesus. This renewed effort has been called the "Second Quest" for the historical Jesus. In many respects, these scholars defined many of the issues examined in contemporary discussions about the life of Jesus.

Beginning in the mid-1980's, another flood of material reflecting on historical and sociological issues related to the life of Jesus issued from scholarly circles. The "Third Quest," as it is now known, is characterized by a much wider diversity of scholars, many of whom have focused on the Jewish context of Jesus' life and ministry. A sizeable number of these scholars are much more open to the possibility of the supernatural at work in the life of Jesus than were the representatives of the first two quests. In some respects, this third quest has evolved into a search for the historical Galilee, as archaeology and the study of extra-biblical sources have freshly examined the Roman influence, social and cultural setting, and ethnic diversity of the region. This quest, however, has not been without its more marginal figures, who have captured the attention of popular audiences. The Jesus Seminar is one example of a rather unusual venue for examining Jesus' life. A small group of scholars, almost exclusively from North America, in a sort of "road show" fashion meet in various cities to discuss and ultimately cast ballots on what Jesus did, or did not, say or do.

One clear fact has emerged from over two centuries of historical critical reflection on the historical Jesus. Often the presuppositions and ideological motivations of the interpreters are more clearly revealed than are lasting conclusions made regarding this enigmatic individual who had such a brief but profoundly influential life during the Second Temple period. Where scholars begin is often where they end in the life of Jesus research. If, for example, an individual contends that there is indeed such a thing as the miraculous, then many of the crucial events in the life of Jesus are much easier for that individual to accept. However, if one begins with the assumption that miracles do not exist, then that particular individual is liable to find little or no historically verifiable evidence for the healings, nature miracles, and most notably, the resurrection of Jesus.

What differences between Hillel and Jesus emerge from an examination of these troublesome sources? The most obvious difference: the Jews highly revered Hillel. On the other hand, the Jews rejected Jesus and supported Rome's crucifixion of him. Unlike Hillel, Jesus was not married and had no descendants. While Hillel was associated with the Jewish establishment, Jesus directly conflicted the leaders of the Pharisees and the power brokers of first-century Palestinian Judaism. Recent literature has portrayed Jesus as a much more marginal figure than Hillel. For example, Jesus is only briefly mentioned in Jewish and pagan literature, he was a jobless itinerant whose style of teaching often appeared obnoxious and even dangerous to the Jewish establishment, and his death by crucifixion was the ultimate marginalization. Hillel was most interested in formulating rules for daily life, but Jesus instead, told many parables and was more interested in apocalyptic themes. Perhaps one of the major ethical differences between these two leaders was their position on divorce. Hillel rather broadly permitted divorce while Jesus issued a strict ruling on it, permitting it only on the condition of adultery (Matt 5:27-30). Their varying positions are indicative of the disparate perspectives among Jews in the first century C.E.

In spite of these differences, no evidence suggests that the strife between Rabbinic Judaism and early Christianity can be attributed directly to animosities between Hillel and Jesus. The major difference between these two influential figures is how their disciples chose to pass on their messages to future generations. Hillel's followers were content to portray Hillel as an exceptional teacher, while the Jesus Movement was convinced that Jesus was a teacher—but much more, the Messiah, the Son of God, who had taken away the sin of humanity. Miracle narratives, then, are central to the activity of Jesus on every level of the oral and written traditions of the Jesus Movement. Both friends and enemies viewed Jesus as an exorcist and healer, not just a spinner of ethical maxims or a preacher of theology. The first half of the Gospel of Mark, for example, is little more than a catalog of miracles performed by Jesus. Both Matthew and Luke contain several chapters of miracle stories, and the Gospel of John organizes his entire work around seven "signs" performed during Jesus' ministry. Even later Jewish literature categorized Jesus as a wonder worker. His resurrection, however, was the hallmark of early Christian literature, from the earliest of Paul's letters, to all of the gospels and the apocalypse.

Rabbinic Judaism

Hillel is regularly cited as one of the most influential forerunners of Rabbinic Judaism. Rabbinic Judaism also has been called "talmudic," "normative," or "classical" Judaism, because of its dominant status in the history of the Jewish faith. In many ways, rabbinic Judaism was an interpretive supplement to the foundational scriptural text of ancient Israel, the Torah. Rabbinism's driving force was exegesis, but it was much more than that. The movement's interest in Scripture was primarily a beginning point of discussion for how the Law might relate to even the minutest detail of life.

Destroying the Second Temple opened a door for a new way to practice the Torah. Preoccupations with issues such as food, purity, kinship, taboos, and holy days compensated for the loss of the temple. The traditions and institutions of Israel were radically transformed as a result of the temple's demise. Centuries earlier, when the first temple was destroyed in 586 B.C.E., Jews in Palestine and the Diaspora began to develop new modes of worship and piety. The rise of the synagogue and the reinterpretation of Torah, for example, which began after the first destruction, set a precedent, providing a mechanism for recreating ancient traditions already in place when the Second Temple was destroyed. Consequently, like the destruction of the Temple of Solomon, the destruction of the Second Temple drastically changed Judaism in almost every respect.

Because of the destruction of the Temple, new preoccupations emerged regarding how the faithful might protect their sacred traditions. Shortly thereafter, the text and the canon of the Hebrew Bible was fixed and closed. The canonization of the Hebrew Bible led to new and innovative ways of interpreting and transforming Scripture. Early rabbinic sages gathered in academies to fervently discuss the application of Torah to the daily life of the Jews, particularly because the temple no longer existed. In a sense, the academy became the new Temple with the rabbis being the new priesthood. Eventually, at least in some respects, the study *of* the Torah became equivalent to faithfulness *to* the Torah.

These rabbis perpetuated the notion that Yahweh actually revealed two Torah's at Sinai: one written and one oral. Moses received only one revelation, but two torahs. Both were authoritative. Another account of Shammai and Hillel bears this out:

A certain heathen once came before Shammai and asked him, 'how many Torahs have you?' 'Two,' he replied, 'The Written Torah and the Oral Torah.' 'I believe you with respect to the Written Torah, but not with respect to the Oral Torah. Make me a proselyte on condition that you teach me the Written Torah only.' He scolded him and repulsed him in anger. When he went before Hillel, he accepted him as a proselyte. On the first day he taught him, *alef, bet, gimmel, dalet* [=A,B,C,D]; the following day he reversed them to him. 'But yesterday you did not teach them to me thus,' he said. 'Must you not rely upon me? Then rely upon me with respect to the Oral Torah too.' (*b. Sabb* 30b-31a)

This concept of two Torahs lay at the heart of the later development of the Oral traditions of Judaism. The rabbis recorded these laws and normative behavior of the Oral Torah as the Mishnah and its supplements. This collection of the teachings of the Pharasiac sages from 100 B.C.E. to 200 C.E. is divided into six major orders: Seeds, Feasts, Women, Damages, Holy Matters and Purities. *Seeds* deals with the production of crops in accordance under Scriptural rules, as well as paying appropriate offerings and tithes to priests. *Feasts* legislates issues of Sabbath, festivals and other appointed times in the Hebrew calendar. *Women* relates to legal stipulations affecting women in Israelite society, temple, marriage, divorce, and sexual relations. *Damages* deals with civil law and takes as its goal preserving the established wholeness of the social economy. *Holy Matters* covers rules for the temple altar and temple servants. *Purities* specifies sources of uncleanness and modes of purification. Supplementary legislation in the Mishnah, called the Tosephta, includes a number of additional decrees and rulings, and the Pirqe Avot is a collection of practical sayings by the rabbinic masters on how to conduct one's life. The purpose of the Mishnah was to distinguish Israel in all its dimensions from the surrounding cultures. This distinction involved temple and table, field and family, altar and hearth, and other relationships with the world. The framers of the Mishnah never tried to imitate the language of the Torah, yet its authority virtually stood on the same plane as Scripture. Consequently, both Oral Torah and Written Torah provided stability, regularity, and predictability for Israel.

Rabbinic dialogue did not end with the Mishnah. From the second century to the sixth century C.E., further generations of sages discussed the meaning and application of the Hebrew Bible and the Mishnah. The results of these discussions were the two Talmuds. The Palestinian Talmud, called the Yerushalmi, dates from around 400 C.E., while the Babylonian Talmud, or the Bavli, dates from roughly 500-600 C.E. The redactional construction of these two collections formed the foundational documents of modern Judaism. Both collections received authority and status, but the Babylonian Talmud eventually dominated all legal discussions of Judaism for many further generations. Abstract and incredibly complex, the Talmud determined to wrestle with the relationship of the Mishnah to the Hebrew Bible, but went much further than that, including a smothering array of additional theological, homiletic, and legislative material.

Table 9.1

Important Rabbinic Literature		
Title	**Date**	**Description**
Mishnah	2nd Century	Product of Rabbi Judah the prince. Six *Sedarim* or Sections Commentary on the Torah.
Pirqe Avot	3rd Century	Collection of practical sayings of the rabbinic masters on human conduct.
Tosephta	3rd- 4th Cent.	Supplement to the Mishnah
Yerushalmi	4th Century	Classical rabbinic discourses on the Mishnah. Includes legendary, homiletical and theological matters. (Palestinian Talmud)
Bavli	5th Century	Commentary on the Mishnah. Over seven centuries of cultural growth. (Babylonian Talmud)

Early Christianity

It is a mistake for modern Christianity to neglect the essential Jewishness of early Christianity. Early Christianity began as a movement within Judaism. Jesus was a Jew; all of his disciples were Jewish. Initially, all Christianity was Jewish Christianity. The gospels were written, in large part, to demonstrate the way Jesus culminated Israel's history. Early Christians shared with Judaism a Bible, a common history, rituals, and messianic expectations. In fact, Christians were persecuted as Jews until the second century. Nascent Christianity emerged from the eschatological conviction of Judaism. Consequently, understanding Jesus as a Jew serves more than mere historical curiosity; it influences an informed comprehension of Christian and Jewish self-understanding, since both religions in some sense came to self-definition through dialogue and debate with one another. The reductive view that Jesus merely represented an opposition to Judaism cannot stand in light of the plurality of Judaism in the Second Temple period, and the many parallels in the life and work of Jesus with the divergent forms of classical Hebraic faith. Such an approach inevitably leads to anti-Semitism. For the Jesus Movement, the final age of history began in the ministry, death, and resurrection of Jesus. Christ was the new Moses, who reinterpreted the Torah for the new age; the Passover Lamb, he was the perfect sacrifice for sin; and the new Joshua, he led his people to establish the new Kingdom of God.

Two primary tenets eventually led to the division of early Christianity from Rabbinic Judaism: the incarnation and the resurrection. The belief that God himself had uniquely entered history through the God-man, Jesus the Messiah, and the perspective that this Messiah would suffer, die, and rise from the dead, were the unlikely foundations of Jewish Christianity. The destruction of the temple of Jerusalem in 70 C.E. provided significant impetus for the initial separation of Christianity and Judaism. Historically, Jerusalem had been the focal point of early Christianity, but the destruction of the Temple and city in 70 C.E. and again in 135 C.E. accelerated divergent paths of Christianity and Judaism. Many Christians interpreted the destruction of the temple as a sign of God's displeasure with the Jews. As a result, Christianity spread instead to the Gentiles, leading to a emerging dichotomy between Christianity and Rabbinic Judaism.

As the Jesus Movement developed, significant differences between Christianity and its Jewish roots began to emerge. The designation, Christianity, like Judaism, was an umbrella term encompassing diverse and often competing religious ideologies. In fact, the social boundaries of the Jesus Movement were much more open than were many of the boundaries of similar socio-religious groups of the Second Temple period. Christians came from many backgrounds, both as Jews and as Gentiles. Their worship involved a ritual meal, but not the dietary laws previously associated with Judaism. They observed a special day of worship, but celebrated the resurrection of Jesus each Sunday, instead of worshiping on the traditional Sabbath day, Saturday. The question of circumcision, a quintessential marker of Jewishness, was answered "yes" and "no" by these early Christian communities. Some felt the need to identify with (and not offend) their Jewish brethren, while others were enraged to think a believer in Christ would submit to circumcision, contending that those who were circumcised had completely abandoned their new heritage as believers in the free grace of Jesus Christ. The Jerusalem Council in Acts 15 responded to the "gentile problem" by affirming these new believers as brothers and sisters, without requiring the rite of circumcision. Yet other aspects of Jewish Law were not so easily abandoned. Even the apostle Paul had conflicting opinions on the issue. Paul's personal practice was to have some of the leaders of the early church under his authority circumcised, while his writings themselves indicate circumcision was valueless to the believer (Gal 6:15).

The open boundaries between inside and outside the community extended well beyond issues of circumcision and uncircumcision, Jew and Gentile, male and female, slave and free (Gal 3:28). No rigid hierarchy appeared in the leadership of early Christianity, though this level playing field would change over time. Even women enjoyed a degree of authority as prophets and teachers.

In the end, Rome eventually replaced Jerusalem as Christianity's primary locus. Theological discussion shifted from matters deriving from Jewish morality to problems framed by Greek philosophy and Roman governmental rule. Christianity migrated northward from Jerusalem to Antioch, Asia Minor, and, ultimately, to Rome. Relations between Christianity and Judaism were often hostile, as what once were two factions within Judaism separated to become two distinct world religions. Jesus, to be sure, was much more at the heart of Christianity than Hillel was at the heart of Judaism, but both strongly influenced the direction of these two emerging systems of faith.

Bibliography

Part Two: Pluralism and the Jewish Communities

Cohen, Shaye J.D. *The Beginnings of Jewishness: Boundaries, Varieties, Uncertainties.* Berkeley: University of California Press, 1999.

Gowan, Donald. *Bridge Between the Testaments.* Pittsburgh: Pickwick Press, 1976.

Hengel, Martin. *Judaism and Hellenism: Studies in their Encounter in Palestine during the Early Hellenistic Period.* 2 vols. Trans. J. Bowden, Philadelphia: Fortress Press, 1974.

Horsley, Richard A. *Bandits, Prophets, and Messiahs: Popular Movements in the Time of Jesus.* Harrisburg, PA: Trinity Press International, 1999.

Jaffee, Martin S. *Early Judaism.* Upper Saddle River, NJ: Prentice Hall, 1997.

Kraft, Robert A. and George W. E. Nicholsburg, eds. *Early Judaism and Its Modern Interpreters.* Atlanta: Scholars Press, 1986.

Neusner, Jacob. *Judaism in the Beginning of Christianity.* Philadelphia: Fortress Press, 1984.

Neusner, Jacob. *Rabbinic Judaism: Structure and System.* Minneapolis: Fortress Press, 1995.

Porton, Gary G. "Diversity in Postbiblical Judaism." Pages 57-80 in *Early Judaism and Its Modern Interpreters.* Edited by R.A. Kraft and G.W.E. Nicholsburg. Philadelphia: Fortress, 1986.

Saldarini, A.J. *Pharisees, Scribes, and Sadducees in Palestinian Society: A Sociological Approach.* Wilmington, DL: Michael Glazier, 1988.

Sanders, E.P. *Judaism: Practice and Belief 63 BCE-66CE.* Philadelphia: Trinity Press International, 1994.

Smith, Morton. *Palestinian Parties and Politics that Shaped the Old Testament.* New York: Columbia University Press, 1971.

Stemberger, Günter. *Jewish Contemporaries of Jesus: Pharisees, Sadducees, Essenes.* Translated by Allan Mahnke. Minneapolis: Fortress, 1995.

Vanderkam, James C. *An Introduction to Early Judaism.* Grand Rapids, MI: Eerdmans, 2001.

Part Three

Literary Creativity: From Religious Literature to Sacred Text

Chapter 10

Scripture and Canon

The Evolution of the Hebrew Bible

Early Judaism and nascent Christianity emerged during a time of significant literary activity. Some of the religious works written during the Second Temple period were transmitted to subsequent generations, but many eventually were lost. These writings ordinarily are divided into two general categories: canonical and non-canonical literature. The word *canonical* refers to those works that eventually became part of the authoritative collection, or canon, of sacred literature for the Jewish or Christian communities. The term *non-canonical* refers to those pseudepigraphical works that did not become a part of the canon of sacred scripture. Roman Catholic and Orthodox communities consider a number of books authoritative that are not included in the Protestant canon. Protestants refer to these books as the Apocrypha, while Catholicism prefers the term *deuterocanonical* or a "second canon." Scholars refer to the process by which collections of sacred scripture develop as *canonization*. Ordinarily, a canon usually arises from a historical situation that heightens a need for a collection of authoritative literature. What kind of stimuli might create such a social condition? History would indicate that the destruction of the Second Temple and the uncertainties associated with the Roman occupation created an impetus for a canon-consciousness among the Jews. Additionally, tensions between Christianity and Rabbinic Judaism accelerated the closing of the canon. One thing is certain; the canon consciousness did not develop all at once. Centuries of reflective activity led to the Hebrew canon that emerged after the close of the Second Temple period.

No historical reconstruction of the origins of Scripture commands universal acceptance. During the first half of the twentieth century, the common consensus was that the rabbis fixed the canon of the Hebrew Bible around 90 C.E. as a result of decisions rendered by Johannon ben Zakkai and his associates in Jamnia, a village along the Mediterranean coast of Palestine. Recently, this consensus has been strongly challenged. One view gaining acceptance is that the canon had been fixed much earlier in the first century C.E. The councils at Jamnia and elsewhere had little extrinsic authority, particularly outside of Palestine. Some scholars go so far as to question whether such a council ever existed in the early Rabbinic period.

The Hebrew Bible was a product of the community of Israel emerging over hundreds of years. The scriptures of Judaism were never rigidly distinct from the process of tradition that gave them life. For generations, the ancestors orally passed down many of the traditions, poems, songs, prophetic oracles, and stories of the Israelite nation before ever recording these traditions. As centuries progressed, succeeding generations embellished and refined these traditions. Such oral transmission of a people's heritage is common to many cultures of the past and present alike. This is not to say that all of the written materials came late in Israel's history. Some of oral traditions may have been encoded in written form very early in Israel's existence. Evidence indicates that at the time of David and Solomon in the tenth century C.E., and particularly during and after the exile, Israel entered a period of prolific literary creativity. Shortly thereafter, religious leaders gathered these writings into coherent collections.

Three main canonical units compose the Hebrew Bible: the Law (*Torah*), the Prophets (*Nebiim*), and the Writings (*Kethubim*). But how did these individual books and collections evolve from religious literature to sacred texts, authoritative for the religion and faith of Israel and Early Christianity? It is misleading to place explicit dates with the canonization of any one section of the Hebrew Bible. The process of canonization was primarily an unconscious one. No evidence exists of any official or public activity that concluded that the Law, Prophets, or Writings were added to the sacred canon at any given date. In fact, historians know little about the exact process of how some books were lost and others were preserved. What does appear, however, is that the additional units of the Prophets and the Writings over the final four centuries B.C.E. supplemented the central nucleus of the Law.

Table 10.1

Principle Sources of Ancient Israelite Traditions
Oral Traditions: 　Heroic Epics 　Prophetic Oracles 　Priestly Ritual Practices 　Psalms Written Traditions 　Royal Law Codes 　Priestly Regulations 　Royal archival history

The Law (Torah) came first, both chronologically and ideologically. The first five books of the Hebrew Bible, Genesis, Exodus, Leviticus, Numbers, and Deuteronomy, were composed of multiple sources and edited over successive generations. Portions of the Law may have been considered authoritative much earlier (Exod. 24:4, Josh 24:26), but during the Second Temple period all Jewish communities recognized the Torah as authoritative. This recognition was perhaps due to the reforms of Ezra and Nehemiah in response to the perils of the exile. For whatever the reason, most scholars agree that by 400 B.C.E. at the very latest, the Torah reached roughly its present form.

The next major section of the Hebrew Bible is the prophets (*Nebiim*). The prophetic collection of the Hebrew Bible is divided into two sections: Former Prophets (Joshua, Judges, Samuel, Kings) and the Latter Prophets (Isaiah, Jeremiah, Ezekiel, The Book of the Twelve). The Hebrew prophets did not read from a text to proclaim their message, but spoke from the heart. These early prophets originally proclaimed their messages orally. Only later did their followers record their utterances. Hebrew prophetic literature includes both biographical materials and prophetic speeches. By the time the Law was given authoritative status, many of these prophetic books also were extremely popular as well. It is conceivable that the collection of the canon now designated as "Prophets" may have been fixed almost as early as the Torah. The prologue of the apocryphal book, Ben Sira (c. 132 B.C.E.), for example, states that the "prophets and other books" had been translated from Hebrew into Greek, indicating that by the second century B.C.E., the Jewish community had affirmed this collection of prophetic books as authoritative, perhaps as early as 200 B.C.E.

The final section of the Hebrew Bible, the Writings, contains history (Chronicles, Ezra, Nehemiah), poetry (Job, Psalms, Proverbs), the *Megilloth* (Ruth, Esther, Ecclesiastes, Song of Songs, Lamentations) and the book of Daniel. While many of the songs, traditions, and proverbs of this collection certainly were quite ancient, the boundaries of the collection remained undefined for several centuries after the Law and Prophets. Evidence from the New Testament Gospels supports this possibility. In Matthew's gospel, for example, Jesus refers to the Law and the Prophets only (Matt 5:17). In the Gospel of Luke, he speaks of the Law, Prophets, and Psalms (Luke 24:44). Indeed, the New Testament never specifically mentions the Writings as a coherent collection.

Certain peculiarities characterize this portion of the Hebrew Bible. No specific consensus exists in the rabbinic period regarding the authority of several of the books contained in the Writings. Early rabbinic literature indicates that the Rabbis hotly debated the sacred nature of Ecclesiastes, Esther, and Song of Songs. A second century Mishnaic tractate speaks of debates among the rabbis as to which books "defiled the hands." Individuals who handled books that were sacred required ceremonial washing after contact. Literature that was not sacred did not require such action. There appears to have been no rabbinical consensus regarding the sacred nature of these three books. The discoveries of the Dead Sea Scrolls confirm this ambivalence. The book of Esther is the only biblical book not found at Qumran. The pessimism of Ecclesiastes, the secular tone of Esther, and the vivid sexual imagery of Song of Songs may have contributed to the lack of consensus. The New Testament also seems to support this uncertainty, as it never quotes Esther, Ecclesiastes, or the Song of Songs.

The Book of Daniel poses an additional canonical problem. Many students familiar with the canon of the English Old Testament are surprised that the Book of Daniel is not placed in the prophetic section of the Hebrew Bible, but in the Writings. Many scholars today speculate that this is either due to the late date of the composition of Daniel, to the apocalyptic genre of the book, or both.

Exactly when the rabbis finally standardized the canon is unclear. Given the diversity of Jewish literature in the Second Temple period, it is remarkable that any uniform collection of Jewish Scripture emerged at all. Josephus indicates that the Jews had 22 books of special status (*Ag. Ap.* 1:37-43). These 22 books are probably the same 24 of the current Hebrew canon, since Lamentations was often associated with Jeremiah, and Ruth with the book of Judges. The apocalyptic work, 2 Esdras, also delineates two groups of authoritative writings. Its author indicates that there were 24 books to be read by everyone, and 70 books were reserved for the "wise" among the people. While the process is difficult to trace, the end of the Second Temple period records the transition from simple tradition to authoritative Scripture.

Early Versions of the Hebrew Bible

Scholars call the received text of the Hebrew Bible the Masoretic Text (MT). The original textual tradition of the Hebrew Bible contained only consonants. The authoritative teachers of Scriptural tradition, called the Masoretes, preserved this consonantal text, but also punctuated and furnished vowel points. Beginning as early as 500 C.E., and becoming dominant in the 9th and 10th centuries, the Masoretic families of ben Asher and Naphtali provided notations at the end of each book and in the margins relaying information regarding how to read the consonantal text. In the 14th century the two traditions from ben Asher and Naphtali united to form a mixed text called the *textus receptus,* (received text). Translators base most modern English editions upon this received text of the Hebrew Bible.

Important early versions of the Hebrew Scriptures began to emerge in the Second Temple period. A version is simply a translation of the Bible from its original language to another. The Septuagint, for example, is one of the most important early versions. The impact of Alexander the Great and Hellenism already has been mentioned as being extremely significant. As Greek culture and language spread to Palestine, Babylon, and North Egypt, Jewish communities came under the influence of Hellenism. One thriving Jewish community existed in Alexandria, Egypt. This community produced a highly influential translation of the Hebrew Scriptures in the Greek language. The Letter of Aristeas is a legendary account of the origins of this new translation.

It indicates that the director of the famous library of Alexandria, one of the largest in the world, reported to King Ptolemy Philadelphus that the Law of the Jews was worthy of inclusion. The king consented and petitioned the High Priest in Jerusalem for competent scholars to work on a new translation. The High Priest, Eleazar, responded by sending seventy-two men (six from each of the twelve tribes) to Alexandria. These scholars were taken to the Island of Pharos, and there they translated the Torah in seventy-two days. Each scholar worked in strict isolation. The translation was presented and approved by the Jewish community, and was added to the collection in Alexandria. The above story was evidently quite popular among the Jews, being retold by Aristobulus, Philo, and Josephus. In spite of the popularity of the tale, its legendary character is well known today. The actual reason for the translation was most likely because younger generations of Egyptian Jewry no longer understood Hebrew, and the translators were probably Alexandrian Jews, not scholars from Palestine.   Rather than being a single translation completed by a group of scholars at a specific time, the Septuagint is not even a single version, but instead a variety of versions produced over an extended period of time.

The Greek Septuagint differs considerably from the Masoretic text in several instances, most notably the books of Samuel, Jeremiah, and Job. Until recently, scholars thought the differences were due to certain liberties taken by the translators of the Septuagint. Findings at Qumran, however, indicate that the Septuagint may in many cases derive from an original Hebrew textual tradition that differed from the textual tradition preceding the Masoretic Text. The Septuagint also contains a different ordering of biblical books, as well as some fifteen additional books not a part of the Hebrew Bible.

Table 10.2

Important Early Versions of the Hebrew Bible			
Version	**Composition Date**	**Oldest Copy**	**Significance**
Masoretic Text	ca. 100 CE	1000 CE	standard Heb. text
Septuagint	300-200 BCE	300-500 CE	Early Greek Translation. Important early witness.
Samaritan Pent.	200-100 BCE	1100 CE	Early witness of the Pentateuch
Dead Sea Scrolls	200-100 BCE	200-100 BCE	Earliest witness of every book of OT except Esther.
Targums	500-1000 CE Some earlier	150 CE	Aramaic paraphrase of various OT books

The Samaritan Pentateuch is another common version of the Hebrew Bible. Samaritan origins have been discussed in an earlier chapter. Scholars debate whether there was a specific break or a gradual separating of the ways between Jews and Samaritans. These Samaritans held an intriguing view of sacred scripture. The canon of the Samaritans was limited to the Pentateuch alone, written in a special archaizing script derived from the Hasmonean period. It differs from the Masoretic text in some six thousand instances, though admittedly many of these variants are minor. In nearly two thousand instances, the Samaritan Pentateuch agrees with the Septuagint *against* readings in the Masoretic Text. Some differences are clearly alterations, such as the revision of the Ten Commandments to include an injunction stating that true worship may only take place on Mt. Gerazim, but discoveries at Qumran demonstrate that the Samaritan textual tradition enjoyed more widespread use that earlier believed.

The twentieth-century discovery of the Dead Sea Scrolls and other scriptural finds at Masada, Wadi Murabbaa't, Nahal Hever, and elsewhere in the Judean desert have also shed light on the process of the development of the canon of the Hebrew Bible. Modern translations are based on the Leningrad Codex, an edition of the Hebrew Bible that dates to 1008 C.E. The Aleppo Codex dates about a century earlier, but does not contain the entire corpus of the Hebrew Bible. Other ancient fragments of the Hebrew Bible were found in a Genizah in Cairo, Egypt, dating from 600-900 C.E. All of these conformed exactly to the Masoretic textual tradition, the received text of the Hebrew Bible that was punctuated and furnished with vowel points by the Masoretes. Even the textual discoveries at Masada and Wadi Murabba'at dating from the late first and early second century C.E. adhere in every detail to the Masoretic textual tradition.

The discovery of the Dead Sea Scrolls added perplexing new evidence to the question of the canon. These scrolls date from 150 B.C.E. to 100 C.E., a century earlier than the finds in the Judean desert at Masada and elsewhere, and over a millennium earlier than Codex Leningradensis. At Qumran, the caves yielded over 170 biblical manuscripts, plus two fragments from apocryphal writings, many pseudepigraphical texts, as well as numerous manuscripts specific to the sect that inhabited the site. Among these biblical manuscripts, no single textual tradition emerges. There appears to be, at a minimum, several distinct textual variations, each roughly paralleling one of three traditions: the Masoretic Text, the Greek Septuagint, or the Samaritan Pentateuch. Consequently, if there was no established text in this period, there could hardly be an established canon, as the delineation of a canon ordinarily succeeds the fixing of a textual tradition. Unlike the evidence from the rest of the Judean desert, manuscript evidence indicates that Qumran existed in a proto-canonical setting. The fluid text and diverse collection of writings demonstrates that both text and canon were not yet fixed. A number of non-canonical works appear to have at least some degree of authority as sacred literature for the community, but were not a part of a clearly defined and closed set of writings.

The Apocrypha

Both the Greek Septuagint and the discoveries along the Dead Sea at Qumran included selected books of the Apocrypha. In the common vernacular, the word "apocryphal" carries the connotation of "false." Actually, the term comes from the Greek, meaning, "hidden." Why these books are considered "hidden," however, is unclear. In the apocryphal book, 2 Esdras, God commanded Ezra to re-write all the sacred books of Israel (*2 Esd.* 14:45-46). Twenty-four of these books, presumably the same 24 currently in the Hebrew Bible, were to be published and seventy were to be "hidden". Perhaps this connection is the reason for the terminology used to refer to these fifteen additional books.

Table 10.3

The Apocrypha	
Tobit	Prayer of Azariah and The Song of the Three Jews
Judith	Susanna
The Additions to Esther	Bel and the Dragon
The Wisdom of Solomon	1 and 2 Maccabees
Ecclesiasticus (Ben Sirah)	1 Esdras
Baruch	The Prayer of Manasseh
The Letter of Jeremiah	2 Esdras

In modern contexts, Protestants employ the term *apocrypha* to refer to those books found in the Christian Greek and Latin Bibles, but not in the Hebrew Bible. The term *deuterocanonical*, or "second canon," is the designation given by Roman Catholicism to these fifteen additional books.

When Jerome (c. 400 C.E.) prepared his edition of the Bible in Latin, called the Vulgate, he chose to follow the order of the Hebrew canon rather than the Septuagint, placing the apocryphal books in a separate section with their own preface. Later versions of the Vulgate, however, included these books within the traditional sequence of Old Testament literature. Ultimately, the Council of Trent (1556) declared these books canonical and divinely inspired.   In addition to these books, the Eastern Orthodox Church also recognized 3-4 Maccabees and Psalm 151 as authoritative. The books of the Apocrypha belong to several literary genres: religious history, wisdom, moralistic novels, prayers, letters, and apocalyptic literature.

Religious History

1 Esdras, and 1-2 Maccabees belong to the genre of religious history. 1 Esdras reproduces much of 2 Chronicles 35-36, all of Ezra, and Nehemiah 7:38-8:12, beginning with the reforms of Josiah during the monarchy and ending with the reforms of Ezra after the exile. Both the beginning and ending of the book appear quite abrupt, which leads some to speculate that the work might be an excerpt from an early expansion of Chronicles and Ezra. In addition to the material it has in common with the canonical accounts, 1 Esdras exhibits a number of discrepancies, and an additional narrative, the popular story of the three young bodyguards of Darius in 3:1-5:6. In this enjoyable tale, each of three bodyguards was asked to make a written argument for the strongest thing known to humanity. Darius promised that he would then reward the individual whose argument was most convincing. The first bodyguard stated that wine was strongest because wine had the inherent power to lead astray all who drink it. The second said that the king was strongest, because he ruled over land and sea and everything in them. The third of the king's bodyguards was Zerubbabel, leader of one of the early groups of returnees from Babylonian captivity. He advocated that women were the strongest, since a man will do nearly anything for a woman. Yet, in spite of a woman's strength, he further suggests that truth was strongest commodity of all, because unlike wine, kings, and women, there is absolutely no partiality or unrighteousness associated with truth.   Furthermore, truth, argued Zerubbabel, unlike everything else, endures forever. Because of his insightful response, the king rewarded Zerubbabel for his astute answer allowed him to return to Jerusalem to rebuild the temple and city. Consequently, what at first glance appears as a moralistic tale is really an etiology of how God anointed Zerubbabel to lead the exiles to rebuild the temple.

Apart from this popular story, 1 Esdras is for the most part difficult to read, due to the author's telescoped chronologies which collapse diverse accounts occurring over several centuries into a relatively brief period of time. The primary focus of the book, however, is impossible to miss. The restoration of the dominant religious institutions of Israel, particularly the priesthood and sacrificial system just as much a part of the rebuilding process as the physical temple, city walls, and people's homes. These two institutions of temple and home are central in the theology of the writer of 1 Esdras. The writer also pays attention to the problem of mixed marriages with the resultant solution that all who married outsiders must divorce them. The book ends with Ezra's recitation of the Torah to the returnees in Jerusalem. The extant text of 1 Esdras is in Greek, but growing evidence indicates a Hebrew original. The usual dates posited for 1 Esdras are some time during the second century B.C.E.

1 Maccabees is also religious history but appropriately can be referred to as a dynastic history, similar to that in the canonical books of Kings and Chronicles. The book begins with the death of Alexander the Great and ends with the death of Simon Maccabee and the ascension of John Hyrcanus, covering three generations of the Maccabees. Strongly conservative and anti-Hellenistic, the book describes the valiant rise of the Maccabean family to restore religious and political freedom to Israel. The story begins by inaugurating a crisis: the ruthless Seleucid monarch, Antiochus Epiphanes, defiled the temple and abolished many of the cherished institutions of Jewish life. Mattathias and his five sons, known as the Maccabees, led a stubborn resistance against this proscription. When an officer of the king journeyed to Modein to enforce the edict of Antiochus, Mattathias killed him, as well as a Jewish sympathizer. The rest of the book is an account of the exploits of Judas, Jonathan, and Simon, all sons of Mattathias who continued the revolt, which culminated in a successful restoration of political autonomy in 142 B.C.E. The Maccabean family serves as models in 1 Maccabees for all Jews who would resolve to take a stand against unjust governments and compromising religious communities. The success of the rebellion was evidence to the writer that the Hasmonean insurrection was in accordance with the divine will of God. 1 Maccabees has been strongly influential in establishing a working knowledge of Jewish history from 167 to 130 B.C.E. In fact, Josephus, does little more than paraphrase 1 Maccabees when describing this period.

2 Maccabees parallels the first eight chapters of 1 Maccabees, though with a flare for exaggeration and invective lacking in 1 Maccabees. With an interest in polemical religious speeches, the author depicts God's judgment on the Seleucid leaders who are causing the suffering of God's people. This book's unique contribution is that it focuses on several attacks against the temple of Jerusalem during the leadership of Judas Maccabeas. The Jewish people under Judas' leadership successfully defend each of these three attacks. Unlike 1 Maccabees, 2 Maccabees is not at all interested in the Maccabean family *per se*, but is primarily concerned with the defense of the temple under the leadership of Judas. Even though Judas is the physical leader, God alone delivers the temple from the hands of its enemies.

Another unique contribution of the book is in its preoccupation with martyrdom and resurrection. 2 Maccabees relishes the account of the elder scribe Eleazar, who faces death rather than eat the food prohibited by the Torah. Various martyr stories saturate the book, the most famous being the account of the mother and her seven sons. In this narrative, each of this woman's seven sons is brought before her and tortured for resolute support of the Sabbath, circumcision, and observance of dietary food laws. Finally, the mother herself is martyred. In several of these martyr stories, the hope of resurrection gives the martyr the strength to take an unmovable stand against their oppressors. The martyr stories of this book strongly influenced 4 Maccabees, which greatly expands the details of the torture these heroes received. The willingness of these heroes to give up what they most cherished served to inspire readers to take courageous stands that remained faithful to the requirements of the Torah. 2 Maccabees probably was written in Greek in the early first century.

Wisdom

The Wisdom of Solomon and Ecclesiasticus or Sirach are excellent examples of late wisdom literature of the Second Temple period. Originally written in Greek in the late first century B.C.E., the Wisdom of Solomon combines a thorough knowledge of Jewish history with Hellenistic philosophy. Rather than merely being an anthology of practical advise about matters of life, the Wisdom of Solomon is an advocate for the benefits and necessity of wisdom itself.   This attempt to bring together Greek philosophical concepts and the Hebrew Bible, suggests that the work may have originally been written in a major Hellenistic center, such as Alexandria, Egypt. By tackling the issue of immortality, for example, the Wisdom of Solomon covers ground the canonical literature of the Hebrew Bible did not yet occupy (Wis 3:1-9). This emphasis on immortality is perhaps the book's greatest contribution, and also introduces a matter of some controversy. The author appears to believe in the preexistence of souls, a view not advocated in the Hebrew Bible or in the Christian New Testament.

The Wisdom of Solomon easily can be divided into three parts, each with a clear opening exhortation. The book begins with an exhortation to "love righteousness," since righteousness is immortal. This first major section (ch. 1-5) primarily describes wisdom by contrasting it with errors of the wicked (1:16-2:24), discussing the destinies of the faithful and unfaithful (3:1-12), and juxtaposing the righteous and unrighteous (4:16-5:14). Section Two (ch. 6-9) introduces the nature and wonder of wisdom. Like its canonical counterpart, the Wisdom of Solomon personifies wisdom as a radiant woman, inviting the worthy to obtain wisdom and instruction. The author appeals to Solomon in several instances in this section as an example of one who obtained wisdom from God. Wisdom is described further with 21 attributes, concluding with a prayer for wisdom. The final section of the Wisdom of Solomon (ch. 10-19) is a historical survey of wisdom's influence in the history of ancient Israel, from Adam to Moses. Wisdom is instrumental as creating the world, building the ark, rescuing Lot, leading the Exodus from Egypt. The Exodus motif is expanded further with a series of seven contrasts associated with the narrative of the departure. In this series of contrasts, the Egyptians experience one phenomenon while the Israelites experience something quite different. In linking Wisdom with the traditions of Israel, the wisdom literature of the Apocrypha does something that canonical wisdom literature does not do. These important traditions are conspicuously absent in the wisdom literature of the Hebrew Bible, but were obviously incorporated into later wisdom traditions.

Ecclesiasticus, or The Wisdom of Jesus, Son of Sirach, was perhaps one of the most popular examples of the literature of the Apocrypha. It is certainly one of the most influential. Scholars refer to it by one of several titles: in Hebrew it is Ben Sira; in Latin it is Ecclesiasticus; and in Greek it is Sirach. Ben Sira resembles the book of Proverbs in many ways, although it is nearly twice as long, and provides practical advice on how to cope with daily life.   Ben Sira, the wise sage and teacher, instructs the younger student on how one can become wise.   Like the canonical book of Proverbs, Ben Sira is an anthology of many short proverbs on a host of practical subjects.   Unlike the biblical counterpart, however, Ben Sira topically organizes many of these proverbs.   Prominent topics include the nature, discipline, and benefits of wisdom, creation, friendship, speech, wealth, sin, and prayers. There are unique topics dealing with the importance of tradesmen, scribes, and even physicians.   At the heart of the thought of Ben Sira is the relationship between Wisdom and Torah.   Wisdom is identified with the Torah as it is likened to the Jordan River and the life sustaining streams that surround paradise (Sir 24:25-29).   Wisdom dwells in the temple in Jerusalem, and there are great rewards for those who lead a life of devotion to wisdom and Torah.   The climax of the book (chaps. 44-50) is a celebration of the famous ancestors of ancient Israel, beginning with Enoch, and concluding with the high priest Simon, son of Onias.   This recitation of ancestors indicates a general date of composition of the book, around 180 B.C.E. in Jerusalem.

Ben Sira/Ecclesiasticus was strongly influential on the early Christian church.   While it is not quoted in the New Testament, the book was translated into Latin, Coptic, Syriac, Ethioptic, Armenian, and Arabic.   Many of the Greek and Latin Church Fathers quoted directly from the book of Ben Sira in their sermons, commentaries, and letters.   One of Ben Sira's most controversial contributions is its position on women and the treatment of slaves. Ben Sira holds women responsible for the entry of sin into the world (Sir 25:24) and provides several unflattering descriptions of an evil wife (Sir 26:5-12).   Clearly written in a patriarchal setting, the husband is warned about the importance of choosing an appropriate wife (Sir 36:26-31), and the ideal wife emerges as one who is modest, charming, and beautiful--but most of all, quiet (Sir 26:13-18, 36:26-31).   Ben Sira contains several urgent warnings to fathers to keep an exacting watch over one's virgin daughters (Sir 42:9-10, 25:10-12)

Moralistic Novels

Tobit, Judith, Susanna, Bel and the Dragon, and the additions to the book of Esther can be considered as moralistic novels.   The book of

Tobit is a wonderful piece of historical fiction that tells a tale of a pious Israelite and his family.   The story's protagonist, Tobit, a model of biblical piety, was taken captive to Assyria by King Shalmaneser. He lived a life of dedication to the Torah, even though he lived under the authority of a pagan culture, the Assyrians.   God blessed Tobit's obedience, and he became a wealthy buyer for King Shalmaneser. On one of his business trips to Media, Tobit left a large sum of money in trust with his friend Gabael, but due to unstable conditions in the empire after Shalmaneser's death, was never able to retrieve it.

Tobit's vexing dilemma began because of his willingness to bury one of his fellow Israelites who had been killed by the Assyrians. Because of this charitable act, Tobit was guilty of treason against Assyria, and was forced to flee Ninevah from the wrath of Shalmaneser's son, Sennacherib.   Upon Sennacherib's death, he returned to Ninevah.   Later, Tobit mercifully buried another fellow Israelite whose corpse had been thrown callously into the marketplace. In order not to impart ritual defilement of his family by his contact with a corpse, he slept in the courtyard that night. While he slept, droppings from the sparrows on the ledges above his head fell into his eyes, leaving him tragically blind.

Meanwhile, the storyteller develops a second important plot that took place in the neighboring country of Media. Tobit's relative Sarah, had been married seven times, yet with each successive marriage, the groom was slain on their wedding night by an evil demon. Unaware of each other, both Tobit and Sarah simultaneously prayed for God's intervention on their behalf. God responded to their prayers by sending an incognito angel, Raphael, to answer them both: Raphael is to heal Tobit from his blindness and to provide a husband for Sarah. Tobit commissioned his son, Tobias, to retrieve the money Tobit had left in Media. He sought out and found a guide, who unknown to him, turned out to be the angel Raphael.   Through angelic intervention, Tobias retrieved the money from his kinsman, and ultimately gains the ability to cure Tobit. While at the Tigris River, Raphael instructed Tobias to catch a fish, cut out its gal, heart, and liver for medicine.   Prepared properly, these ingredients simultaneously would provide healing of the blind and would also drive away demons. When they arrived at the home of Raguel, Sarah's father, Tobias learns that he was the closest surviving relative and has hereditary claim to take Sarah as his wife. But what would Tobias make of all her fallen husbands? In spite of the likelihood of his own death, Tobias fell in love with Sarah, and after reassurance from Raphael, decided to marry her. Tobias miraculously survived his wedding night, and the happy couple would eventually raise many sons and grandsons for his father Tobit. Tobias returned to his father with the money and the healing ointment, and cured him of his blindness.

The book of Tobit probably was composed in the second or third century B.C.E. The work survives primarily in two Greek versions, each of which differs strikingly from the others. Five manuscripts of Tobit were discovered at Qumran, four being in Aramiac, and one in Hebrew.

The story of Judith is about another pious Israelite. This time the protagonist is a widow who risked her life to deliver Israel from the Assyrian general, Holofernes. The story opens as Nebuchadnezzar, mistakenly identified as the king of Assyria, sought to conquer the Israelites in the same way he had been victorious in the East. He appointed his general Holofernes to coordinate the attack. Holofernes descended upon Israel, and the people were filled with such great terror that the armies fled to the hills for protection and the people desperately prayed for God's deliverance. Holofernes mocked this reliance on a God who, in his words, could not protect Israel any more than the gods of other nations protected them from the great king, Nebuchadnezzar.

Judith then is introduced in the narrative. Much like Tobit, she is also portrayed as a pious Israelite, yet Judith takes extraordinary measures to secure Israel's deliverance. A wealthy widow, Judith trusted in God, but used her beauty and wits to battle against her adversaries. Her plan was to dress seductively and approach Holofernes with a plan whereby he might defeat the entire nation of Israel, without loosing a single soldier. Through outright lies, half-truths, and double entendres, she insidiously secured the lustful general's trust. After a banquet for his attendants, Holofernes "lured" her to his bedchamber so he could seduce her. Drunk and alone, he was easy prey. Judith unceremoniously cut off his head, placed it in a food bag, and returned to her home in Bethulia. The head of Holofernes was raised up on the city wall for all to see and the Assyrian army fled in disarray.

The theme is similar to the biblical book of Esther. In both narratives, women take advantage of their physical beauty to save their people. In these two books, life under foreign rule implies a test of the spiritual loyalty of God's people. Oddly enough, in spite of its wide popularity, no clear evidence exists of direct influence of the book of Judith on early Christianity or the New Testament, though it did influence medieval Christianity and Judaism. While the story is set in the sixth century B.C.E., its composition is much later, perhaps having been written in the second or first century B.C.E.

Susanna, and Bel and the Dragon are two of the three (the other being the Prayer of Azariah and the Song of the Three Jews) additions to the book of Daniel extant in the Septuagint that are not present in the Hebrew Bible. Susanna is an account of a beautiful wife of a Babylonian Jew who was being harassed by two elderly judges. When she refused their immoral sexual advances, they falsely implicated her in an affair with a young man, and she was charged with adultery. The trial began the next day. The elders ordered that she appear in the presence of her parents, husband, and children. They even demanded that she be unveiled, so that she would be shamed further and people looked at her great beauty. As the trial began, Susanna looked to heaven for help from God. Because of the false testimony of the elders, she was ruled guilty and condemned to death. Daniel, for his part, saw though the hypocrisy of the two judges. Daniel demanded a new trial and exposed the evil judges by separately interrogating them. After they presented contradictory evidence, Susanna was released and the deceitful judges were put to death.

If Susanna tells the story of personal fidelity and its rewards, so Bel and the Dragon tells of public and private fidelity. The story of Bel and the Dragon is an account of Daniel's refusal to worship the Babylonian god Bel. The story is actually a parody on idolatry. Each day food was brought before the god and each night it was consumed. The king, Cyrus, questioned Daniel as to why he did not worship the pagan god, Bel. Daniel responded that he only worshiped the living God who created everything that exists. Bel, so said Daniel, was simply an idol made with human hands. To settle the matter, Cyrus proposed that they set out food in the temple and seal the door with his own seal. If the food disappeared before morning, Bel would be vindicated and Daniel would be subject to death. Daniel, of course, suspected that a god had not eaten the food at all. He ultimately proved his case by scattering ashes on the floor of the temple. The next morning the food and drink were indeed gone, but the floor was filled with human footprints. The priests and their families who had taken the food were killed and the king allowed Daniel himself to personally destroy the idol of Bel.

The dragon episode, like the story of Bel, also parodies the folly of idolatry. The story combines three accounts: Daniel and the dragon, Daniel and the Lion's den, and Habakkuk's supernatural transportation to Babylon by the Angel of the Lord. At the beginning of the tale, the great dragon in Babylon is worshipped as a living god. The heroic Daniel, killed the dragon, causing such an uproar that the king reluctantly had him thrown into the lion's den. For six days, Habakkuk the prophet ministered to Daniel, and on the seventh day, Daniel emerged from the den, fit and unmolested by the lions. Consequently those who sought his destruction were themselves thrown to the hungry lions. These three brief accounts demonstrate God's complete superiority over the empty idols of Babylon.

The additions to the book of Esther also fit the category of moralistic fiction. These six additions are clearly intrusive and secondary, and even contradict the Hebrew account in a number of instances. They include Mordecai's dreams; the letter of king Artaxerxes to his governors dishonoring the Jews; Mordecai's and Esther's prayers; details on Esther's appeal to the king; and the letter of Artaxerxes proclaiming freedom to the Jews. The primary purpose of these additions is to make explicit what was left implicit in the canonical account. While coincidences abound in the biblical book of Esther, God is never explicitly mentioned—an irony not overlooked by both ancient and modern interpreters of the book. Mordecai's dream revealed "what God was going to do" (11:12), the prayers reveal an explicit dependence on God for deliverance and protection, and the letter of Artaxerxes decrees that the disobedient will never escape the "evil-hating justice of God" (16:4). In addition to making explicit references to the activity of God in the story, these additions also soften some of the possible objections to Esther's conduct. In one of the additions, Esther explicitly denies ever having had sexual relations with any uncircumcised alien, or having eaten at the table of Haman the Gentile, or of having drunk wine at any of the king's feasts (Esth 14:15-17).

The stories of Tobit, Judith, and the additions to Daniel and Esther all share a common element. They all develop themes of pious Jews in the Diaspora maintaining their faithfulness amidst the idolatrous practices of the foreign nations.

Prayers and Letters

The Apocrypha also includes several prayers. The Prayer of
Manasseh records the repentance of perhaps the most evil king of
Judah. The Prayer of Azariah and the Song of the Three Jews records
the prayer of Daniel's friends while they were in the fiery furnace and
their subsequent song of joy when they were delivered. The additions
to Esther include prayers of Mordecai and Esther, asking for mercy
from on high and protection from the enemies of God's people.

There are also letters included in the Apocrypha. According to
tradition, Jeremiah supposedly wrote The Letter of Jeremiah to the
Jews who were about to be sent into exile. This letter, however, is
dated in the Hellenistic period prior to 100 B.C.E., possibly composed
in Aramaic. Primarily a polemic against idols and idolatrous worship,
the body of the letter contains a series of ten warnings against idolatry.
Each of the ten warnings explains the foolish attempts to worship idols
made by human hands. Similar to the Wisdom of Solomon (chaps. 13-
15) the author presents a case that idols are not at all what the Gentiles
suppose them to be. As evidence, he cites that these gods cannot set up
or depose kings, show mercy to the widow and orphan, send rain,
administer justice, or give sight to the blind. In fact, these gods cannot
even do the things mere humans do: talk, breath, and see. Through
repetition of these ten polemical warnings, the author heaps up
evidence against the existence of idols.

While not a letter, Baruch is one of several works attributed to
Jeremiah's secretary. Sometimes it is called 1 Baruch (Hebrew), to
distinguish it from the pseudipigraphical apocalypses of 2 Baruch
(Syriac), 3 Baruch (Greek), and 4 Baruch (the Paraleipomena of
Jeremiah). The book of Baruch contains four sections: a narrative
introduction, a prayer, and two poems. The two poems share a
common theme of the exile and return, demonstrating that a theological
interpretation of the exile is a central feature of the work. With
theology similar to the Deuteronomistic literature, Baruch argues that
the exile was a direct consequence of Israel's rampant sin. God
summoned the Babylonians to punish Israel for her disobedience to
God. At the heart of the book is a poem about wisdom (Bar 3:9-4:4)
that argues that it is hard for humans to understand why God acts in
certain ways, particularly as to why God would allow the exile to

happen. In spite of this inability of humankind to know the mind of God, because God is good and merciful, a return is possible if God's people will repent. The book ends with the confident hope that the exiles will indeed return to their land. No specific historical allusions in the book occur, making it one of the most difficult in the Apocrypha to date, but it is unlikely that Jeremiah's scribe, Baruch was the author of this piece of literature. Also very little evidence exists that this book directly influenced early Judaism or Christianity.

Apocalyptic Literature

2 Esdras falls into the category of apocalyptic literature. Actually it is three separate compositions (chaps 1-2, 3-14, 15-16), each of which probably was written after the close of the first century, C.E., and it lies outside the chronological framework of this present study. Some of these compositions are Christian (chapters 1-2, 15-16) and others are Jewish (chaps 3-14). The core of the work (chaps. 3-14) is a Jewish apocalypse. Like other apocalyptic literature, it is replete with numerical and animal imagery, and it purports to be a revelation of future events. Ezra laments the destruction of Israel and wonders why Israel deserved such harsh punishment, particularly when those who destroyed her were so much more wicked. Like similar Jewish literature that questioned God's rationale for the destruction of Jerusalem, the blame is laid at the feet of Israel, because of her idolatry. Unlike comparable literature, however, this Jewish apocalypse, also known as 4 Ezra, extends the discussion much further by questioning the very origins of sin. The book is a narrative of six dramatic visions given to Ezra revealing what will transpire as the new age opens. The angel Uriel reveals some of the answers to the questions of sin's origins in three dialogues with Ezra. Sin so dominates this present evil age that the only hope is for a completely new beginning, when in the final age God's justice and wisdom will be revealed for all to see and understand. It seeks to grapple with questions of theodicy and is among the most developed examples of apocalyptic literature. In spite of the fact that the lion's share of the book of 2 Esdras is a Jewish apocalypse, the book ironically had little or no influence in Judaism. It was, however, strongly influential in Christian history.

Summary

The Reformers were perplexed that the original Hebrew Bible contained none of the books of the Apocrypha. They also were troubled that the New Testament never quoted from any of these books. A third concern surfaced in that some of the apocryphal books of the Eastern Orthodox canon were not included in the Roman Catholic canon. These concerns, combined with a pressing discomfort with some of the doctrines taught in this literature and the desire to work back in time to the most ancient traditions of Israel, motivated the Reformers to model the Protestant canon after the Greek Septuagint, minus the additional books of the Apocrypha. While the collection's order differs from the Hebrew Scriptures, the Protestant canon contains the same books as the Hebrew Bible.

In addition to the Apocrypha, Jews wrote many other works during the Second Temple period, particularly in the two centuries prior to the Common Era. Scholars ordinarily give these works the designation Pseudepigrapha, or "false writings." Composed when the limits of the canon were still fluid, many of these writings obtained great popularity in early Judaism. The following chapter considers, then, some of the various genres of literature present not only in the Pseudepigrapha, but also in the period's other works.

Chapter 11

Developments in the Interpretation of Sacred Scripture

For the last two millennia, both Jewish and Christian traditions have been grounded in the interpretation of a set of scriptures. Even in the biblical period, evidence exists of the growing authority of sacred scripture, particularly after the catastrophe of the Babylonian exile. The written word, perceived as having origins in Israel's distant past, came to assume a primacy not held before. While the text and canon of the Hebrew Bible or Christian Old Testament were not fixed until the close of the Second Temple period, the Hebrew Scriptures served as an authoritative source for faith and ethics. Similar to the book of Chronicles' adaptation of its predecessor, the book of Kings, much of the literature of this period adapted and expanded the important texts of the Hebrew Scriptures. This reuse of scripture followed a two-staged process. As interpreters reused an already authoritative text, they created an entirely new work in the process. The enormous literary evidence of this period suggests a surprising liberality in the modification of biblical materials and application of sacred scriptures to present day issues of the Second Temple period. It is impossible to classify all the literature of this period into exactingly concise categories, but the following three groupings provide a useful frame of reference: The Bible Rewritten/Reworked, The Bible Explained, and The Bible Expanded.

The Bible Rewritten/Reworked

Several influential works took popular portions of the Torah and rewrote them with the author's specific audience from the Greek and Roman periods in mind. *Jubilees, The Genesis Apocryphon, Pseudo Philo, The Temple Scroll, the Aramaic Targums,* and Josephus' *Antiquities of the Jews* are some of the better examples of works which began with biblical books as a starting point, and reworked them to suit the author's purposes.

Jubilees

The book of *Jubilees* has sometimes been called "the Little Genesis," because it elaborates Genesis 1 through Exodus 12. The plot begins as Moses is receiving the Law at Sinai. Through angelic revelation, the author recounts the events from the creation to the Exodus, but recasts the narrative in several interesting ways. One of the notable expansions relates to the observance of the Torah. For the author of *Jubilees*, the Torah did not merely come into being with Moses, but was eternal, was preexistent, and was observed by the patriarchs, even before Moses received the Law at Sinai. These ancestors faithfully celebrated the holy days of the priestly calendar and observed the requirements of daily devotion to Yahweh as stipulated in the Torah. Quite often, the writer diverges from the narratives of Genesis to point out how a particular element in the plot of the story supports a specific Torah command. For example, when God provided clothing for Adam and Eve on the eve of their expulsion from the garden, the rationale is given that the Law prohibited nakedness (*Jub.* 3:31), and when Simeon and Levi wreaked their vengeance against Shechem, it was because the Torah prohibited intermarriage (*Jub.* 30:7-23). Other expansions and changes to the biblical narrative reflect hostility against the prevalent Hellenistic cultural practices during the time *Jubilees* was written, such as nudity, uncircumcision, intermarriage, and idolatry. They even condemned following a lunar calendar.

Some of these expansions border on the incredible. The writer transforms the binding of Isaac, for example, from a simple account of Abraham's faithfulness to an extravagantly embellished courtroom scene, prefaced by a heavenly confrontation between a divine angel and a messenger of Satan named Mastema. Through Abraham's righteous act, he defeats the accuser and asserts his integrity.

> And I stood before him and before Prince Mastema. And the LORD said, "Speak to him. Do not let his hand descend upon the child. And do not let him do anything to him because I know that he is one who fears the LORD." And I called out to him from heaven and I said to him, "Abraham, Abraham." And was terrified and said, "here I Am." And I said to him, "Do not put forth your hand against your child and do not do anything to him because now I know that you are one who fears the LORD and you did not deny your firstborn son to me." And Prince Mastema was shamed. (*Jub.* 18: 9-12a)

The book also addresses the age-old question of the identity of Cain's wife, by arguing that she was his sister, Awan (*Jub.* 4:8-9). In another demonstration of the fluidity of these texts, *Jubilees* also contains an interpolation from the book of Enoch (chapters 6-16) into its account of the flood story. This lengthy addition includes a description of the origin of the fallen angels and Enoch's futile intercession on their behalf.

Perhaps the most notable contribution of the book is its chronological framework. Jubilees transforms the Year of Jubilee legislated in Leviticus 25:8 into a technical term referring to an entire 49-year period. The writer divides all of history equally into these Jubilees. Unlike the Hebrew Bible, which follows a lunar calendar, the book of *Jubilees* advocates a solar calendar of twelve, thirty-day months, with an extra day every three months. Many have pointed to the influence and popularity of this work with the community at Qumran, which shares the same calendar. Archaeologists have found no less than 12 copies of the manuscript at Qumran, and many of the religious ideas present in the book of *Jubilees* parallel ideas of that enigmatic monastic community. Allusions to the book of Jubilees appear in some of the literature of the sectarian community. Originally written in Hebrew, the book of Jubilees dates from the second century B.C.E.

The Genesis Apocryphon

The Genesis Apocryphon contains a compilation of narratives about the patriarchs, particularly Lamech and Noah. Composed in Aramaic, the manuscript is 22-columns long, but most of these columns are in very bad condition. This paraphrase of portions of Genesis parallels the book of Jubilees, but *The Genesis Apocryphon* is a much freer revision. Some discussion exists as to whether these two books might in some way be dependent on one another. Since the initial column of the manuscript has been damaged, *The Genesis Apocryphon* begins in Column II with an account, prior to the flood story, of Noah's father, Lamech, and his wife, Bathenosh. The biblical account introduces the flood story with the enigmatic pericope about the sons of God who cohabited with the daughters of men, unions resulting in a race of giants (Gen 6:1-4). But in *The Genesis Apocryphon*, Noah's father Lamech was greatly concerned that the Watchers, those same disobedient heavenly spirits cast down to earth by Yahweh, might have fathered Noah. In spite of Bathenosh's repeated denials, Lamech went to his father Methuselah and asked him to visit his own father Enoch, to learn the truth once and for all. Unfortunately, the answer Enoch gave to this question is missing, as a gap occurs between column II and VI, which begins a first-person account by Noah of the flood and his sojourns, and the division of his inheritance among his sons. After another break, the narrative resumes with an account of Abraham's sojourn to Egypt. Like Jubilees, there are significant differences between the Abraham narrative of *The Genesis Apocryphon* and the Pentateuch. In the tradition of Daniel and Joseph, the author depicts Abraham as a visionary and a seer, one given insight into the mysteries of God, and also he makes Sarai's beauty much more elaborate than in the biblical account. Expanding on the biblical account, the reason for the plague against Pharaoh in *The Genesis Apocryphon* is in part due to Abraham's pious prayer,

> And I, Abram, wept aloud that night, I and my nephew Lot, because Sarai had been taken from me by force. I prayed that night and I begged and implored, and I said in my sorrow while my tears ran down: "Blessed art Thou, O Most High God, Lord of all the worlds, Thou who art Lord and king of all things and who rulest over all the kings of the earth and judgest them all! I cry now before Thee, my Lord, against Pharaoh of Zoan the king of Egypt, because of my wife who has been

taken from me by force. Judge him for me that I may see Thy mighty hand raised against him and against all his household, and that he may not be able to defile my wife this night....(1Qap Gen XX 11-15)

The Genesis Apocryphon probably dates from the turn of the Common Era, but may have been composed as early as the second century B.C.E. It was one of the first of the Dead Sea Scrolls discovered.

Pseudo-Philo

The Book of Biblical Antiquities or *Pseudo-Philo* is a retelling of biblical history from Adam through the death of Saul. The work is present only in Latin, but probably originates from a Hebrew original, written in Palestine shortly before or just after the fall of Jerusalem. In the process of transmission, the work was passed down along with the Latin translations of Philo's works, hence its association with Philo. Modern scholarship denies the unequivocal attribution of this work to Philo, as the text itself makes no claim of his authorship. *Pseudo-Philo* revises the biblical narrative much more radically than *Jubilees* or *The Genesis Apocryphon*, as it bypasses or briefly summarizes some portions of the biblical narrative altogether, expands others by numerous interpolations of speeches and prayers. For example, it omits the creation accounts and the patriarchal narratives from the Genesis narrative, as well as the story of Moses' call and the plagues from the Exodus story. But more significant than these omissions are the interpolations of prayers and speeches, and through these interpolations many of the unique contributions of this document emerge. Like the speeches of Peter and Paul in the book of Acts, these additions not only provide structure to the narrative, but also embellish the content as well. For example, when Moses visits the children of Israel after they sin by fashioning the golden calf, he prays:

Behold now, you O God, who have planted this vine and set its roots into the abyss and stretched out its shoots to your most high seat, look upon it in this time, because the vine has lost its fruit and has not recognized its cultivator. And now, if you are angry at your vine and you uproot it from the abyss and dry up its shoots from your most high and eternal seat, the abyss will come not more to nourish it, nor will your throne come to cool that vine of yours that you have burned up.

> For you are he who is all light; and you have adorned your house with precious stones and gold, and you have sprinkled your house with perfumes and spices and balsam wood and cinnamon and roots of myrrh and costum; and you have filled it with various foods and the sweetness of various drinks. Therefore, if you do not have mercy on your vine, all things, LORD, have been done in vain, and you will not have anyone to glorify you. (L.A.B. 12:8-9a)

Texts like this champion Israel as God's chosen people, even when their own sinfulness threatened their very existence.

Another unique characteristic of the book is the author's adaptation of the Judges cycle of sin, oppression, judgment, and deliverance. The author repeats this cycle numerous times in *Pseudo-Philo*, particularly in the many interpolated speeches of the work. The basic design of the argument is that Israel's vitality is dependent on obedience. However, even in disobedience, Israel has the potential for future blessing. One of the notable examples of the reworking of a biblical narrative comes from the book of Judges, as the narrator replaces the first judge Othniel with his father Kenaz. His first act as leader over Israel was to purge any idolatry among the twelve tribes of Israel. A lengthy tale follows regarding twelve precious stones discovered among the Amorites by one of the tribes of Israel. These stones had miraculous powers of healing and the Amorites used them to seek guidance from their gods. The Amorites burned with fire the idolaters among the tribes who had participated in various forms of spiritual infidelity, along with all of their possessions. Since these stones could not be destroyed by fire, an angel of God cast them into the heart of the sea, because the Amorites had defiled them. God replaced the twelve defiled stones with twelve new stones that he placed in the Ark of the Covenant. They remained there as an eternal testimony against idolatry (L.A.B. 25-26).

Other mind-boggling revisions include the extraordinary testimony that Moses actually was born circumcised, that Job was Dinah's husband, and in a radically revised retelling of the Babel story, Abraham is physically present at the time the tower is built. He and eleven others were the only ones who refused to participate in the project, because of their exclusive devotion to the Lord. The penalty for such refusal was to be thrown into a fiery furnace. Friends secreted away the eleven other dissidents for protection, but Abraham refused the offer of protection and remained confined. When Abraham's enemies threw him into the furnace, God caused a great earthquake, and flames from the furnace leaped out and consumed 83,500 lives. Abraham himself, of course, was completely uninjured.

The Temple Scroll

The Temple Scroll is the longest of the scrolls found at Qumran, over 28 feet in length with 19 sheets of leather containing 67 columns of text. *The Temple Scroll* is basically a rewritten Torah, beginning with the renewal of the Sinai covenant in Exodus 34. This work presents itself as the direct revelation of God to Moses. It is the ultimate pseudegraph, as it were, with God as the author. *The Temple Scroll* contains legal regulations relating to every aspect of sacred space and time associated with the temple. For example, the physical structure of this temple is quite different from the biblical versions in the tabernacle, Solomon's temple, and Ezekiel's temple. Like other temple models, there are concentric spheres of holiness, with the most holy places closest to the center of the temple proper. This temple contains three main courtyards; one for the priests, another for Jewish men, and still another for Jewish women and children. Unlike the temple in Jerusalem, however, no provision for gentiles exists. In fact, a barrier separates the temple proper from the larger Temple Mount, in the likelihood that the temple might be defiled by the sudden entry of an infidel into its domain. Any possible idolatry is to be avoided at all costs and *The Temple Scroll* contains extensive laws to protect the sanctuary from impurity. There are even stipulations requiring special animal hides to carry materials into the temple.

The Temple Scroll also provides instruction for offering the daily, weekly, and monthly sacrifices, according to the solar calendar. Regulations abound regarding the proper conduct of judges, vows and oaths, and rules of proper conduct for the priesthood. Additional regulations describe appropriate practices of kings and the army, laws of warfare, and statutes related to the king's sexual conduct and marriage:

> He shall not marry as wife any daughter of the nations, but shall take a wife for himself from his father's house, from his father's family. He shall not take another wife in addition to her, for she alone shall be with him all the time of her life. But if she dies, he may marry another from his father's house, from his family. He shall not twist judgment; he shall take no bribe to twist a just judgment and shall not covet a field or

a vineyard, any riches or house, or anything desirable in Israel. (11QT
LVI 16-20)

This separate set of laws for the king has many parallels to the biblical
book of Deuteronomy. These commands required that the king refrain
from waging war simply to increase his own wealth, and even demand
that the priests provide a special copy of the Torah for the king's use
(cf. Deut 17).

The Temple Scroll was written in Hebrew, and probably edited in
the Hasmonean period, although the scroll's contemporary editor, the
late Yidael Yadin, assigned it to the late Herodian period. Many have
raised questions regarding whether *The Temple Scroll* had the same
authoritative status at Qumran as the Torah, since it uses the same
square script for the divine name reserved only for the canonical books.
Another matter of debate is whether *The Temple Scroll* was written at
Qumran or whether it was a popular work that originated elsewhere.
The general consensus remains that the community itself probably did
not author the work, as it lacks some of the sectarian polemics common
to some of the other literature from Qumran.

The Targumim

Beginning with Persian dominance and continuing through the
Rabbinic period, Aramaic replaced Hebrew as the vernacular of Jews in
Palestine.   Consequently, Aramaic translations of the Hebrew
Scriptures were produced to accommodate this change. The earliest
translations of the Hebrew Bible composed in Palestine are called the
Targums, or Targumim. Targumim exist for every book in the Hebrew
Bible except Ezra-Nehemiah and Daniel, although, ironically, Jewish
tradition associated the first Targums with the scribe, Ezra (Neh. 8:8).
In the rabbinic period, these Targums became very popular and the
Jews used them not only to translate the Torah readings, but also as a
commentary on the Scriptures. Intended to be read side-by-side with
Scripture, they did more than provide a literal translation, but added
explanatory phrases, reinterpreted texts, and clarified confusing
narratives.   The precise wording of these Targums varied widely.
Some translators interpreted a particular Targum literally, while others
took much more liberty in the translation process.   The Targum
Pseudo-Jonathan, for example, is roughly twice the length of the

original Hebrew sections of the Pentateuch that it translates, as it adds explanations to events and reinterprets the meaning of the biblical text for their contemporary audience.

While the Targums were more commonly employed in the rabbinic and talumidic periods, their origins revert to Second Temple Judaism. Some of the Targums derive from a Babylonian provenance, while others were of Palestinian origin.   Even those from Babylon may have at one point had earlier origins in Palestine. The Aramiac in Targum Onkelos, for example, is similar in date and provenance to that present in the *Genesis Apocryphon*.   The fact that there are fragments of Targums of Job and Leviticus at Qumran (11Q10, 4Q 156-157) indicates that the Targum is clearly a pre-rabbinic phenomenon. These earlier Targums appear to contain much less exegetical explanation than the later examples that became authoritative in Judaism. The Job Targum is the best preserved today, and coincidentally, rabbinic tradition speaks of a Targum of Job that Rabbai Gamaliel preserved during the first century.

Josephus' Antiquities of the Jews

The Antiquities of the Jews was one of several significant works composed by the first-century Jewish historian Josephus, also known for his *Wars of the Jews*, his own personal autobiography, and his apology, *Against Apion*. Written in the last decade of the first century, *The Antiquities of the Jews* follows the biblical account of the history of the Jews from the patriarchs to the invasion by Rome. *Antiquities* contains twenty books. Books one through ten cover the period from the patriarchs to the conquest by Babylon and books eleven through twenty survey the history of Judea from the return from Babylon to the advent of Rome in Palestine. The purpose of the work is to portray the magnificent contribution of the Jews to the cultured Greco-Roman world. Because of this, Josephus presents most of the major leaders of Judaism, Abraham, Joseph, Moses, Samuel, Saul, David, and Solomon, in their best light. Josephus explicitly states that he intends to provide precise details of what is written in Scripture. Following the precept of Scripture (Deut 4:2), his official position is that he will neither add nor omit anything from the biblical account. In actuality what occurs is quite the opposite, demonstrating once again the fluid characteristics of rewritten Scripture found elsewhere. *The Antiquities of the Jews* is indeed a very loose paraphrase of the Septuagint, where significant modifications to the biblical account are commonplace.

For example, Josephus significantly expands the story of Israel's disobedience at Shittim in Numbers 25. The biblical account leaves unsaid exactly how Balaam was directly responsible for Israel's sin at Baal Peor. In Josephus' recollection, Balaam instructs Balak that even though God would not punish Israel through defeat in battle, one possible tactic would be for the Moabite women to entice the Israelite men. The king of Moab summoned many of his most beautiful women to stay temporarily with the Israelite men, and as time passed, these men fell passionately in love with the Moabite women. When the time came for the women to return to Moab, the Israelites protested, promising that because they had fallen in love, they were willing to marry the Moabite women. Consequently, the Moabite women agreed to marry the Israelite men, but only with the condition that the Israelites agree to worship their gods as well. Like the biblical account, those who participated in this blatant idolatry died in a plague. Thus, Josephus expands the biblical account by stating how Balaam conspired with Balak to bring Israel to ruin.

Although Josephus cites the Septuagint as the basis for his work, other textual traditions may have had substantial influence on his historical writings. *The Antiquities of the Jews* also shares many details not present in the Scripture with *Pseudo-Philo*, indicating that they may have shared a common source. Parallels exist with *Jubilees,* the *Genesis Apocryphon*, and some of the writings of Philo of Alexandria, though unlike Philo, Josephus rarely uses allegory. The evidence would indicate, therefore, that Josephus had access to a number of diverse traditions associated with the biblical history of ancient Israel. He drew together all of these sources to supplement the biblical materials and create his own history of Israel.

The Bible Explained

Some of the literature of the Second Temple period did not merely revise or rework the authoritative literature of the Bible, but sought to provide specific and detailed commentary on the Scriptures themselves. Sometimes these commentaries provided ethical exposition on the meaning of biblical texts, and others advocated that a particular community literally fulfilled the ancient teachings of Scripture. Three examples of such commentaries are well worth reviewing. The commentaries, or "peshers" of Qumran, the book of Hebrews of early Christianity and selected examples from the commentaries of Philo of Alexandria suggest much about this type of literature.

The Qumran Peshers

The community at Qumran believed that they were living in the end time. They were convinced that the biblical authors wrote the ancient prophets and psalms specifically for their generation to show their community what would take place in these last days. But who had the wisdom or insight into these unfathomable mysteries? The community at Qumran believed their own leader, the Teacher of Righteousness, had been given special insight by God to interpret the meaning of these ancient texts for fulfillment by their own community in the last days,

> And God told Habakkuk to write down that which would happen to the final generation, but He did not make known to him when time would come to an end. And as for that which He said, 'That he who reads may read it speedily': interpreted, this concerns the Teacher of Righteousness, to whom God made known all the mysteries of the words of His servants the prophets. (1QpHab:1-2)

The result of such contemporizing exegesis is called the "pesher." The Hebrew term pesher literally means, "to explain or expound." These peshers or pesharim (plural) found at Qumran are verse-by-verse quotations of selected portions of Isaiah, Hosea, Micah, Nahum, Habakkuk, Zephaniah, and Psalms. No extant peshers on the Torah exist. These quotations are followed by a specific interpretive commentary, prefaced by the words, "the interpretation is," or "its interpretation concerns." For the Qumran community, the efficacy of prophecy depended almost entirely on its proper interpretation, and it was the leader of the community who served as the sacred gatekeeper of official interpretation. Consequently, prophecy became a two-staged process, the first stage founded on the written prophetic text of the Hebrew Scriptures, and the second being the communal leadership's authoritative application. For example, Habbakuk 1:5 states, "Look among the nations, and see; wonder and be astounded. For I am doing a work in your days that you would not believe if told." The interpretation of this text from the *Habbakuk Pesher* reads as follows:

> Interpreted, this concerns those who were unfaithful together with the Liar, in that they did not listen to the word received by the Teacher of Righteousness from the mouth of God. And it concerns the unfaithful of the New Covenant in that they have not believed in the Covenant of God and have profaned His holy Name. And likewise, this saying is to be interpreted as concerning those who will be unfaithful at the end of days. They, the men of violence and the breakers of the Covenant, will not believe when they hear all that is to happen to the final generation from the Priest in whose heart God set understanding that he might interpret all the word of His servants the Prophets, through whom He foretold all that would happen to His people and His land. (1QpHab II 1-9)

Another lasting contribution of the pesher is that the genre provides some of the rare direct historical allusions to the life of the Qumran community in the second century B.C.E. Thus, the words of the prophets are unequivocally linked to the unique setting of the community. For example, the prophet refers to the origins of the community in a comment on Habbakuk 2:15 which states, "Woe to him who makes his neighbors drink of the cup of his wrath and makes them drunk to gaze on their shame." The interpretation in the Qumran Pesher is as follows:

> Interpreted, this concerns the Wicked Priest who pursued the Teacher of Righteousness to the house of his exile that he might confuse him with his venomous fury. And at the time appointed for rest, for the Day of Atonement, he appeared before them to confuse them, and to cause them to stumble on the Day of Fasting, their Sabbath of repose." (1QpHab XI 5-8)

Another specific historical reference is present in the Nahum Pesher, which specifically mentions Antiochus and Demetrius, as well as Rome, called "the Kittim" in the literature of Qumran,

> Interpreted this concerns Demetrius king of Greece who sought, on the counsel of those who seek smooth things, to enter Jerusalem. But God did not permit the city to be delivered into the hands of the kings of Greece, from the time of Antiochus until the coming of the rulers of the Kittim. But then she shall be trampled under their feet (4Q169 I:3-4).

The best-preserved pesher is the *Habakkuk Commentary* (1QpHab). Among the first of the discoveries of the Dead Sea Scrolls, the *Habakkuk Commentary* consists of twelve columns, virtually all of Habakkuk 1-2. *The Habbakuk Commentary* describes the struggle of the Teacher of Righteousness with the Wicked Priest, set firmly in the context of the terrible things that were transpiring in Jerusalem and Judah by the Romans. Thus, the commentary has little value in interpreting the meaning of what was in the mind of the original prophet. One of the more unusual characteristics of the *Habakkuk Commentary* is the type of script used when referring to the divine name. Four times in the book, the book uses old Paleo-Hebrew script where the word YHWH would have been present in the original Habbakuk text of the Hebrew Bible.

Although the prophets and the book of Psalms provide the only extant examples of pesharim, it is impossible to determine whether these works were the only subjects of this kind of exegesis or whether literature from the Torah might have also been the object of this kind of analysis.

The Book of Hebrews

Like Qumran, the early Christian community also perceived that they were living in the last days. Furthermore, they firmly believed that the prophecies of the Hebrew Bible applied directly to the coming of the Messiah, Jesus, having been ultimately fulfilled through his life, death, and resurrection. The book of Hebrews is one of the best examples in the New Testament of how the early Christians interpreted texts in the Hebrew Bible to demonstrate their fulfillment through the life and work of Jesus Christ. In many ways, it is a commentary on the book of Leviticus. While not specifically a commentary, the book of Hebrews is a systematic overview of the major institutions and offices of the religion of Israel, arguing that the ministry of Jesus the Messiah is superior to all of these ancient institutions.

The book begins by demonstrating how Jesus, as mediator of the new covenant, is superior to angels, Moses, and the prophets. Since Jesus is the Son of God, unlike his predecessors, his mediation comes directly from God. "In ages past, God spoke through the patriarchs and prophets in many ways, but in these last days has spoken through his

Son, who is the exact representation of the divine nature" (Heb 1:1-3). It continues by claiming that Jesus is superior to the angelic mediators of the covenant as well as the human mediator, Moses.

At the heart of the book of Hebrews is the claim that the ministry of Jesus is superior to all the major institutions of the Hebraic sacrificial cult: the Sabbath, the tabernacle, priesthood, covenant, and sacrifice. As high priest, for example, Jesus was not limited as earthly priests, who were obligated to offer year after year the same sacrifices for sin, but he is a high priest who has passed through the heavens. But just how could Jesus be a priest if he was from the tribe a Judah and the family of David the King? To demonstrate the superiority of this priesthood, the author of Hebrews appeals to a rather popular figure in Second Temple Jewish literature, the priest, Melchizedek. This enigmatic figure appears only once in the Pentateuch, as priest of Salem. Before there was ever an Israelite priesthood, Abraham gave a tenth of all he had to this priest who "without father or mother, without genealogy, having neither beginning of days nor end of life, but made like the Son of God, he abides a priest perpetually" (Heb 7:3). Jesus, likewise, is a priest according to this ancient order of Melchizedek, not that of Aaron, Zadok, or Abiathar.

For early Christianity, Jesus was the perfect priest because he also offered the perfect sacrifice. Rather than being limited to offering the blood of bulls and goats year after year that can never take away sin, Jesus, according to Hebrews, offered his own life, once for all time. After having offered this sacrifice for sin, he sat down at the right hand of God, ending the need for further sacrifice.

> When he said above, 'You have neither desired nor taken pleasure in sacrifices and offerings and burnt offerings and sin offerings' (these are offered according to the law), then he added, 'See, I have come to do your will.' He abolishes the first in order to establish the second. And by that will we have been sanctified through the offering of the body of Jesus Christ once for all.
>
> And every priest stands day after day at his service, offering again and again the same sacrifices that can never take away sins. But when Christ had offered for all time a single sacrifice for sins, he sat down at the right hand of God, and since then has been waiting until his enemies should be made a stool for his feet. For by a single offering he has perfected for all time those who are sanctified. (Heb 10:8-14)

According to the author of the book of Hebrews, by one offering, then, Jesus abolished the entire sacrificial system and everything involved in it.

The book of Hebrews also demonstrates that the earthly tabernacle and temple were simply models of what in reality existed in the heavens. Unlike the earthly high priest, who annually entered the Holy of Holies to offer the appropriate sacrifice, Jesus did not enter an earthly temple at all, but entered heaven itself, the true temple, a tabernacle not made with hands (Heb 8:1-6). Thus, the offering of his own blood in the eternal temple initiated a new covenant that superceded and replaced the old covenant of the Law--a new covenant based on grace and forgiveness.

Hebrews refers to activities in the temple in the present tense as though the temple cult continued to exist. The destruction of the temple never is mentioned to support the argument that this institution was evidence of an outmoded sacrificial system. Therefore, a date prior to the destruction of the temple would seem possible, though many have opted for a later date. That 1 Clement refers to the book of Hebrews in his letters (95 C.E.), necessitates a date prior to the second century C.E.

Philo

One of the most prolific and influential Jews of the Second Temple period was Philo. Philo was a prominent Jew from Alexandria, Egypt, and perhaps one of the wealthiest men in the city. His adult life can be placed in the first half of the first century C.E., but the exact details of his birth and death cannot be determined. To say that his writings were numerous is an obvious understatement, with over 40 separate works extant. These writings fall into two main categories. The first is similar to those works categorized previously as reworked scripture. For example, in his *Exposition of the Laws of Moses*, he paraphrases and expands biblical law to suit his purposes. This work includes a systematic effort to take the miscellaneous laws of the Torah and associate them with one of the Ten Commandments. It also includes biographies of many of the patriarchs who predate the Law.

The second category, however, includes two different types of commentaries on the Scriptures of the Torah. The first, *Questions and Answers on the Books of Genesis and Exodus*, is exactly what the title indicates--commentary on these two books employing a question/answer format. However, due to the fragmentary nature of the sources scholars find his exegetical methodology difficult to define. The second type of commentary includes a number of verse-by-verse commentaries dealing with the book of Genesis. The unique contribution of these commentaries is their use of allegory in interpretation, a kind of exegesis for which Philo is notorious. For Philo, the primeval history does not necessarily render a literal account of Adam, Eve, Cain, Abel, and Noah, but instead it depicts these individuals as symbols of the religious and moral development of the human soul. Philo's writings reflect a first-hand knowledge of Hellenistic culture. On one hand, he demonstrates loyalty to the institutions and religion of Judaism, yet on the other hand draws deeply on Greek philosophy. This fusion of Judaism and Hellenism has made Philo most famous. The goal of human existence is similar to that expressed by Plato. As humans ascend through the spheres, they move beyond mere matter, ascending to pure form:

> For God, being God, assumed that a beautiful copy would never be produced apart from a beautiful pattern, and that no object of perception would be faultless which was not made in the likeness of an original discerned only by the intellect. So when He willed to create this visible world He first fully formed the intelligible world, in order that He might have the use of a pattern wholly God-like and incorporeal in producing the material world, as a later creation, the very image of an earlier, to embrace in itself objects of intelligence. (*Creation* 4.16)

The Bible Expanded

Another example of the way the scriptures influenced Second Temple Judaism is through parabiblical texts. These texts were not revisions or commentaries, but were tied nonetheless to famous or confusing persons and events in the Hebrew Bible. Any Bible student will confess that some of the narratives of the Hebrew Bible actually raise more questions than they answer. This effect is particularly true with the primeval history in the book of Genesis. What else might one know about Adam and Eve, about Enoch, and Melchizedek? One specific example is notable. The patriarchal narratives of Genesis address the origins of the wives of the patriarchs in some detail, with the glaring exception of Joseph. The book of Genesis, then, mentions

Asenath, but says nothing about her life and faith. Who was Joseph's wife Asenath, and how is it that a righteous Jew could be approved for marrying an Egyptian? This particular issue was especially troublesome for Jews struggling with clarifying socio-religious boundaries. Questions like these were dealt with in many of the parabiblical expansions to biblical narratives written during the Second Temple period. Four such works demonstrate how the writers of this period expanded the scriptures to confront troublesome narratives in the biblical text: *Joseph and Asenath*; *The Testament of the Twelve Patriarchs*; *The Life of Adam and Eve* or the *Apocalypse of Moses*, and the book of *1 Enoch*.

Joseph and Asenath

One of the most enjoyable works produced near the turn of the Common Era is the Jewish romance, *Joseph and Asenath*. The story describes how Asenath, daughter of an Egyptian priest, converted to Judaism and married Joseph, a prominent model of Jewish piety and faith. This book is one of the best-attested and widely distributed books of the Pseudepigrapha. The story opens just as many of the nobles of Egypt are desiring the hand of Asenath in marriage, including the son of the Pharaoh. Asenath rejects all suitors, content to live in a lavish tower, served by maidens and worshiping numerous idols. On a trip to gather corn during the seven years of plenty, Joseph plans a visit to Asenath's father, Pentephres. Pentephres keenly observes that this as a perfect opportunity to marry off his daughter to someone of indisputably high standing. When Pentephres announces his intentions to Asenath, she flatly refuses. But when she actually sees the splendor and handsomeness of Joseph with her own eyes, she is stricken, not only with guilt for her rash words, but with love for the virgin Joseph. When she later advances for Joseph to kiss her, it is he who refuses, unwilling to kiss a heathen woman who worships idols. He does find it in his heart to pray for her conversion and leaves to return at a later time. Meanwhile, Asenath is so moved by Joseph's prayer that she repents, breaks her idols, and for seven days, prays for forgiveness. On the eighth day, she is visited by an angel, who announces that her sins have been forgiven. Furthermore, the angel proclaimes that she would now be an example to anyone who repents like her. He feeds her a piece of honeycomb, which is equated with the breath of life, and announces that she will be the bride of Joseph. Shortly thereafter, Joseph returnes, discovers that she has been converted, immediately falls in love, and marries Asenath. In the course of time, Asenath ultimately gives birth to their two sons, Ephraim and Manasseh.

Eight years later, Pharaoh's son gazes on Asenath and is consumed with the idea of making her his bride. He tries to persuade Joseph's brothers, Simeon and Levi to help him kidnap Asenath and kill Joseph, but they refuse. He later, however, succeeds in enlisting the help of two of his half brothers, Dan and Gad. Joseph's other brothers foil the plot, and Joseph's full brother Benjamin kills Pharaoh's son. His father, the Pharaoh, is so stricken by grief that he dies as well, paving the way for Joseph to become Pharaoh, reigning over Egypt for forty-eight years.

This work can be characterized as a Greek Romance, but with a small "g." The romance is thoroughly Jewish in its allusions, purposes, and nature. It presupposes knowledge of the Hebrew ancestral traditions, as well as the way of the Torah. The genre gives the work an inoffensive and entertaining character to deal with the touchy issues of exogamy and proselytism. It also addresses the thorny theological dilemma as to how one of the biblical ancestors could lower himself to marry a foreigner.

The Testament of the Twelve Patriarchs

One of the common, although admittedly variegated genres of the Second Temple period typically involves a famous Hebrew ancestor gathering together his family prior to his death for blessings, curses, and predictions of the future. While other examples appear in pseudepigraphical literature, one of the best is *The Testament of the Twelve Patriarchs*. *The Testament of the Twelve Patriarchs* is a collection of twelve independent testimonies by each of Jacob's twelve sons. Each testament is self-contained. The Testament models the closing chapters of Genesis, as Jacob exhorts each of his sons. Most of the testaments in this work follow a common pattern. The sequence of events begins introducing the ancestor and a describing that individual's life. On the ancestor's deathbed, he delivers a number of ethical exhortations to his children, along with a prediction of what will happen to the tribe itself or to the nation of Israel. These stereotypical predictions are examples of *prophecy ex eventu,* nearly always describing events that had already taken place by the time of the writer. Another set of ethical commands follows the predictions. The work ordinarily ends with the death and burial of the ancestor.

One of the hotly debated questions is whether *The Testament of the Twelve Patriarchs* is a Jewish or Christian work. In present form, the collection is clearly Christian, with a number of explicit references to the Christian Messiah. Most of the Christian passages, however, appear to be later interpolations. At the very least there appears to be a thoroughgoing Christian redaction, and at most, the work is a Christian composition. Striking thematic parallels exist with some of the sectarian works from Qumran, such as the *Damascus Document*, the *Community Rule*, and the *War Scroll*. The metaphor of light and darkness as symbolism for good and evil and other dualistic notions of two spirits and two ways are shared with the literature from Qumran. These similarities do not necessarily suggest that *The Testament of the Twelve Patriarchs* was written by the sectarians of Qumran.

The Apocalypse of Moses and The Life of Adam and Eve

The book of Genesis is silent over the fate of some of its most central figures. In particular, there are numerous Jewish legends regarding the ultimate fate of the first human couple, Adam and Eve. *The Apocalypse of Moses* and *The Life of Adam and Eve* are two translations of the same work, a testamentary genre deriving from a common Hebrew source. The shorter *Apocalypse of Moses* is a Greek text and *The Life of Adam and Eve* is a Latin recension. Both books describe what presumably happened to Adam and Eve after their expulsion from the Garden of Eden.

The Greek version begins by recounting the murder of Abel by Cain, but is primarily concerned with introducing the birth of Seth. A devastating illness inflicts Adam and he calls Seth and Eve to his bedside. In order to explain what death was, Adam recounts his sin in the garden and asks them to return to Paradise to get oil from the tree of Life. As they approach Paradise, a wild beast attacks Seth. The beast charges that because of Eve's sin, its nature had changed and enmity had been introduced, allowing it authority over humankind. Seth reproves the beast, prohibiting it from contact with the image of God until the Day of Judgment. Michael the archangel then appears to Seth, informing him that the oil of healing would not be available until the end of times. When Adam learns that the possibility of delaying his death does not exist, he instructs Eve to recount in exacting detail the story of the fall in Paradise and the subsequent consequences of the fall. After recounting these things, Eve, who suffered the primary responsibility for the fall, repents and Adam dies. After a time of cleansing, Adam's soul is taken to Paradise and Eve dies six days later. The narrative ends with her burial.

About half of the content of the Latin version (*Life of Adam and Eve*) overlaps with the *Apocalypse of Moses*. The Latin version begins with a lengthy description of the couple's repentance and search for food after being ejected from Paradise. Before Eve's repentance was complete, however, Satan tempts her again and she consequently interrupts her repentance. Adam confronts Satan and Satan provides an account of his own expulsion from heaven, ironically because he refused to worship the image of God, Adam. In a lengthy discourse Satan expresses resentment that it was because of a human, Adam, that he was expelled from heaven. After Satan's soliloquy, Adam appeals to God for deliverance and Satan flees from his presence. Next the work describes the birth of Cain and Abel, followed by Adam's fatal illness. Adam recounts the story of the fall and instructs his son Seth and his wife Eve to leave in search of the oil of mercy, so that he might be anointed and healed. As in the Greek version, Eve and Seth make the discovery that the healing oil was to be reserved only for the last days. Adam, therefore, dies and for seven days the sun, moon, and stars are darkened. Eve dies six days later after a final testament to her sons and daughters. So, like the *Apocalypse of Moses*, *The Life of Adam and Eve* ends with Eve's burial. The book was written between 100 B.C.E. and 100 C.E.

1 Enoch

Students of the Old Testament or Hebrew Bible know Enoch from his cameo appearance in Genesis 5:24, where Enoch "walked with God, and he was not, for God took him." In the course of later Israelite history, particularly in the Second Temple period, all kinds of speculative and legendary material arose around the character of Enoch. The books of *Jubilees*, *The Genesis Apocryphon*, the New Testament book of Jude, and many others portray Enoch as a wise sage who has insights into the secrets of heaven, a faithful scribe who recorded God's divine judgments and grand movements in history, and a priestly figure who intercedes on behalf of men and angels alike. The books that bear his name, *1 and 2 Enoch*, were extremely popular, not only in Early Judaism, but particularly in the early church.

1 Enoch is an apocalyptic work, known only in Ethiopic and Greek until the discovery of the Dead Sea Scrolls. When the Dead Sea Scrolls were discovered, many Aramaic fragments of the book were present among the finds, indicating that the work was probably originally written in Aramaic. 1 Enoch was a composite work of five parts, probably on the analogy of the Torah, the Psalms, and the Megilloth, each of which also contained five literary units. The first of the five sections, "The Book of the Watchers" (ch. 1-36), dates from the second century B.C.E, or perhaps earlier. As the title indicates, the story expands upon the enigmatic Genesis 6 account about the sons of God, interpreted here as 200 fallen angels called 'the Watchers', who had sexual relations with the daughters of men. The resultant offspring were men of renown, giants among the human race. Enoch pronounces judgment against these rebels in the Book of the Watchers. The second section of 1 Enoch, "The Parables of Enoch" (ch. 37-71), is almost certainly an independent book. This was the only section of the book not found at Qumran. Dated in the first century CE prior to the destruction of Jerusalem, The Parables of Enoch relates three parables Enoch saw in a vision. These parables deal with the coming judgment when the chosen one will reign along with the righteous. "The Book of Heavenly Luminaries" (ch 72-82) is an astounding astronomical primer as Enoch is escorted through the heavens by the Angel, Urial. There, like *Jubilees* and other literature of the period, a solar calendar is proposed, with blessings on those who follow this solar year. Here, God's providence over the universe is in direct relation to the movement of the stars and the correct reckoning of the solar year. The obvious implication is a judgment against the lunar calendar. The fourth section of 1 Enoch, "The Book of Dream Visions," dates from the second century B.C.E., and contains two visions. The first is a revision of the flood story and the second is an account of the history of the world from Adam through the Maccabees. Like "The Book of the Watchers," "The Book of Dream Visions" examines the fallen angels and their well-deserved punishment. Finally, "The Book of Admonitions" (ch. 91-105) divides history into ten epochs, seven of which have passed and three which are in the future. The Book of

Admonitions predicts resurrection and a final judgment at the end of the age, when God will eliminate all evil and bless the righteous.

As one of the best examples of apocalyptic literature, the book of *1 Enoch* illustrates of how the life of a famous character in the Hebrew Scriptures was expanded to meet the needs of a contemporary audience. Perhaps, due to its affinities with the Book of Revelation in the New Testament, *1 Enoch* became extremely popular in the early church. Partially due to its popularity among Christians, the book fell out of favor with the Jews until the Middle Ages.

Conclusion

The enormous corpus of religious literature written by Jews in Palestine, Babylon, and Egypt during the turn of the Common Era bears witness to the tremendous creativity and innovative spirit of these communities. The reflective nature of this literature also points out the importance of the sacred traditions of Israel present in the Torah. Scholars find it impossible to determine the level of authority that these texts had. Obviously some were more readily accepted than others, and with few exceptions, none of these texts attained the same level of authority that was held by the Torah and the Prophets. The creators of this material grappled with some of the same questions, perplexities, and inconsistencies that lovers of Scripture have wrestled with for generations. This love for Scripture, coupled with a yearning for answers to questions that were left unresolved by the Torah, fueled new theological and philosophical speculation.

Chapter 12

Theological Innovation in the Second Temple Period

The same creative spirit that fostered a rise in Jewish literature in the Second Temple period also gave impetus to fresh theological innovation. Exposure to cultural diversity in the Diaspora, as well as Palestine itself, led to new concepts about God and divine relations with the human community. Old traditions were investigated, challenged, and given new vitality. Additionally, new traditions emerged as various covenant groups sought to encourage and challenge their followers and confound their foes. While the Torah served as the bedrock for testing these new insights into God's ways in the world, other external factors led to new ways of understanding God's revelation to the people of God.

Sin, Evil, and the Human Dilemma

One of the emerging preoccupations of the Jews and early Christians of the Second Temple period was considering the nature and origin of evil. While the reality of evil is present in the texts of the Hebrew Bible, the emphasis on the origins of evil and its personifications of Satan and demons is minimal, or many would argue, nonexistent. In the Second Temple period, external conditions of social life prompted renewed concerns about theodicy. After the exile, the returnees rebuilt the temple and reinstated Torah worship. The prophets Haggai and Zechariah had promised blessing and prosperity beyond description. But this long-awaited period of peace did not happen as promised, or at least as was hoped in the minds of the faithful. Sin still appeared to be rewarded and evil was a dominant force, despite divine providence. God's people suffered while those with little concern for the commands of God prospered. How could God allow this?

One of the logical directions their inquiries took them was to speculate about the human and supernatural origins of evil. Would it even be remotely conceivable that God is the ultimate origin of evil? The texts of the Hebrew Bible are strangely silent on this subject. Evil is simply assumed. Many of the sources from the Second Temple period, not surprisingly, revert to the Genesis narratives of Adam and Eve for an answer to the origins of evil. In some cases, Eve is given the primary responsibility for bringing sin into the world. Ben Sira 25:24, for example, claims, "From a woman sin had its beginning and because of her we all die." Additionally, in *The Life of Adam and Eve*, which dates from the turn of the Common Era, Eve willingly confesses that she, and not Adam, sinned first.

'And Eve said to Adam, "Live out your life, my lord. You are granted life, since you are guilty of neither the first nor the second error. But I have erred and been led astray, for I have not kept God's commandment. Cut me off now from the light of your life and I will go westwards and remain there until I die." And she began to weep bitterly and groan aloud. And she made there a booth, having been pregnant for about three months.' (*L.A.E* 18:1-3)

On the other hand, other sources indicate that Adam is the chief culprit introducing sin into the human race. The book of 2 Esdras charges the sin to Adam, but adds the qualification that both good and evil initially resides in Adam's heart. Once the evil way is chosen, good departs.

Yet you did not take away their evil heart from them, so that your law might produce fruit in them. For the first Adam, burdened with an evil heart, transgressed and was overcome, as were also all who were descended from him. Thus the disease became permanent; the law was in the heart of the people along with the evil root; but what was good departed, and the evil remained. (2 Esd 3:20-22)

The book of *2 Baruch* also faults Adam for the origin of sin, but adds a qualification that there was legitimate freedom of choice among humans as willing participants,

> for though Adam first sinned and brought untimely death upon all men, yet each one of those who were born from him has either prepared for his own soul its future torment or chosen for himself the glories that are to be (*2 Bar.* 54:14).

Early Christians also grappled with this thorny problem. The New Testament addresses the origins of human sinfulness with ambivalence. On one hand, Eve is the first to succumb to the Devil's wiles, while on the other hand sin's actual entrance into the world is through the man, Adam. Thus, the blame falls on both Adam and Eve. The author of 1 Timothy states, "for Adam was formed first, then Eve; and Adam was not deceived, but the woman was deceived and became a transgressor" (1 Tim 2:13-14). Yet in the book of Romans, Paul adds,

> Therefore just as sin came into the world through one man and death came through sin, and so death spread to all because all have sinned...therefore just as one man's trespass led to the condemnation for all, so one man's act of righteousness leads to justification and life for all." (Romans 5:12, 18)

Jesus did not directly address the issue of the origins of evil in the Gospels. His teachings simply assume its existence and reality. In Luke 13, for example, Jesus indicates that the misery that often accompanies life is not necessarily because of sin. He points to two terrible first century C.E. events, Pilate's execution of the Jews and the collapse of the Tower of Siloam. Jesus argues that those who died in these unfortunate circumstances are no more or less righteous than those whose lives are spared.

One of the most interesting developments during the Second Temple period in the discussion regarding the origins of evil lies in the seeming fascination with the peculiar passage in Genesis 6. In this infamous text, the Sons of God have intimate relations with the daughters of men, producing a race of giants. Several books from the Second Temple period address this enigmatic topic (*1 En.* 6:1-16:4, 40:7, 54:6, *2 En.* 18, *Jub.* 7:21). The book of *1 Enoch* 6:1-16:4 contains a narrative depicting the Sons of God, which are interpreted as fallen angels who had sexual intercourse with human women. Enoch unsuccessfully attempts to intercede on their behalf and the corruption of all humankind is the unfortunate but inevitable result. Consequently, evil enters the world through this race of men who corrupted humanity in all sorts of ways, specifically by introducing long-held taboos like making weaponry and cosmetics. When his intercession fails, Enoch is instructed to predict the doom of these fallen beings, or "watchers." The term, "watcher," is also found in Daniel 4:13,17,23 referring to a specific celestial being who serves as a heavenly council to do the bidding of the deity. Most of the Apocryphal and Pseudipigraphical literature, however, depicts these Watchers negatively. Enoch, for example, equates the Watchers with evil spirits,

> Enoch scribe of righteousness, go and make known to the Watchers of heaven who have abandoned the high heaven, the holy eternal place, and have defiled themselves with women...neither will there be peace with them nor the forgiveness of sin. (*1 En.* 12:4-6)

The origins of evil were also considered at Qumran. The writings found there indicate that the community envisioned two separate spirits who were brought into being at the time of creation, a good spirit and an evil spirit. Each had human and angelic followers referred to as "the lot." The behavior of individuals in this life was determined in some way by which group or "lot" one belonged to. While good would ultimately prevail, evil was characterized as a persistent and enduring reality in this present age (1QSb 3:17-21).

Numerous sources question how God can seemingly allow sin to be rewarded, the righteous to suffer, and good to be thwarted in the world. In the Hebrew Bible, the books of Job and Habakkuk grapple with the problem of evil. Neither really gives an answer except to say that God will in his own time and his own way bring the world to its appropriate and just end. Second Temple Jewish literature such as 2 Esdras, *2 Baruch*, the *Apocalypse of Abraham*, and *3 Baruch* also partially address this topic. In the end, like their biblical counterparts, these materials appeal to the ultimate mystery of God,

> Who can equal your goodness O Lord
> For it is incomprehensible?
> Or who can fathom your grace,
> Which is without end?

Or who can understand your intelligence?
Or who can narrate the thoughts of your spirit?
Or who of those born can hope to arrive at these things? (*2 Bar.* 75: 1b-5a)

Messianism

Second Temple Judaism did not espouse any unifying messianic expectation. For that matter, neither did the Hebrew Bible. This statement sometimes comes as a shock to Christians familiar with the central messianic hope of the New Testament. The Hebrew word for Messiah (*mashiah*) means, "anointed one," and can refer broadly to one who is a chosen agent of God or narrowly to a specific reference to an eschatological hope of an ideal king. Evidence exists that both kings and priests were anointed in ancient Israel. In the Hebrew Bible, the specific term, "messiah," and the fully developed messianic concept did not always go together. Allusions to this concept emerge from texts in Isaiah 9:2-7, 11:1-9, Jeremiah 23:5-6, Jeremiah 33:14-22, Micah 5: 2-4, Zechariah 9:9-10, Ezekiel 34:20-31 and 37:24-28, but scholars cannot demonstrate conclusively which if any of these instances use the word as a technical term. While the Hebrew Bible does teach that a descendant of David would always be on the throne of Israel (2 Sam 7, 23:1-3), the concept of a messiah ruling over an ideal messianic kingdom has only minimal attestation in the Hebrew Scriptures, at least until the Assyrian conquest of the northern kingdom. A growing hope of a future messianic king who would lead in triumph and usher in a reign of peace flourished briefly during the time of Zerubbabel (Hag 2:23, Zech 3:8, 6:12), but was met with disappointment. The book of Daniel is unclear as to whether readers should envision a priestly or a kingly messiah,

> Know therefore and understand: from the time that the word went out to restore and build Jerusalem to the time of an anointed prince, there shall be seven weeks. And for sixty-two weeks it shall be built again with streets and moat, but in a troubled time. After the sixty-two weeks, an anointed one shall be cut off, and shall have nothing, and the troops of the prince who is to come shall destroy the city and its sanctuary. Its end shall come with a flood and to the end there shall be war. Desolations are decreed. He shall make a strong covenant with many

> for one week; and for half of the week he shall make sacrifice and
> offering cease; and in their place shall be an abomination that desolates,
> until the decreed end is poured out upon the desolator. (Dan 9:25-27)

The messianic idea was extensively developed in the Hellenistic
and Roman times, particularly in the Pseudepigraphical literature.
Among these writings, however, no clear consensus emerges on most
issues. Would the Messiah be of human or supernatural origins?
Would he come at the end of time or in the midst of present day
history? Would he be primarily a monarch or a priest? How long
would the Messianic age last? Would the Messiah crush Israel's
enemies and judge the nations? The Jews met these questions with a
variety of responses. Not all Jews of the first century were obsessed
with Messianic expectations, particularly in the 20's and 30's when
Roman oppression was less noticeable than several decades later. No
single definition of who the anointed one would be ever decisively
dominated alternative perspectives. Some sought messianic
deliverance through angels, prophets, kings, military leaders, priests, or
even revered figures like Enoch and Elijah. The most common
messianic notions appeared to involve one (or both) of two ideals. On
one hand, the messiah would have a restorative function that would
bring Israel the ancient glory she once had during the golden age of
Israel's history. On the other hand was a utopian dream that provided
an even better future than Israel had ever experienced, or even dreamed
of, at any point in her history.

Most of the pseudepigraphical literature with specific messianic
content is from the late first century C.E. One of the few pre-Christian
descriptions of the Messiah comes from *The Psalms of Solomon* in the
middle of the first century B.C.E. *The Psalms of Solomon* depicts "the
Lord Messiah" who gathers his holy people, purges Jerusalem, and
judges the nations with wisdom and righteousness *(Pss. Sol.* 17:21-46).
This influential text continues,

> He shall be compassionate to all the nations who reverently stand
> before him. He will strike the earth with the word of this mouth
> forever; he will bless the Lord's people with wisdom and happiness.
> And he himself will be free from sin, in order to rule a great people. He
> will expose officials and drive out sinners by the strength of his word.
> *(Pss. Sol* 17:34-36)

The Sibylline Oracles, which date from around 140 B.C.E., also mention a Messianic King who would end all war,

> And then God will send a King from the sun who will stop the entire earth from war, killing some, imposing oaths of loyalty on others; and he will not do all these things by his private plans but in obedience to the noble teachings of the great God (*Sib. Or.* 3:652-656).

After this, *The Sibylline Oracles* proclaims that God's judgment will be brought against the earth and all who live in it, and the elect will be saved.

Written at roughly the same time as the New Testament, the book of *2 Baruch* contains a more clearly defined messianic expectation. It presents a number of kingdoms, following one upon another, with each becoming increasingly powerful. At the end of time, truth will hide itself and the entire earth will be polluted with unrighteousness (*2 Bar.* 39-42). At that time the anointed one will come. He will summon all the nations and judge them, a judgment, based on how each nation treated the Jews. Every nation that has not trodden down the people of Israel will live. Those who violated Israel in any way will be destroyed. Baruch declares that God will then usher in a reign of peace in which "health will descend in dew, and illness will vanish, and fear and tribulation and lamentation will pass away from among men, and joy will encompass the earth" (*2 Bar.* 73:2).

A similar presentation of the messianic theme is found in *4 Ezra*. Composed around the turn of the first century C.E., 4 Ezra depicts the inaugural revelation of the Messiah followed by a time of rejoicing for four hundred years. After this, the Messiah will die, along with the entire created order, and the world will be returned to primeval silence. After a period of seven days, God will miraculously rouse the world, and the earth will give up those who are asleep in it, and all will be judged, some to the pit of torment and some to Paradise (*4 Ezra* 7; 11:37-12:34; 13:3-14:9).

Much of the pseudepigraphical literature, however, does not have clearly developed messianic conceptions. The Messiah plays no role whatsoever in the eschatology of *Jubilees*, *1 Enoch* 1-13, 91-104, *2 Enoch*, or the *Assumption of Moses*. *1 Enoch* 37-71 depicts figures such as the Son of Man, the Righteous One, and the Elect One, but does not directly attribute messianic functions to these characters. The book of *3 Enoch* mentions the Messiah as a Son of David and as a Son of Joseph, so it is difficult to tell whether a dual concept of messiah is depicted.

The literature present from the community at Qumran indicates a definite messianic expectation, though the evidence at hand does not permit categorical statements about their belief. At least some degree of pluralism existed within the sect over beliefs about the anointed one. This pluralism may be because of differing approaches held concurrently, or evolution of the sect's self understanding over the course of their existence. *The War Scroll*, *Habakkuk Commentary*, and *Psalms Scrolls*, for example, say nothing about the Messiah, although there is an emphasis on eschatology where a final battle would take place, ushering in the messianic age. Elsewhere in the literature from Qumran, there appears to be two Messiahs, a messiah of Aaron and a messiah of Israel. In addition to a priestly and kingly messiah, some have even argued the possibility of a third prophetic messiah taught in these texts. The injunction in the *Community Rule* states,

> They shall depart from none of the counsels of the Law to walk in all the stubbornness of their hearts; but shall be ruled by the primitive precepts in which the men of the Community were first instructed until there shall come the Prophet and the Messiahs of Aaron and Israel. (1QS IX:11-12)

This multiple messianic concept also is present in the text 4Q175. It refers to a prophet like Moses who would have the words of God in his mouth, a royal messiah who would crush the borderlands of Moab, and a future priestly figure who would handle the Urim and Thummim. The final portion of the text depicts two or three wicked figures who would also be raised up as instruments of wrongdoing, creating a stronghold of evil. In *The Messianic Apocalypse*, the author presents a single messiah, "the heavens and earth will listen to His Messiah, and none therein will stray from the commandments of the holy ones" (4 Q 521 II 1-2).

One of the most unusual Qumran texts is the so-called "pierced Messiah" text. Since the release of the scrolls in 1991, some have employed this fragmented text to draw a link between the Qumran community and early Christianity. After intense debate, scholarly consensus overwhelmingly has rejected the dying messiah interpretation in favor of one whereby the leader of the nation, the Branch of David, condemns the forces of evil to death:

> the Branch of David and they will enter into judgment with...and the Prince of the Congregation, the Br[anch of David] will kill him [...by strok]es and by wounds. And a Priest [of renown?] will command [...the salin of the Kittim...]. (4Q285, fr.5)

The early Christian community probably had the most fully developed messianic consciousness of the period. Nascent Christianity unequivocally viewed Jesus as the Messianic king. The title freely given to him, *Christos*, is a literal Greek translation of the Hebrew word, *meshiah*. The Gospels depict that Jesus himself, however, was suspicious of the term, and rarely used it to refer to himself. In fact, the Gospel of John's narrative of the feeding of the five thousand ends with Jesus retiring from the crowds to avoid being proclaimed as king. However, several points in his ministry stand out as he asserted his identity as the messiah (Matt 14:61-62, 16:13-23, 22:42, John 6:15). His actions in the triumphal entry, the cleansing of the temple, and the transfiguration, all confirmed the identification of Jesus as Messiah. Even these three crucial events are dramatically presented in a way that altered the traditional views of messiahship. Jesus did not come as a triumphant warrior against Rome, but instead as a peaceful leader, one who proclaimed the Kingdom of God, a kingdom in which God reigns in the human heart, not over a political state. The new theme of a suffering messiah was certainly unique to the life and ministry of Jesus, as the death and resurrection of the Messiah was a notion unprecedented in Judaism.

During the first century C.E., several rebel leaders claimed to be the Messiah. Among those was Judas the Galilean and his descendant, Menaham. Messianic leaders such as these were largely responsible for a growing hatred for Rome that fueled the fires of revolt and led to the destruction of Jerusalem in 70 C.E. Even after the destruction of Jerusalem, the longing for a deliverer continued.

Table 12.1

Early Messianic Movements	
Name	*Date*
Judas of Galilee	6 CE
Simon	6 CE
Athronges	6CE
Jesus of Nazareth	30-32 CE
Menachem, son of Judas	66 CE
Simon ben Giora	ca. 66-70 CE
Simon bar Kosiba (bar Kochba)	132-135

In the Second Jewish Revolt of 132-135, Rabbi Akiba believed Bar Kochba to be the messiah. The failure of this final revolt and metamorphosis of Jerusalem into a Roman City, Aelia Capitolina, may have severely hampered much of the messianic expectation present in the first century C.E. The Mishnah, the record of the Oral Torah associated with Rabbinic Judaism, contains very little messianic expectation. The many changes in Judaism associated with the destruction of the temple and the failure of Jewish revolts against Rome somehow transformed this nationalistic longing for deliverance.

Resurrection and Paradise

The Hebrew Bible contains virtually no significant mention of the resurrection. It does include stories of restoration to life (1 Kgs 17:17, 2 Kgs 4:19, 13:21) and narratives mentioning that some never died at all (Gen 5:21-24, 2 Kgs 2: 1-12). None of these instances, however, clearly depict a final state that depends on a resurrection. Admittedly, hints of resurrection occur in the book of Job, Isaiah 26 and Daniel 12, but no fully developed doctrine of resurrection emerges in the Hebrew Bible or Christian Old Testament. Life in the Hebrew Bible can be described more as vitality than mere existence. The vitality of life is directly related to *shalom* or wholeness. Upon one's death, God gathered the faithful and unfaithful alike to Sheol, the realm of the dead. Sheol was not a place of reward or punishment, but was primarily a way that, upon death, an individual gathered to his or her ancestors.

This situation changes in the Second Temple period. The apocalyptic literature of the Apocrypha, Pseudepigrapha, and the Dead Sea Scrolls contain numerous references to resurrection. One of the earliest explicit references to resurrection comes from 2 Maccabees in the Apocrypha,

> When he was near death, he said, "One cannot but choose to die at the hands of mortals and to cherish the hope that God gives of being raised again by him. But for you there will be no resurrection to life!" (2 Macc 7:14)

The Wisdom of Solomon, portrays the soul as essentially immortal, a thoroughly Greek philosophical concept,

> The beginning of wisdom is the most sincere desire for instruction, and concern for instruction is love of her, and the love of her is the keeping of her laws, and giving heed to her laws is the assurance of immortality, and immortality brings one near to God; so the desire for wisdom leads to a kingdom. (Wis 6:17-20)

The reason for such an interest in resurrection may have been due to the marginalization of the Jews by other nations in the period. Belief in resurrection may have provided the only real hope for Jewry in dire circumstances. In *1 Enoch*, for example, after all of Israel's enemies are destroyed, once-despised Israel gathers together to rebuild the temple. After the completion of this new temple the resurrection comes (*1 En.* 6-36).

It spite of some variation, much the literature of the Second Temple period provides a theological bridge between the Hebrew Bible's minimalist concept of the afterlife and the fully developed doctrine of the resurrection as found in the Christian New Testament. Whether the delay to put such a concept in writing was due to lack of acceptance of general populace or other circumstances is impossible to say. Even considering the diversity of teachings present in the literature, a definite fascination with the resurrection hope emerged. For example, some writers of the period rejected the idea of a resurrection for the wicked altogether (2 Macc 7:14). Others envisioned a temporary kingdom on earth followed by eternity in heaven (*2 Bar.* 72:2, 30:1-2). Although written much later, the Mishnah also testifies to the validity of resurrection hope, "And these are they that have no share in the world to come: he that says there is no resurrection of the dead prescribed in the Law." (*Sanh.* 10.1). The Mishnah also discusses classes of sinners not raised for judgment (*Sanh.* 10.3).

As stated above, the focus of some texts is not on resurrection at all but rather on the immortality of the soul:

> But the souls of the righteous are in the hand of God, and no torment will ever touch them. In the eyes of the foolish they seemed to have died and their departure was thought to be a disaster and their going from us to be their destruction; but they are at peace. For though in the sight of others they were punished, their hope is full of immortality. (Wis 3:1-4)

For most of Judaism, however, the Greek concept of the immortality of the soul was not accepted without at least some participation of the body. The soul, therefore, could only be united with the body in resurrection. Exactly what kind of body that was open to all kinds of speculation (2 Macc 14:46, *2 En.* 22:8-9, 38:5, 40:2, 56:2, 64:2-3).

Of course, the resurrection was absolutely a fundamental necessity for the life of the early Church. Because of the confidence in the resurrection of Jesus the disciples boldly abandoned their timidity and proclaimed the gospel of Jesus Christ. It was the resurrection that gave the believers who were alive, hope for those who had already died. This belief lay at the core of the teaching of the early church. The apostle Paul queries,

> Now if Christ is proclaimed as raised from the dead, how can some of you say there is no resurrection of the dead? If there is no resurrection of the dead, then Christ has not been raised; and if Christ has not been raised, then our proclamation has been in vain and your faith has been in vain...For if the dead are not raised, then Christ has not been raised. If Christ has not been raised, your faith is futile and you are still in your sins. Then those who also who have died in Christ have perished. If for this life only we have hoped in Christ, we are of all people most to be pitied (1 Cor 15:12-14, 16-19).

The early Christian church, like other movements within Judaism, held to the idea of marriage of spirit and body at the resurrection.

Wisdom

The wisdom literature of the Second Temple period grew out of a much larger movement in ancient Israel and in the Ancient Near East. Virtually every Ancient Near Eastern civilization experienced influential currents of wisdom traditions and wisdom schools. Nonetheless, identifying wisdom literature in the Hebrew Bible and elsewhere is a perplexing task. Although Job, Proverbs, and Ecclesiastes are universally acknowledged as wisdom literature, no specific wisdom section exists in the Hebrew Scriptures. Until relatively recently, wisdom literature suffered benign neglect by scholars, perhaps due to the uniqueness of the wisdom corpus. Many common themes from the Hebrew Bible, for example, are conspicuously absent in the wisdom tradition. References to the patriarchs, the exodus from Egypt, the covenant at Sinai, conquest of Canaan, centrality of Jerusalem, and Davidic covenant are absent in the wisdom literature of the Hebrew Bible. In place of these themes, the Hebrew Bible advocates a broader, more universal orientation to faith and ethics. Another characteristic that sets the wisdom literature of the Hebrew Bible apart is its experimental attitude toward daily life. A fundamental order in the world is observable in creation and society that provides guidance for moral life. Because the universe follows an observable order that should be characterized by justice and integrity, individuals bear primary responsibility for their own destiny. People must choose wisely and responsibly. The wisdom literature in the Hebrew Bible included both practical and speculative elements. The book of Proverbs focused on these practical elements while Job dealt with larger concerns of theodicy, and Ecclesiastes considered the broad issues of the purpose and meaning of life.

In the Second Temple period, two major apocryphal works have been characterized as deriving from the wisdom tradition, Ben Sira and the Wisdom of Solomon. In addition, recent releases of discoveries at Qumran have disclosed the sect's numerous sapiental texts. While all of these Qumran texts are fragmentary and their study is still in its infancy, they promise to yield more exciting information about the wisdom tradition in the Second Temple period.

Ben Sira is a wisdom anthology, similar to the book of Proverbs. It contains practical advise on the family, raising children, conduct in business, and general ethical practice. While many of its teachings are remarkably similar to its counterpart in the Hebrew Bible, Ben Sira's teaching on women has generated a great deal of attention in the modern world. As it claims, "Any iniquity is insignificant compared to a wife's iniquity, may a sinner's lot befall her" (Sir 25:19). Unlike the wisdom literature of the Hebrew Bible, Ben Sira succeeded in incorporating some of the historical traditions of Israel into the focus of the work. His hymn in honor of the ancestors provides a virtual roll call of famous figures in the Israelite history, beginning with Enoch and ending with the Hasmonean leader Simon II. The book also breaks new ground by taking up the topics of the importance of the offices of the physician and the scribe (38:1-15, 24-26), prescribes moderation in eating and drinking (31:12-31), and discusses the paradox of divine sovereignty and free will (10:19). One of the most widely celebrated contributions of the book is its identification of wisdom with the Torah, a new development in the Second Temple period. Devotion to wisdom thus is the equivalent of devotion to Torah. In "The Hymn in Praise of Lady Wisdom" is states,

> All this is the book of the covenant of the Most High God, the law that Moses commanded us as an inheritance for the congregations of Jacob. It overflows like Pishon, with wisdom, and like the Tigris at the time of the first fruits. It runs over, like the Euphrates, with understanding, and like the Jordan at harvest time. It pours forth instruction like the Nile, like the Gihon at the time of vintage. The first man did not know wisdom fully, nor will the last one fathom her. For her thoughts are more abundant than the sea, and her counsel deeper than the great abyss. (Sir 24:23-29)

The Wisdom of Solomon is quite different from Ben Sira. It uses Greek language and thought to convey new dimensions in the wisdom tradition. Written in the first century, B.C.E., the Wisdom of Solomon is clearly the product of Hellenistic culture, possibly coming from the hand of a hellenized Jew in Alexandria. Some scholars have pointed to the influence of Ben Sira on the author of the Wisdom of Solomon. Wisdom is personified here, much like the book of Proverbs (8:22-31). Yet wisdom is extended to include broader concerns. What some might consider as wisdom's core curriculum reads thusly,

For it is he who gave me unerring knowledge of what exists, to know the structure of the world and the activity of the elements; the beginning and end and middle of times, the alternations of the solstices and the changes of the seasons, the cycles of the year and the constellations of the stars, the natures of animals and the tempers of wild animals, the powers of spirits and the thoughts of human beings, the varieties of plants and the virtues of roots; I learned both what is secret and what is manifest, for wisdom, the fashioner of all things, taught me. (Wis 7:17-22)

This kind of wisdom was not the exclusive domain of some secret mystery as was common in much of Greek culture, but was broadly available to all who aspired to seek wisdom and to know her fruits. A number of fragments from Caves 1 and 4 at Qumran contain various poems and compositions of wisdom literature. Most of these date from the first century B.C.E. One such poem has parallels to the teaching on the false attractions of the adulteress in Proverbs 7. The text from Qumran adapts a metaphor with a twist: "harlotry" represents the lures of false teachings,

In the city's squares she veils herself and she stands in the gates of the towns. She will never re[st] from wh[orin]g, her eyes glance hither and thither. She lifts her eyelids naughtily to stare at a virtuous man and join him, and an important man to trip him up, at upright men to pervert their way, and the righteous elect to keep them from the commandment, at the firmly established to bring them down wantonly, and those who walk in uprightness to alter the statute; to cause the humble to rebel against God, and turn their steeps away from the ways of justice, to bring insolence to their heart, so that they march no more in the paths of uprightness; to lead men astray to the ways of the Pit, and seduce with flatteries every son of man. (4Q184 10-15)

Several other sapiental works with terminology and worldviews similar to the sectarian community at Qumran are found in a number of fragments. These poems deal with proper business dealings, warnings against borrowing money, repayment of debts, and the fleeting nature of riches. Many of these poems address the concerns and temptations of the poor. For example,

Do not give money in pledge for your inheritance lest it impoverish your body. Do not satiate yourself with bread while there is not clothing. Do not drink wine while there is no food. Do not seek luxury when you lack bread. Do not glorify yourself in your need if you are poor lest you degrade your life. Also do not treat with contempt your ordained instrument.... (4Q416, fr. 2 i-ii, 20-25)

Another work that bears an unmistakable acquaintance with the Hebrew Bible and its wisdom literature is the Greek work, *Pseudo-Phoclydes*. Written in Greek some time from the first century B.C.E. to the first century C.E., this work is an example of non-proselyting, religious propaganda. Written as a Greek hexametric poem, this work seeks to attract Jewish sympathizers from the Greek world. It takes those ethical injunctions in the Torah that might be acceptable to the Greeks and states them in palatable ways. The work shows influences of the book of Proverbs and Ben Sira. Beginning with a summary of the Ten Commandments, *Pseudo-Phoclydes* broaches such subjects as the importance of justice, mercy, the dangers of the love of money, the importance of modesty, and moderation in all things. Similar to Proverbs and Ben Sira, it tackles the subjects of the importance of proper speech, the usefulness of labor, and family life in the context of an ethic of universal monotheism.

Apocalyptic

The words "apocalypse" and "apocalyptic" derive from a Greek word meaning "to unveil." The root word has a wide range of meanings in the diverse literature from the Second Temple period, but it also serves as a technical term. An "apocalypse" refers to a specific literary genre dating from 250 B.C.E. to 100 C.E., with roots going back to the Persian Period, and even into the prophetic tradition of the Hebrew Scriptures. This literature is keenly interested in the heavenly world and the fulfillment of history in the next age. Written as a direct revelation from God, an apocalypse reveals God's ultimate intentions for this world, the unbelieving nations, and God's people. The term "apocalyptic" refers, then, to the specific perspective and ideology associated with these writings. Scholars have speculated that the roots of apocalyptic thought may derive from a community that became excluded from power and influence in society. As the community became more and more marginalized, interest in vindicating God and the restoring their community to its rightful place became paramount in their collective thinking,

Table 12.2

Second Temple Apocalyptic Literature	
Book	**Date**
Daniel	5th century BCE to 2nd century BCE
Revelation	1st century CE
I Enoch (Ethiopic)	3rd century BCE to 1st century CE
II Enoch (Slavonic)	late 1st century CE
Apocalypse of Zephaniah	1st century BCE- 1st century CE
Testament of Moses	2nd century BCE or 1st century CE
II Esdras (4 Ezra)	1st century CE
Apocalypse of Abraham	1st century CE
II Baruch (Syriac Apocalypse)	2nd century CE

Apocalyptic literature is present in the Hebrew Bible, the New Testament, the Apocrypha, Pseudipigrapha, and in the literature from Qumran. In the Hebrew Bible, the book of Daniel is considered apocalyptic literature as the book uses elaborate symbols and stories to demonstrate God's control of History. In the New Testament, the book of the Revelation is also an apocalypse. In this book the persecuted Christian church longs for God's final deliverance in the return of Jesus Christ, and the judgment of the wicked, plus the creation of a new heaven and a new earth. In the Apocrypha, the book of *2 Esdras* was a very influential apocalypse. In the Pseudepigrapha, there a number of books counted in the genre of apocalypse: *1 and 2 Enoch*, the *Apocalypse of Zephaniah*, the *Apocalypse of Abraham*, and *2 Baruch*, most of which date from the first century C.E. Other books from this period such as the book of *Jubilees*, and *Testament of the Twelve Patriarchs*, and the *Testament of Moses* have an apocalyptic style. Recent publications of materials from Qumran has also revealed several fragments which may derive from apocalyptic writings such as 4Q247, 4Q248, 1Q27, 4Q299-301, 4Q521.

One of the distinguishing characteristics of apocalyptic literature is the mode of divine revelation. These works are often pseudonymous, as the author assumes a name of a popular figure from Israelite history. Such a task was an acceptable literary convention that could trace back in time a certain character in antiquity, thus creating a greater authority. Prominent figures such as Moses, Enoch, Ezra, and Daniel were awarded a glimpse of God's activity in heaven and in the future, creating *ex eventu* prophecy, or prophecy after the event. Such a revelation usually took place in the form of a dream, a vision of an otherworldly journey, or through an angelic mediator. This revelation appears as a mystery that God once hid but now revealed to the one who understands. Imagery of secret, sealed books opened to the protagonist convey God's divine message of his current and future actions in this world.

Symbolism is a common rhetorical devise of apocalyptic literature. The use of coded language provided some protection as these disenfranchised communities strongly criticized the religious and social establishments of the day. The symbolism of numbers regularly was employed to depict the timing of God in bringing about his long-awaited justice. The literature frequently favors the numbers 3, 4, 7, 10, 12, and 70. The author uses these numbers to calculate the unfolding of history when the ultimate activities of God would be revealed. Such history is highly schematized, and numbers play a prominent role in the presentation of this history. Animal symbolism in highly exaggerated proportions is common, using animals known to people or elaborate mythic creatures of otherworldly origins. The New Testament book of Revelation, for example, is replete with images of winged creatures, evil beasts, conquering horsemen, and bowls containing various displays of divine judgment, as well as mythological creatures such as the dragon and the serpent.

In apocalyptic literature, God reveals the divine secrets of what will transpire on this earth, in human history, and at the final judgment. This literature contains strong dualisms between God and Satan, good and evil, angels and demons, this present evil age and the age to come, light and darkness, life and death, yet within the strict confines of Jewish monotheism. The authors of apocalyptic literature believed that there was another world, far removed from the present visible cosmos. Because of the distance of this spiritual world, mediation was necessary through contact spiritual angelic beings, heavenly dreams and visions.

This mediation provided the author a glimpse of what God was doing in history and of what God's plans were for the future.

Apocalyptic literature was influential, then, particularly in Christian circles. Even literature not specifically considered apocalyptic assumes and shares some of the same literary symbols of this literature. The opposite also is true. Apocalyptic literature drew on the heritage of the literature of the Hebrew Scriptures, from the historical events portrayed in the Torah and historical books, and even upon the messages of the Hebrew prophets.

Eventually apocalyptic literature eventually fell out of favor in Jewish circles. Its fall may have been because Judaism was so thoroughly transformed by the crisis of the destruction of Jerusalem in 70 C.E. Some also speculate that the rather revolutionary nature of apocalyptic literature may have been too dangerous for Jewish communities to embrace after the fall of the temple. Perhaps, however, the most convincing reason for the Jew's disenchantment with this enigmatic literature is that the Christian church adapted many of the apocalyptic writings of the Second Temple period, as well as writing some of their own, such as the highly influential book of Revelation. These Jewish writings were well suited to the message of the early Christian church and the triumphalism of the gospel. The popularity of this literature with early Christianity may also explain why many of the extant documents of this genre have been passed down in Greek, rather than Hebrew or Aramaic.

Bibliography

Part Three: Literary Creativity: From Religious Literature to Sacred Text

Charlesworth, James H., ed. *The Bible and the Dead Sea Scrolls*. N. Richland Hills, VA: Bibal Press, 2000.

Charlesworth, James H., ed. *The Old Testament Pseudepigrapha*. (2 vols.) New York: Doubleday, 1983.

Collins, John J. *The Apocalyptic Imagination*. New York: Crossroad, 1984.

Coote, Robert B., and Mary P. Coote. *Power, Politics and the Making of the Bible*. Minneapolis, MN: Augsburg Fortress, 1990.

Hanson, Paul D. *The Dawn of Apocalyptic*. Philadelphia: Fortress Press, 1975.

Harrington, Daniel J. *Invitation to the Apocrypha*. Grand Rapids, MI: Wm. B. Eerdmans, 1999.

Jobes, Karen J. and M. Silva. *Invitation to Septuagint*. Grand Rapids, MI: Baker, 2000.

Kraft, Robert and George W.E. Nickelsburg, eds. *Early Judaism and Its Modern Interpreters*. Atlanta: Scholars Press, 1986.

Kugel, James L., and Rowen A. Greer. *Early Biblical Interpretation*. Philadelphia: Westminster, 1986.

Kugel, James L. *Traditions of the Bible: A Guide to the Bible as it Was at the Start of The Common Era*. Cambridge: Harvard University Press, 1998.

Metzger, Bruce M. *An Introduction to Apocrypha*. New York: Oxford Press, 1957.

Neusner, Jacob. *Scriptures of the Oral Torah*. San Francisco: Harper and Row, 1987.

Nickelsburg, George W.E. *Jewish Literature Between the Bible and the Mishnah*. Philadelphia: Fortress, 1981.

Russell, D.S. *Divine Disclosure: An Introduction to Jewish Apocalyptic.* Minneapolis, MN: Fortress Press, 1992.

Schiffman, Lawrence H. *Reclaiming the Dead Sea Scrolls: Their True Meaning for Judaism and Christianity.* New York: Doubleday, 1995.

Stone, Michael E. and Theodore A. Bergren, eds. *Biblical Figures Outside the Bible.* Harrisburg, PA: Trinity Press International, 1998.

Stone, Michael, ed. *Jewish Writings of the Second Temple Period: Apocrypha, Pseudepigrapha, Qumran Sectarian Writings, Philo, Josephus.* Assen: van Gorlcum; Philadelphia: Fortress Press, 1984.

Ulrich, Eugene. *The Dead Sea Scrolls and the Origins of the Bible.* Grand Rapids, MI: Wm. B. Eerdmans, 1999.

Vanderkam, James C. *An Introduction to Early Judaism.* Grand Rapids, MI: Wm. B. Eerdmans, 2001.

Vermes, Geza. *The Complete Dead Sea Scrolls In English.* New York: Penguin Books, 1997.

Wise, Michael, Martin Abegg, and Edward Cook. *The Dead Sea Scrolls: A New Translation.* San Francisco: Harper, 1999.

Index